The Random House Atlas of the
OCEANS

The Random House Atlas of the
OCEANS

Introduction by Jacques Cousteau

Published in association with the
World Conservation Union (IUCN)

Random House　New York

General Editors
Dr Danny Elder and Dr John Pernetta

Research Assistant
Sarah Humphrey

Contributors
Jill Bailey
Dr Danny Elder
Dr Tony Hare
Sarah Humphrey
Dr John Pernetta
Dr Andrew Price

Edited and designed by Mitchell Beazley Publishers, Michelin House, 81 Fulham
Road, London SW3 6RB

Senior Executive Editor **Robin Rees**
Senior Editor **Annabel Else**
Editor **Simon Ryder**
Editor **Alfred LeMaitre**
Editor **Julia Gorton**
Editor **Sue Dyson**
Proofreader **Mark Hendy**
Cartographic Editor **Andrew Thompson**
Senior Art Editor **Sean Keogh**
Art Editor **Siân Protheroe**
Picture Research **Brigitte Arora**
Picture Research **Jackum Brown**
Production **Ted Timberlake**

Maps by Euromap Limited, Pangbourne, England

Library of Congress Cataloging-in-Publication Data

The Random House atlas of the oceans / produced in association with the
World Conservation Union (IUCN).
   p. cm.
 " U.K. edition: Oceans, a Mitchell Beazley world conservation
 atlas" – CIP data sheet.
  Includes index.
   1. Oceans–Maps. 2. Marine biology–Maps. 3. Marine resources
conservation–Maps. 4. Man–Influence on nature–Maps. I. Random
House (Firm) II. Mitchell Beazley Publishers. III. International
Union for Conservation of Nature and Natural Resources. IV. Title: Atlas of
the oceans. V. Title: Oceans.
G2800.46'0022'3–dc20   1-675019
                                             CIP
                                             MAP

1 2 3 4 5 6 7 8 9

First U.S. Edition

Typeset in Sabon by Kerri Hinchon for Evolution
Printed and bound in West Germany by Mohndruck GmbH, Gütersloh

Measurements – both metric and imperial measurements are given throughout.

Billions – because of the differing usage between the United Kingdom and the
United States, billions here correspond to thousand millions.

CONTENTS

Foreword

Oceans and their resources, once seen as beyond the reach of man's destructive capabilities, are showing the first serious signs of mismanagement. Thousands of kilometres of coastal ecosystems are badly mauled, some virtually beyond recovery; many fish stocks are severely depleted; and pollution is spreading at an alarming pace. Nowhere are these signs more ominous than in the near-shore waters and in the narrow zone where the sea meets the land.

The notion that something will have to be done to halt and reverse the present trend and thus safeguard the use of the oceans on a sustainable basis, is gaining strength. The general public, the scientists, the managers and policy makers are all aware, more than ever before, that solutions can only be found through a common global strategy. Wise and rational management of the oceans and their resources, as opposed to reckless exploitation in the interest of short-term gains, seems to be the cornerstone for such a strategy.

One of the basic impediments to rational management of the oceans is still our inadequate understanding of the full complexity of interactions between the physical, chemical and biological processes which maintain the oceans in a healthy and productive state. Science has only been seriously applied to the study of the oceans during this century. We still do not adequately understand the significance of the changing biological and chemical composition of the oceans, or the resilience and recovery power of oceanic ecosystems, hence we cannot predict the possible long-term consequences of today's interventions by people. Without a sound scientific insight based on critical thinking, modelling and adequate data there can be no rational management.

The readers of this ocean atlas will find it a useful guide to the application of science in management of the oceans. The book is much more than an atlas in the conventional sense of the word. It is also much more than a standard description of the oceans. Instead of allowing the deluge of data to obscure the facts, it tries to analyse the problems of the oceans, still believed by many to be the frontier of man's common heritage, and to suggest measures which may alleviate these problems. It is written not for experts in a particular narrow field but for those who are looking for a balanced view on which meaningful actions could be based.

S. Keckes, Former Director, Oceans & Coastal Areas Programme Activity Centre, United Nations Environment Programme
G. Kullenberg, Secretary, Intergovernmental Oceanographic Commission of UNESCO

Introduction

The health of the global water system rooted in the ocean is vital to the future welfare of our planet, and is of particular concern to me as an ocean explorer. The future needs of society will be well served, however, only if we change our short-term mentality and often arrogant indifference to the results of our actions and focus on long-term considerations and a sound attitude in the use of all our resources.

It is an unavoidable fact of international life that the decision-makers in governments everywhere are most influenced by vested interests with extravagant lobbying budgets and by organizations with enormous memberships. Those of us who love the sea, who recognize the blood relationship of all earth's beings, who see on this Water Planet a growing threat to our most fundamental biological machinery, do not command the money and the power of even a single major multinational corporation. But we can wield the formidable power of our numbers, the strength of a great unified crowd of citizens of the planet.

The rate of environmental devastation is alarming. We ourselves are increasingly threatened by toxic debris and lethal miscalculations. This is unbelievable and unacceptable. We must stop this stupidity, and the most effective weapon we have as citizens – as parents – is the sheer force of our numbers. That is the strategy of the dolphin when threatened by an animal armed with greater strength and size. Pursued by a large shark, a pack of dolphins will suddenly turn en masse, dive below the shark and drive their blunt noses into its belly, one after another. It is the perfect strategy. With no ribs or diaphragm to protect its vital organs, the shark is vulnerable. For all its power, the shark is defeated by intelligence and the force of numbers. It is the weaponry of the peacemakers and the common people throughout history.

For all the darkness that presently confronts us and our descendants, there is no reason to give up. There is every reason to take up the fight, because we have within our grasp the power of the people to force the right decisions. The more people, the more power, the more hope. On behalf of future generations whose legacy we are squandering, let us begin to make waves – forcing decision-makers to protect and to nurture the environment. How can we accomplish this? We can rise as a human family and compel the powerful and the profit-only-minded to consider life the greatest priority. We can take our inspiration from the dolphins, who defend themselves and their offspring through an instinct to mass together in the face of danger...and to attack power with wisdom.

de l'Academie Française

Living on the Edge

People have always been attracted to coasts as places to live, trade and travel. Today, six out of every ten people inhabit coastal regions. Communications and transport have opened up trade links between East and West, North and South, the Old World and the New. The oceans are being exploited for food, energy and minerals as never before, and human impacts are felt globally. Average sea levels are already rising at a rate of 1.5 millimetres per year, and as the climate warms and sea levels continue to rise during the 21st century, coastal populations will feel serious impacts.

In Bangladesh, around six million people live within 1 metre (3.3 feet) of the present sea level.

Living on the Edge

The oceans cover three-fourths of our planet and greatly influence the world's climate. In coastal areas the sea interacts directly with the land, eroding and depositing sediments and occasionally causing major floods. It is in the coastal zone that as many as two-thirds of the world's population may be living by the year 2000. In the past, human uses of the oceans have been limited largely because of low levels of demand and simple technologies. Rapidly expanding populations, combined with improved technologies, threaten the quality of the ocean environment and the survival of many of its species.

The oceans are a rich source of food, of energy, minerals and medicines, which are growing in importance as technology improves and land-based resources become more scarce. In some respects present human use of marine resources parallels the hunter-gatherer stage of development on land: we exploit wild populations of fish until they can no longer support continued harvesting. Our management systems are inadequate, partly because we cannot understand and model marine animal populations, and partly because of the long tradition of free and open access in all uses of the ocean. The history of whaling illustrates the failure of such approaches to rational and sustainable management of the world's marine resources.

It is a sobering thought that the current world catch of marine fish has reached what many informed scientists consider to be the limits of production: 100 million tonnes a year. By the year 2000, world demand is likely to outstrip supply by around 20 million tonnes per year. As a result, world fish prices will rise and inevitably many of the poorer people in developing countries will lose their major source of protein, as their governments sell more marine products to finance development and to meet their international debt repayments.

Although marine living resources only supply around ten per cent of total world food, the dependence of human populations in tropical and subtropical countries on protein from fish is high. The open access to marine resources is seen as a solution to the problems of rural poverty in some developing countries. As coastal populations grow, increasing numbers of people become dependent on the diminishing resource base. Sixty per cent of the present populations of these countries obtain between 40 and 100 per cent of their animal protein from this source. Despite this reliance on fish protein, per capita consumption of fish in developing countries is low – 7.7 kilograms (17 pounds) per person per year – compared with developed countries – 25 kilograms (55 pounds) per person per year – reflecting the different standards of living. Consumption of marine fish and shellfish reaches as much as 74.5 kilograms (164 pounds) per person in Japan. The prospects for expanding our harvest of natural fish and shellfish are distinctly limited. With the possible exceptions of deep-ocean squid and Antarctic krill, new resources are just not there to exploit. At present the technology to harvest these squid resources does not exist, and it seems likely that krill will not sustain extended and heavy exploitation.

As our technologies improve and the search for more and different ocean resources accelerates, we stand on the threshold of a revolution as great as that which occurred on land when people exchanged the way of life of the hunter-gatherer for that of the settled agriculturalist. The Neolithic revolution in western Europe saw a dramatic change in the land-

Landing the catch (left) *from a nearby coral reef is a common scene in many parts of the tropical world. Coastal societies worldwide depend on the bounties of the oceans to supplement their livelihood. In many tropical countries, a high percentage of protein is derived from the local fishery. A variety of techniques are used, including fish traps, beach seines, hook and line, and spearfishing.*

In Tokyo's fish market (above), *the evenly sized, frozen tuna on sale are in sharp contrast to the wide variety of caught fish shown in the main picture. Tuna is so sought after in Japan, particularly for use in sushi dishes, that it has a very high market value. Many yellowfin tuna, caught off the coast of Massachusetts, are bled, frozen and air freighted to Japan, to be eaten within 3 to 4 days of capture.*

scape, with forests being felled to make way for farms, and the human population growing at an accelerating rate. Modern western European society is living in landscapes greatly modified by human activity. The people of the temperate zones are fortunate that the clearance of the forests did not result in the rapid soil degradation which so often accompanies the felling of tropical rainforests for agriculture. Without sound management the oceans and their resources will be unable to withstand the accelerating demands of society and, like tropical soils, may soon reach the point of no return. Without the incorporation of the concept of sustainability into future ocean management, the productivity of the oceans may become a thing of the past. The need for new approaches is urgent if fisheries are not to decline drastically.

The continued growth of human populations – we will almost certainly exceed six billion by the year 2000 – is placing increasing pressure on the ocean margins. Already 20 per cent of the world's population in both developing and developed countries live in coastal urban centres. One might reasonably ask why so many people live on the edge of the ocean, and although the answers vary from place to place, one answer lies in the productivity of the coastal zone. Much of the world's richest agricultural land is found along the flat coastal plains, while the coastal waters above the continental shelf are the sites for productive fisheries. Combined with the ease of long-distance maritime transport, and the consequent development of ports, these plentiful resources make the coasts attractive areas in which to settle.

Living on the edge is not without its problems. Violent storms at some distance from the coast may cause swells which result in flooding and damage. Often such damage is made worse by improper design of wharfs, piers, groynes and sea walls, by the destruction of habitats which protect the coastline, and by mining of offshore reefs and sand banks, which interfere with the normal patterns of current and wave movements along the shore. Many coastal cities are already below present sea level, and some are continuing to sink, requiring large capital and technological investment to prevent flooding. Such solutions are not possible in poorer countries, where urban centres are expanding rapidly as populations grow, and people migrate to such areas in search of education, medical care, and economic opportunities.

Many coastal cities are located on major river estuaries and deltas, and the resulting destruction of productive wetland habitats places such environments under severe threat worldwide. Damming of rivers reduces sediment inputs, makes barrier islands more vulnerable to erosion, and reduces coastal fisheries production because nutrient inputs are reduced. All these problems are evident in the Nile Delta. Dredging and canalization of waterways, as has happened in the Mississippi Delta, causes erosion elsewhere in the delta system and irreversible habitat modification in sensitive wetland communities of plants and animals. Clearance of coastal mangroves for fuelwood, wetland rice production and fish farming, destroys coastal protection, resulting in severe flooding and erosion under storm conditions. Reclamation of land on atoll reefs, such as the Maldives, increases the risk of catastrophic flooding, and destroys the natural protection afforded by the coral reef system.

The annual influx of tourists to beaches, small islands and coastal resorts in both developed and developing areas often exceeds the "carrying capacity" of the local environment, and adds to the problems of coastal settlements. As coastlines are modified in one area, problems arise elsewhere. Building on coastal dunes interferes with the natural movement of sediments, and has resulted in severe erosion of coastal beaches on the east coast of America. To counter beach loss and to maintain tourist revenue, expensive "beach replenishment" projects involve further interference with natural processes by pumping sand from deeper, offshore waters back onto the beach. All of these changes result in accelerating rates of coastal degradation and pollution, so the margins of the oceans are now showing obvious signs of deterioration worldwide. Historically, when coastal populations were low, and natural rather than artificial harbours were in use, human impact on coastal zones was also low. Perhaps more import-

Villages built on stilts over shallow water, such as this one in Borneo (right), *are common throughout Asia and the Pacific. In the densely populated countries of South-East Asia, open access to marine resources is often seen as one of the solutions to rural poverty.*

antly, the impacts of one person's activities had little effect upon his neighbour, and development of one coastal port did not affect adjacent settlements. Unfortunately, today's reality is different. Coastal populations have now reached the point where one kind of coastal use conflicts with another, simply through a lack of space. All too often one person's solution becomes another person's problem. The need for integrated planning and management of human use of the environment is perhaps nowhere more obvious than on the ocean's edge.

Ipanema Beach, near Rio de Janeiro (above) is a popular tourist destination, with resort hotels separated from the beach only by the width of a boulevard. Hotel construction and the sheer numbers of visitors add to environmental problems in some areas.

15

Human use of the oceans is not merely confined to exploiting a few resources, or modifying a few coastal habitats; nor is it confined only to parts of the ocean. The influence of human activities is felt in all parts of the seas, from the most isolated beaches contaminated with plastic litter to the ocean deeps, which are used as dumping grounds for wastes we cannot or will not dispose of on land. The 1972 Conference on the Human Environment in Stockholm expressed concern about the impacts of pollution on the world's oceans. Although the problems of pollution of the open ocean are less severe than was thought to be the case at that time, pollution of the coastal zone is a growing problem. Overall, it is estimated that 40 per cent of ocean contamination is derived from land-based sources; 30 per cent via the atmosphere; 11 per cent from maritime sources; 10 per cent via dumping; and around 8 per cent from natural sources.

Various estimates suggest that as much as 90 per cent of the contaminants entering the world's oceans remain in coastal waters, where most human use of the marine environment is also concentrated. Coastal waters are being polluted as a consequence of the dumping and discharge of industrial, domestic and sewage wastes, which not only appear as unsightly refuse along the shore, but also interfere with the natural functioning of ecosystems, and cause toxic algal blooms, fish kills, and unsightly algal scum in tourist areas. Long-lived toxic chemicals used in agriculture and industry on land, such as DDT, PCBs, and organochlorine compounds, accumulate in marine organisms. Chemicals such as TBT (tributyl tin) used in antifouling paints on ships interfere with the reproduction of marine molluscs. Sewage and nutrient runoff from agricultural activities may temporarily increase production, but in many areas have led to excessive plant growth, die-back and oxygen depletion in enclosed and semi-enclosed areas. Considerable efforts have been made both nationally and internationally to control various sources of pollution during the last two decades. Unfortunately, pollution from most sources except shipping is increasing despite these efforts.

Ironically, mariculture, hailed in the 1970s as a potential solution to the shortage of protein in poor, developing countries, and as a source of export earnings for development, is now itself the source of many environmental problems. While the much vaunted potential of mariculture has not yet been realized, many of the environmental problems of the coastal area have been highlighted by mariculture developments. There have been outbreaks of cholera, typhoid, infectious hepatitis and gastroenteritis when shellfish grown in water polluted by sewage have been used for human consumption. Shellfish beds have themselves been destroyed by increased sediment runoff, resulting from poor agricultural practices and forest clearance inland. Algal blooms have been caused in some areas by nutrients that originated in fish or shellfish farms. Destruction of coastal mangroves in tropical developing countries to construct prawn mariculture ponds has destroyed the very habitats on which the wild populations depend, resulting in a decline in the number of juveniles available to stock the ponds.

The evidence shows clearly that human influence on the marine environment is both extensive and increasing. It is also clear that many developments in coastal areas around the world will increase their vulnerability to the impacts of global climate change. Few people realize the important role that the world's

The Panama Canal (below) represents a major engineering feat which links the tropical Atlantic and the Pacific. It is one of the busiest shipping routes in the world, but it also acts as a pathway for animal and plant dispersal.

San Francisco Bay (left) illustrates the high level of development which results from access to harbour facilities and the rich natural resource base of coastal areas.

In these regions, the boundary between land and sea is entirely artificial. Activities inland cause changes to offshore currents and marine ecosystems.

oceans play in the climate of the Earth. The oceans serve as a mechanism for the transport of heat from the tropics to higher latitudes, and directly affect the climate and weather of neighbouring land. As the world warms under the greenhouse effect, dramatic alterations to the ocean circulation could occur, resulting in extensive changes to the climate and weather of various regions of the world. Perhaps better known is the potential rise in sea level which will occur as a consequence of the expansion of the surface waters of the oceans. Storms will increase in frequency and may increase in violence, flooding will occur, salt water will intrude into coastal freshwater supplies, erosion will increase, and all these changes will be enhanced by our failure to manage properly the productive coastal regions on which human society depends.

The challenge for this generation is to devise planning and management methods which will reduce the intensity and extent of present coastal problems, enhance and protect marine habitats and biodiversity, prepare the next generation for future climate changes, and leave the oceans in a productive and attractive state. Living on the edge is what we presently do, but is it the edge of disaster or the edge of a new and productive relationship between people and the seas? The choice is ours.

Martin Holdgate, Director General, IUCN
John Pernetta and Danny Elder, General Editors

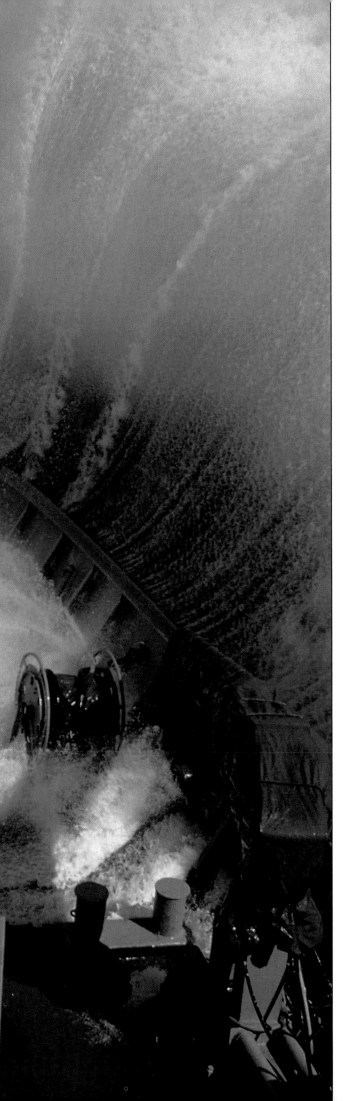

The Turbulent Oceans

The power of the sea is familiar to everyone: its power to erode and build up coastlines, its unpredictable dangers for those who spend their lives at sea, and its devastating ability to flood low-lying coasts. Its waters are in constant motion, circulating heat, salt and nutrients, and its environments range widely, from the sunlit, warm waters of a tropical lagoon to the frozen seas of polar regions or the dark abysses of the ocean deeps. As the ultimate store of the Earth's water, the oceans play a hidden but crucial role in determining the climate and weather on land.

A ship crashes through heavy seas.

Ocean Origins

Radioactive dating of rocks indicates that while the oldest igneous rocks on the planet solidified around 4,200 million years ago, the oldest rocks under the ocean floor are only 200 million years old. But it does not follow that oceans have only been a feature of the Earth since this time. The first water probably appeared as vapour, one of the many gases expelled from the Earth as it began to cool, later condensing to form the oceans. The appearance of the first photosynthetic life forms in the oceans, between two and three billion years ago, had a profound effect on the chemistry of the oceans, of the atmosphere, and on the evolution of all organisms. The early atmosphere lacked oxygen, so the photosynthetic production of oxygen, and the subsequent development of an ozone shield in the upper atmosphere, set the scene for the evolution of present life forms.

The drifting of the continents

The way in which the present-day continents can superficially be fitted together into a single landmass like pieces of a jigsaw puzzle, combined with geological evidence, led Alfred Wegener, a German meteorologist, to propose the theory of continental drift in 1912. He suggested that the existing distribution of the continents about the globe resulted from a process in which they moved to their current positions following the break-up of a single landmass, the supercontinent of Pangea, more than 200 million years ago. There is now a wealth of geological, fossil, and biogeographical evidence to support this theory, which explains the changes in the size of existing oceans and the formation of new oceans. However, it was not until the 1960s that a mechanism for continental drift was proposed (see pp. 22-23), which also provided an explanation for the relatively young age of the rocks that underlie the oceans.

The break-up of Pangea into two major continents, Gondwana in the southern hemisphere and Laurasia to the north, began around 200 million years ago. Panthallasia, the single ocean which surrounded Pangea, began to shrink and a new, shallow ocean, the Tethys Sea, was formed between the new continents. A further split divided Gondwana into two parts, one of which was ultimately to form Australia and Antarctica, while the other was to become Africa. By about 65 million years ago, the Atlantic and Indian Oceans had appeared, but the North American and European continents remained joined in the north. The Pacific became separated from the Atlantic and Indian Oceans when the North and South American continents became joined and Australia drifted northwards away from Antarctica towards its current position; while the separation of Greenland from North America, and the widening of the North Atlantic, completed the encirclement of the Arctic Ocean. The Caribbean took shape when South America moved into its current position and the Central American land bridge was formed.

The division of the world's oceans by landmasses has influenced the distribution and evolution of marine fauna and flora. Where a land barrier prevents mixing between different populations of the same species, the two populations may evolve into separate species. A barrier may also prevent a species from occupying all of its potential range. If it is removed, the species may spread out into new areas, coexisting with or outcompeting species that already reside in these areas. The Suez and Panama Canals have reopened links between oceans long separated and enabled species to spread into new habitats.

Along with dust and smoke, water vapour is released into the atmosphere by volcanic eruptions (right). Much of this comes from water which originally fell on the land as rain and was stored underground before being heated and expelled through the volcano. A very small proportion of this vapour is "new" water that has not been part of the water cycle before. It is released from the volcanic rocks in a similar way to the water that formed the oceans many millions of years ago.

At its northern end, the Red Sea (above) splits into the Gulf of Suez (situated in the centre of this satellite photograph), which connects to the Mediterranean through the Suez Canal, and the Gulf of Aqaba on the right. The Red Sea is a relatively new sea. It began to appear about 50 million years ago when Africa started to drift away from Arabia. The Gulf of Suez opened up around 35 million years ago, followed by the northern part of the Red Sea 10 million years later. On the other side of the Arabian peninsula, the Persian Gulf began to appear between 3 and 4 million years ago. Today, the Red Sea is widening at a rate of about 2 cm (0.8 in) a year.

The Ocean Floor

If it were possible to remove the water from the oceans to expose the floor beneath, a truly remarkable landscape would be revealed: long mountain ranges, vast plains covered in a thick layer of sediment, volcanoes and deep trenches. It was not until the late 1960s that the theory of plate tectonics provided an explanation of the way in which the formation and destruction of the Earth's crust accounts for the topography of the ocean floor and for continental drift (see pp. 20-21).

According to this theory, the Earth's surface is made up of about 12 rigid crustal plates, which overlie and move about on the semi-molten rock beneath. The driving force behind this movement is believed to be thermal convection in the Earth's interior. Where these plates meet, three types of border form: constructive borders, where magma rises up to the surface forcing the plates on either side apart, and forming new oceanic crust in between; destructive borders, where two plates collide and one is overridden by the other; and conservative borders, where plates move past one another, the friction between the two causing faults and fractures.

Oceanic ridges and sea floor spreading

The constructive boundary between two oceanic plates is marked by an oceanic ridge, one to four kilometres (0.6-2.5 miles) high, along the central rift of which molten lava rises up from the mantle. Lava also emerges from smaller vents on the slopes of the ridge, forming submarine volcanoes which may break the surface as volcanic islands, or remain under water as seamounts. Chains of such islands of increasing age can be traced away from ridges as a result of the plates moving apart. Farther from the ridge, the remains of submerged islands are present as guyots, their peaks truncated by wave action.

Evidence for sea floor speading is to be found in the magnetism of basaltic minerals in the floor itself, the direction of which is fixed according to the prevailing direction of the Earth's magnetic field when the rock solidified. Owing to the periodic reversal of this field, a symmetrical pattern of magnetic bands with alternating polarity is produced, with the bands running parallel to the ridge. Since the time between the reversals in magnetic north are known, the rate of sea floor spreading can be calculated: spread rates are estimated to range from less than one centimetre (0.4 inch) per year from the Mid-Atlantic Ridge, to as much as 16 centimetres (6.3 inches) a year for the East Pacific Rise. The divergence of plates and formation of new crust may also occur beneath continents. This leads to the formation of a rift valley, such as the Great Rift Valley in East Africa, and in some cases to the subsequent formation of a new ocean.

The addition of new crustal material at constructive boundaries is compensated for by the destruction of oceanic crust at destructive boundaries; otherwise the surface of the Earth would be continually expanding. This accounts for the young age of oceanic crust. Where two continental plates collide, dramatic folding of the land and the upthrust of mountain chains such as the Himalayas occurs. Where continental and oceanic plates collide, the continental plate overrides the more dense oceanic plate in a process known as subduction. Subduction zones are characterized by oceanic trenches which can be a staggering ten kilometres (6.2 miles) deep, and mark the line along which the oceanic plate is forced downwards. At a depth of 700 kilometres (435 miles), the leading edge of the subducted plate melts and dissolves back into

the mantle. The magma may then rise back up through the continental plate above, forming a chain of volcanoes along the continental margin, as has happened with the Andes. The build-up of such mountain chains is added to by sediment from the ocean floor, which is scraped off the subducting plate and accumulates on the continental margin.

Sediments on the sea floor come from three main sources: the land, from which material is eroded by water, ice and wind; the surface waters of the ocean, from which organic matter, both living and dead, falls to the floor beneath; and deep-ocean waters, from which there is a very gradual production of material by crystalization. Terrigenous materials are mostly deposited near to the continental margin, and some of them may become incorporated in the sediments on the ocean floor as a result of ocean currents and underwater "landslides". The pelagic sediments consist of clays, which are often a rich, red-brown colour owing to a coating of iron oxide and oozes of various colours consisting of biogenic materials accumulated over millions of years.

The topography of the ocean floor (above) is in many ways far more dramatic than that of the land. The Pacific Basin is surrounded by deep trenches, representing the zones of subduction where the spreading ocean floor meets the continental plates. The Pacific is also characterized by a myriad of mountains, some of which originated as volcanic peaks, which developed where thinning of the ocean crust allowed molten material to penetrate the ocean floor. The Hawaiian Islands formed over such a "hotspots", and as the ocean crust moves north-west, new islands appear such that the youngest Hawaiian Islands are found at the south-eastern end of the chain.

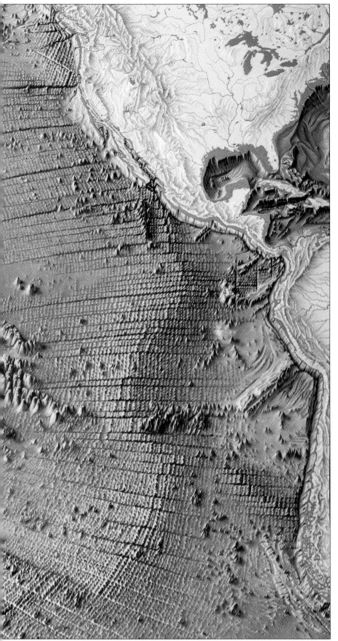

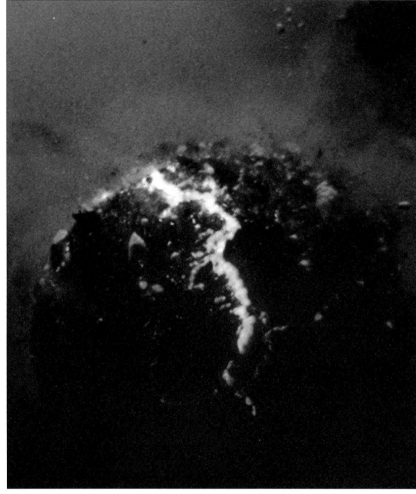

Seen through a cloud of fine black sand particles, this picture (above) is one of the first ever taken of lava erupting under water. The occasion was the eruption of the Hawaiian volcano Kilauea in March 1971, which poured dark pahoehoe lava into a network of hardened lava tubes leading down into the sea. Surprisingly, the entrance into the sea of the hot basaltic lava was not accompanied by vast clouds of steam. The surface of the molten rock cooled on contact with the sea water to form a brittle tube through which the molten lava continued to flow. Many oceanic islands such as the Hawaiian chain and the islands of Micronesia and Polynesia have been formed by submarine volcanic activity which occurs along oceanic ridges as a result of upwelling of molten rock from the Earth's interior. Mountain building on the ocean floor as a result of volcanic activity and movement of the ocean crust results in a rugged underwater topography, which affects deep-water currents in the ocean basin.

This diagram (right) illustrates the process of sea floor spreading and the origin of typical features of the ocean floor. Where two convection cells in the molten magma underlying the crust rise towards the surface, the ocean floor is pushed upwards to form a mid-oceanic ridge. On each side of the ridge the material flows in opposite directions, until it meets the continental plates at the ocean margins. The ocean floor materials pass under the continents, becoming molten once more.

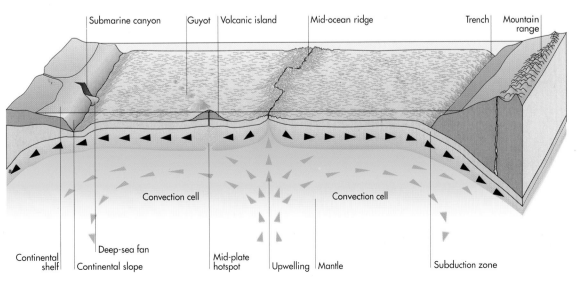

Submarine canyon | Guyot | Volcanic island | Mid-ocean ridge | Trench | Mountain range

Continental shelf | Continental slope | Deep-sea fan | Mid-plate hotspot | Convection cell | Upwelling | Mantle | Convection cell | Subduction zone

The Moving Waters

The sea is never still: it moves in different directions, at different speeds and is influenced by many forces. Understanding the ways in which oceans move is a complex task for oceanographers. Even though the basic processes causing these movements are each quite simple, their combined interaction results in regional differences in current patterns which are strikingly varied in each of the world's oceans.

Convection currents drive surface waters from the warmer equatorial regions towards the poles, where the water becomes colder and more dense, sinking to great depths before moving back towards the Equator. Vertical movements of water in the oceans are influenced by water density, itself a function of salt content and temperature. When heated, surface water in the tropics expands, becoming less dense. This is countered by evaporation which increases salinity and therefore density. The balance between these forces determines whether the water sinks or remains at the surface.

In the tropical Atlantic, water losses through evaporation are greater than gains from rivers and rainfall. The upper layer of the sea becomes warm and saline, flows north as the Gulf Stream, and gives off heat to the atmosphere as it moves north. When it reaches the Greenland Sea this highly saline water is near freezing and has become more dense than the deeper water below it. As convection sets in the water sinks to the bottom, where it spreads out and flows southward. Deep, cold water masses are also formed in the seas near the Antarctic continent, and some of this water moves northwards along the western coasts of the continents before being forced to the surface in certain areas, which form productive upwelling zones. Deep-water currents are influenced by the shape of the ocean floor, with submarine ridges deflecting currents and trenches channelling water flow.

Powered by the wind

The atmosphere above the oceans is not still and winds that blow strongly in one direction for extended periods of time, such as the trade winds which occur around 15°N and 15°S, move the surface waters of the oceans. As surface water moves, the underlying water as far down as 450-750 metres (1,500-2,500 feet) is also affected. Wind-driven surface currents move water across the ocean basins where it piles up against the continental land masses and flows along the coasts. In latitudes where the winds are less strong, the water starts to flow back in the opposite direction.

Because the Earth spins on its polar axis, the direction of these major currents and the winds above them are deflected to the right in the northern hemisphere and to the left in the southern hemisphere.

Atmospheric changes also influence the sea surface; in areas of high pressure the surface is depressed, in areas of low pressure it is raised. Atmospheric pressure varies greatly, setting up waves and short-term surface currents of varying strengths, and influencing local weather patterns.

To all these different influences must be added the effect of the gravitational pull of the Moon, the Sun, and the Earth. Where the Earth's gravity is higher than average, the surface of the sea is lower than where it is less strong. The gravitational pull of the Moon, and to a lesser extent the Sun, are stronger on the surface of the sea which is directly facing these celestial bodies, causing the daily cycle of tides, with intervals of approximately 12 and 24 hours.

The sudden appearance of rough seas along a coast (right) when the weather is bright and clear can be due to storms far out to sea. Strong storm centres over the ocean can set up long-distance swells which may have devastating effects when they reach land some considerable distance from the storm centre itself. In one recorded instance, waves caused by a storm in the Indian Ocean travelled some 20,000 km (12,400 miles) to Alaska. In 1987, extensive flooding in the Maldives in the Indian Ocean was the result of long distance swells from a storm centre off the south-west coast of Australia. The power and energy contained in moving water bodies is also seen when two strong currents meet. In the Saltstraumen channel off the north-west coast of Norway (inset), dangerous eddies are produced as the result of colliding currents and strong tides. The power of the conflicting forces involved is apparent from the thundering noise that is produced, which can be heard as for as 5 km (3 miles) away.

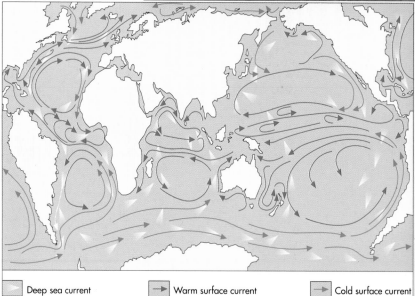

| Deep sea current | Warm surface current | Cold surface current |

When the major ocean currents are mapped (above), the effects of some of the forces that produce them become apparent. These include the swirling pattern of surface currents in each ocean basin which result from the action of winds, the Earth's spin, and convection currents.

The Underwater World

Popular perceptions of our planet as illustrated by its name, Earth, have only recently begun to change as satellite pictures have brought home the extent to which the Earth is in fact a "blue" planet, covered by water. The oceans contain some 1,370 million cubic kilometres (330 million cubic miles) of water which act as a giant store of minerals, nutrients and dissolved gases such as oxygen and carbon dioxide, that provide the essential basis for life in the oceans.

These essential elements vary in their concentration, from area to area and with depth. The movement of the water in the oceans mixes water masses of different composition, and living organisms themselves alter these concentrations by taking up some elements and producing others.

The influence of the oceans goes far beyond their own boundaries, shaping the physical conditions and biological processes of the planet on local, regional and global scales. Gas exchange with the atmosphere, climate and weather (see pp. 30-33), the carbon and hydrological cycles, and other atmospheric and physical processes are all critically influenced or determined by the oceans.

The importance of light

Although living organisms are found throughout the oceans, their diversity and abundance vary considerably from area to area. The basis of all life is light energy, which is converted into chemical energy by photosynthetic organisms. Because most of the light falling on the oceans is absorbed within the surface layers, the zone of highest productivity in the tropics occurs within 30 metres (100 feet) of the surface. The surface waters are also where the oxygen needed for respiration and the carbon dioxide needed for photosynthesis are absorbed into the seas from the atmosphere above.

In deeper waters, life is less abundant, limited by the absence of light and lower oxygen concentrations. In some specialized deep-sea environments, underwater volcanic vents release sulphur-bearing chemicals which are used by chemotrophic bacteria as a source of energy. Another source of energy and food in deeper waters is "faecal rain", falling from the upper layers of the ocean. This rain is made up of the remains of dead animals and plants and the waste products of organisms living near the surface.

At first sight, red may not seem to be a suitable colour for the prawn Notostomus gibbosus *(right) to use as camouflage from its predators. However, because this animal lives 700 m (2,300 ft) below the ocean surface, where red light does not penetrate, none can be reflected to give a red appearance; thus it will appear black against a dark background. Although black pigmentation would be equally effective, many deep-water animals are bright red, the red pigment being derived from their food.*

When sunlight strikes the sea surface (right) between 3 and 30 per cent of it is immediately reflected. The amount of reflection depends on the angle at which the light strikes the surface – the smaller the angle the greater the reflection – which varies with latitude and with the season of the year. The characteristic blue colour of the ocean (left) comes from the fact that penetration of sunlight is attenuated selectively according to wavelength. Attenuation is due to absorption and scattering of the light – scattering being particularly strong in water containing suspended particles. The red end of the spectrum is the first to be lost, and only blue light penetrates to any great depth, while below about 1,000 m (3,300 ft) there is virtually no light at all.

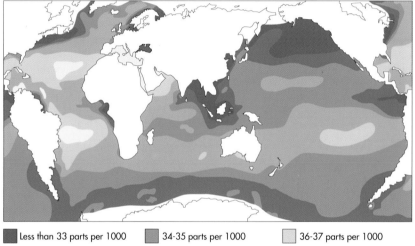

50m

100m

150m

200m

This map (right) shows the variations in surface salinity throughout the world's oceans for the month of February. Although salinities do change during a year, the overall picture remains fairly constant. The most saline water is found in semi-enclosed seas such as the Mediterranean, while the least saline water occurs in areas of high freshwater discharge such as river mouths.

■ Less than 33 parts per 1000 ■ 34-35 parts per 1000 ▢ 36-37 parts per 1000

■ 33-34 parts per 1000 ■ 35-36 parts per 1000 ▢ More than 37 parts per 1000

In the surface waters of the tropics and subtropics, where the water is warm and light is available all year round, biological production is limited by nutrients without which planktonic organisms cannot grow. In some areas nitrogen, phosphorus and silica limit growth. In others such as the Sargasso Sea, dissolved iron is also limiting. As a result of low nutrient concentrations, most open ocean areas are the watery equivalent of deserts. Where ocean currents bring deeper, nutrient-rich water to the surface in zones of upwelling, productivity is high. The same is true in coastal areas, where nutrients are constantly flushed into the sea from the land. At higher latitudes, where water temperatures and light intensity vary seasonally, so does productivity.

In semi-enclosed seas such as the Baltic, parts of the Mediterranean and the Bay of Bengal, stratification of the water column may develop during the summer when warm, lower-salinity water floats on the surface of colder, higher-salinity water. If mixing through wind or current action does not occur then a sharp boundary, the thermocline, may become established between the two water masses. Below the thermocline, bacterial decomposition of the faecal rain on the sea bed can result in most of the oxygen being used up, until animals such as fish cannot survive. As the wastes and dead bodies of the plankton sink below the thermocline they carry with them nutrients, leaving the surface waters with fewer nutrients, which limits further primary production.

In temperate latitudes the thermocline is seasonal, breaking down in the autumn and permitting mixing of the two water bodies during the winter months. This restores oxygen to the deeper layers and nutrients to the surface, ready for the spring bloom of phytoplankton. In the tropics, where production is year round, nutrient availability in surface water is generally low.

Recent events in various parts of the world suggest than human impacts on the marine environment are beginning to affect some of the physical and chemical processes which occur in the coastal seas (see pp. 28-29). The apparent increase in frequency of algal blooms worldwide may be the result of the introduction of nutrients into coastal waters in human sewage and agricultural fertilizer runoff.

Coastal Processes

The shorelines of the world form a transition between the land and the sea and consist of two zones, the intertidal and subtidal. The daily cycle of the tides exposes the intertidal zone alternately to the action of both the air and the water. Below the extreme low-water level, the environment of the subtidal zone grades into the ocean proper, passing through the continental shelf, which generally terminates at a depth of around 200 metres (660 feet) in submarine cliffs which drop to the ocean deeps. The waves, currents and chemistry of these shallow coastal waters differ markedly from the more uniform conditions in the open ocean.

Because of the proximity of land, coastal and near-shore waters receive huge inputs of sediment, nutrients and freshwater. These alter the chemistry of the water and contribute to the high biological productivity of these regions. With the exception of the zones of upwelling, coastal and near-shore waters are the most productive parts of the ocean environment. Their animals and plants display remarkable adaptations to the enormous range of physical factors which characterize these regions.

There are two types of shore. On eroding shores, the action of the waves and tides removes material from the land. On depositing shores, eroded material from the land is deposited, and forms both sandy and muddy beaches, dunes, spits and beach ridges. In general, rocky shores are found in areas of past or present erosion which are exposed to strong wave action, while depositing shores are usually found in more sheltered areas.

In areas of comparatively high wave action, shingle beaches form where large pieces of rock are continuously rolled and moved by the waves. These areas are generally inhospitable environments for animals and plants owing to the continuous grinding actions of the shingle. Pebble, sand or muddy beaches form in areas where the actions of waves and currents are less strong. Depending on the size and composition of the deposited particles, these areas are home to a wide variety of organisms. Some burrow in the sand or mud, while others are so small that they slide through the microscopic water film surrounding each particle. Farther from the shore, the sediments become much finer, so continental shelves are covered by very fine mud and clay.

Waves are a feature of both the open oceans and coastal waters, but it is on coasts that they "break", dissipating their energy. As a wave moves through the sea it represents a large store of energy, with individual particles moving in a circular path beneath the wave peak. The water close to the surface moves faster and in a larger circle than the water deeper down. As a wave approaches shallow water, the friction of the submarine surface slows the deeper water, while the particles at the wave's crest move ahead. Eventually the water at the crest is so far in front that the wave breaks against the shore.

The action of water

Contrary to popular belief, water itself does not cause erosion. It is the particles of sand, pebbles, rocks and other debris caught up in the wave which crash against the beach and erode the shore. The slope of the beach affects the way in which the energy contained in the waves is absorbed. On gently sloping shores, the energy is dissipated over long distances, reducing the erosive force of the wave.

If every coast underwent continuous erosion, then the sea would eventually cover all the land. In coastal areas where wave action is small, deposition of sedi-

Boulder and shingle beaches (right), *like this one in Rackwick Bay on the island of Hoy in Scotland's Orkney Islands, are characteristic of exposed coastlines where the action of the waves is strong. The largest boulders are found in the upper part of the intertidal area. The boulders gradually decrease in size towards the low tide level. Constant movement, under the influence of the waves, grinds the surface of these rocks smooth, and makes such beaches inhospitable environments for animals and plants.*

The Twelve Apostles (left), located in Australia's Port Campbell National Park, are outlying fragments of harder rock left standing after wave action has eroded the softer materials. The waves will eventually undermine the portion of rock above the water level, as in the pillar in the foreground, causing it to collapse and to fragment into smaller pieces.

A broad fan of river-deposited sediment (below) *spreads outward from the estuary formed by the confluence of the Ashley and Cooper rivers, in this satellite view of the Atlantic port city of Charleston, South Carolina. Rivers carry huge loads of sediment, nutrients and fresh water to the sea, a process which makes coastal waters highly productive.*

ments occurs. In this way, dunes, spits and beach ridges are formed. In addition, rivers bring a considerable quantity of sand, silt and clay into coastal areas. Material eroded inland is often deposited in river estuaries and deltas. In areas where currents run parallel to the shore, sediments may be carried along the coast before being redeposited – a process known as longshore drift.

Inputs from rivers

Along with their load of sediments, rivers carry nutrients and freshwater. The nutrients increase the amount of food production in coastal waters. The mingling of freshwater with the saline water of the sea results in flocculation, in which particles of organic and inorganic matter stick together and slowly sink to the bottom, forming sources of food for benthic, or bottom-dwelling, organisms.

Where there are flat coastal plains, rivers may form wide deltas when they reach the coast. In the temperate zones, deltas are characterized by distinctive fresh- and salt-water communities of marsh plants. In the tropics, mangrove communities dominate such areas. The growth of this coastal vegetation slows down water movements, and the roots of the mangroves trap the mud carried downstream by the river water. This causes silt to be deposited, and helps to build up the land.

Coastal wetlands are important habitats for many migratory birds. As areas of distinctive vegetation they are important conservation areas, and are also vital to many marine animals as nursery areas. The growth of human populations in deltas which are used as centres of mariculture, agriculture, trade and commerce threatens such habitats. In other areas, coastal developments including the construction of harbours, sea walls, groynes and piers interferes with the natural process of sediment transport in the coastal zone, and can lead to the "export" of environmental problems to neighbouring areas.

Oceans, Climate and Weather

The oceans have been referred to as "the flywheel of the climate system", since like a flywheel they store energy in the form of heat when it is in plentiful supply, during the day or summer, and release it to the atmosphere when sunshine is absent or in short supply at night or during the winter. But this analogy is inadequate because the oceans do not just act as a passive energy store, but also play an active role, with ocean currents moving thermal energy from the warmer, tropical and subtropical regions to higher latitudes (see pp. 24-25).

As warm ocean currents move towards the poles they lose heat to the atmosphere, and the warm air, when carried by winds over neighbouring land masses, warms the land at night or during the winter. The oceans therefore modulate climates on a local or subregional scale, reducing the extremes of temperature which would otherwise arise. For example, the moderate climate of western Europe compared with central and eastern Europe is in part due to the transfer of heat from the Gulf Stream to the atmosphere which then carries it eastwards towards Europe.

The temperature differences between land and sea reflect the different rates at which they absorb and lose heat. The land surface heats up faster than the sea during the day, but loses heat faster during the night or in winter. This is because the upper layers of the ocean mix with those below, passing some of the heat gained during the day downwards, and so reducing the rate at which it is lost to the atmosphere. Through such vertical mixing and mixing over longer distances as a consequence of the major currents, the temperature range of the whole ocean is small – from about -2°C (28°F), the freezing point of salt water, to 30°C (86°F), although temperatures as high as 35°C (95°F) are found in some semi-enclosed seas. During the course of a day ocean temperatures rarely vary by more than one degree, and usually no more than 10°C (18°F) during the course of a year. For comparison, the range of temperature experienced in the middle of a continent over the course of a year can be as great as 80°C (144°F), and deserts may be scorching during the day but freezing at night.

The oceans and weather

The interplay between the oceans and the atmosphere is complex, with each affecting the other in different ways. For example, wind direction is determined in part by temperature differences between land and ocean, which result in onshore breezes at night when the land is cooler and offshore breezes during the day when the sea is cooler than the land. Ocean surface currents are in turn affected by wind speed and direction (see pp. 24-25). Another important role of the oceans in weather and climate is as a store of water, which evaporates from the surface under high temperatures, forming clouds and ultimately falling again as rain when the atmospheric conditions change.

Tropical ocean areas, which lie outside 5°N and 5°S of the Equator, are also the breeding grounds for violent storms, including hurricanes, which cause extensive damage when they pass over the surface of neighbouring land. On a larger scale, changes in ocean circulation have marked effects on regional climates and weather, as happens during the El Niño Southern Oscillation (see pp. 170-171), when rainfall is reduced in Australia and South-East Asia. If climates change under the influence of the "greenhouse effect" or from other causes, then changes in ocean circulation may be expected with possible major consequences for marine and terrestrial ecosystems.

Unlike a hurricane, which grows from the surface of the ocean upwards, a waterspout (inset) grows downwards from its parent cloud. Waterspouts originate in thunderstorm clouds in much the same way as a vortex of water forms when you stir water in circles in a beaker. The spin in a waterspout develops very rapidly, and is thought to be initiated by strong lateral winds that blow into the parent thundercloud, causing the rising columns of air to be deflected into a spiral. As this rotation accelerates, the vortex extends downwards and becomes narrower and more intense, with wind speeds up to 80 kph (50 mph). It whips up the surface of the sea into a misty ring of spray. The spout moves with its parent cloud, swaying from side to side, and seldom lasts longer than 15 minutes. Hurricanes, on the other hand, often last for days, gaining strength all the time. Such storms are fuelled by the transfer of heat energy from the sea to the atmosphere above. This sets up a convection current with the warmed air rising and being replaced by cooler air from higher latitudes. Spin is imparted to the rising air by the rotation of the Earth, and as more and more air is heated, the storm gathers in intensity, ultimately forming a hurricane.

Tropical rainstorms (left), such as this one near the island of Mahé in the Seychelles, are a feature of the weather in the late afternoon near many small islands. The very high rate of evaporation from the sea during the day results in a build-up of water vapour in the air, and increases the salinity of the surface water. As the air cools during the late afternoon, thunderclouds form and rain falls, often in short, sharp bursts. Every year about 380,000 cu km (91,500 cu miles) of water are evaporated from the surface of the Earth, about 85 per cent of which comes from the oceans. This eventually returns to Earth as rain, with 25 per cent falling on the land, replenishing ground water supplies, rivers and lakes.

Oceans and Changing Climates

Climate change and the "greenhouse effect" have been much in the news recently, with different scenarios of rising seas, hotter climates and melting icecaps being produced on an almost weekly basis. The scenarios range from the probable to the impossible, which reflects the fact that there is still a lack of sound scientific facts and models to explain the way in which the oceans, atmosphere and climate interact.

The "greenhouse effect" is not a new term, but has been used by scientists for more than a hundred years to describe the role of gases in the atmosphere that trap heat close to the Earth's surface, acting in the same way as the glass of a greenhouse. The major greenhouse gases include carbon dioxide, methane, chlorofluorocarbons (CFCs), and of course water vapour. The oceans play an important but little understood role in climate change through their exchange of water vapour and carbon dioxide with the atmosphere, and through their role as a heat store (see pp. 30-31). Given the importance of carbon dioxide in the "greenhouse effect", we still know too little about the role of the oceans in the global carbon cycle. It is known that they act as a massive carbon sink, but just how much carbon dioxide is absorbed from the atmosphere is unclear, as is what happens to it once in the oceans.

The fact that the average temperature at the surface of the Earth has risen by about 0.5°C (0.9°F) over the last century is now widely accepted. Similarly, measurable increases in the concentrations of greenhouse gases have occurred over the same time period, and recent research shows that the global sea level is rising at approximately 1.5 millimetres (0.06 inch) a year. Climate models suggest that these changes could be the result of human activity, including the burning of fossil fuels and the destruction of the rainforests, both of which put more carbon dioxide into the atmosphere.

Predicting future climates

While the evidence tends to support the greenhouse theory, a causal relationship is not proven and the human impact on global climate remains a scientific hypothesis. Nevertheless, scientists at the Second World Climate Conference in 1990 agreed that without action to reduce emissions of greenhouse gases, global warming could reach 2-5°C (3.6-9°F) over the next century, and that the sea level may rise by about 65 centimetres (25 inches) by the end of the next century, but it could be as little as 30 centimetres (12 inches) or as much as 100 centimetres (40 inches). This rate of warming is unprecedented in the past 10,000 years.

The wide range of these estimates is a reflection of uncertainties concerning various components of the global climate system, including the role of the oceans. Most of the predicted rise in sea level will be due to expansion of the surface waters of the oceans as they warm up, and any significant melting of the Antarctic ice sheet would add considerably to these estimates (see pp. 172-173). The best models available at present suggest that warming in the tropics may be less than the global average, while at higher latitudes the rise in temperature may be greater than average. The implications of this for the way in which the oceans circulate and transfer heat are unclear. What is clear is that any increase in the surface temperature of the oceans will increase the rate of evaporation and hence cloud formation. This will in turn affect global surface temperatures because clouds and water vapour in the atmosphere trap heat.

Some scenarios of future climates suggest that the frequency and intensity of hurricanes and tropical storms may increase as a consequence of warming of the sea surface. In addition, it seems likely that the areas in which tropical storms are generated will shift and possibly even expand as a consequence of the expansion of the tropical and subtropical realms.

Given the important role of the oceans in transporting heat around the globe, any changes in sea surface temperature as a consequence of global warming can be expected to alter the existing balance between the oceans and the atmosphere, which in turn may alter ocean current patterns at least on local and medium scales. However, if significant melting of polar icecaps were to occur (an unlikely event on the basis of present models) then this would alter the salinity and hence density of the seawater in these regions. This, for example, could lead to extensive changes to the circulation patterns of the North Atlantic, with dramatic effects on the climate of western Europe.

Several coastal ecosystems are likely to suffer considerably as a consequence of predicted changes, particularly coral reefs, mangroves and salt marshes. Such changes may have significant consequences for marine biodiversity, particularly if widespread changes to coral reef systems occur. Coral reefs are extremely diverse marine communities, equivalent in biological terms to tropical rainforests as sources of species, genetic and habitat diversity.

If global warming is taking place, then there is a possibility that the Antarctic icecap (left) could begin to melt. As 80 per cent of the world's ice is locked into this icecap at present, even a partial melting would have major consequences on the sea level. However, there is conflicting evidence that global warming might result in increased snowfall over Antarctica, which could increase the size of the icecap.

In 1988, 60 per cent of Bangladesh was flooded (above) as the Ganges and Brahmaputra once again broke their banks following monsoon rains, depositing tonnes of silt in their deltas. At the moment it is this sediment, in some places 5 km (3 miles) thick, that keeps large parts of Bangladesh above sea level. But if the sea level were to rise, Bangladesh and many other low-lying areas would be inundated, and if monsoon patterns were to change then the effect on countries in the monsoon belt could be dramatic.

The Living Seas

A nimals and plants which live in the sea display remarkable adaptions for living, breathing, moving, communicating and reproducing under water. Adaptations reflect conditions which vary from the warmth and calm of the Mediterranean to the icy and turbulent waters of the South Atlantic; and from the shallows of the coastal zones to extremes of pressure in the total darkness of the great ocean abysses. Regions where waters well up from the deeps are rich in nutrients which fuel the food chain and can support large numbers of plants and animals, while much of the surface of the open ocean is relatively barren. Whatever its position in the food chain, every species is, in its own way, fighting to survive.

Eel grasses grow on fine sediments which are easily disturbed by a passing lobster.

Biodiversity: Plants and Lower Animals

Biodiversity is a complex concept which means different things to different people. Most simply it can be interpreted as the numbers of species occurring in a particular area – the greater the number of species, the greater the diversity. More recently, biodiversity has been used to describe the extent of genetic variability present in a given community or population.

The number of species found in the oceans is generally considered to be less than that on land. This is partly because the most numerous group of land animals, the insects, are, with the exception of a few specialists such as water striders, absent from marine habitats, and partly because the seas provide an inhospitable environment for higher plants which dominate the land. The environmental stability of the deep oceans results in many species having wide geographic distributions, and animals are easily dispersed over long distances by major current systems. However, if the numbers of major taxa are considered, diversity is greater in the marine environment since several groups of animals are only found there.

Simple organisms, algae and higher plants

Single-celled organisms, both dinoflagellates and diatoms, are diverse and important in the marine environment, forming the basis for much of the primary production. When diatoms die, their silica shells sink to the bottom and accumulate as diatom oozes covering vast areas of the ocean floor. Some species of dinoflagellate are symbiotic, some are toxic causing red tides, while others luminesce at night. The single-celled radiolaria have silicaceous shells of extraordinary beauty, while the foraminifera have skeletons of calcium carbonate or build shells of sand grains, they are so small that in a single gram of ooze there may be as many as 50,000 skeletons.

The blue-green algae are among the simplest forms of life on the planet and are the oldest plant-like organisms that still exist. They are widely distributed and are found from the upper reaches of tidal areas to the subtidal environment as members of the bottom-dwelling community. The higher algae – the green, brown and red seaweeds – reach their greatest diversity and largest size in surface waters. They range from small, green filamentous forms which grow as an algal turf in shallow water to the large, strap-like beds of kelp at depths of 12 to 15 metres (40-50 feet). The green algae, which can withstand high light intensities, tend to dominate the higher intertidal, with brown seaweeds occurring from the mid-tidal to the subtidal, and the reds being found as deep as 180 metres (600 feet) or more below the surface. Coralline forms of red algae are important in cementing together loose fragments on coral reef flats.

The typical flowering plants found on land are confined to the margins of the seas because of the salinity. Higher plants need specializations for removing excess salt, conserving freshwater and breathing in the anoxic, waterlogged soils characteristic of aquatic habitats. The mangroves and sea grasses have also developed vivipary (see pp. 156-157), apparently as a mechanism to ensure survival of the seedlings in this hostile environment. Because of the paucity of higher plants in the marine environment, the basis for life in the oceans is quite different from that on land (see pp. 50-51).

Primitive animals, corals, anemones and jellyfish

With the exception of a few freshwater species, the sponges and cnidarians (corals, anemones and jellyfish) are confined to the marine environment.

Sponges, which represent the simplest of all multicellular animals, are little more than colonies of individual cells, although there is some development of differences in function between individual cells within the body of the animal.

In the case of the cnidaria the body form is simple, consisting of two major tissues separated by a non-cellular layer. Each individual is basically a tube-like animal with a central, dorsal mouth, surrounded by a ring of tentacles which carry the diagnostic stinging cells or nematocysts used to immobilize small planktonic prey. The Hydrozoa, a group which contains a few freshwater species, demonstrates another peculiarity, the alteration of generations in which the plant-like polyp generation produces medusae, small jellyfish which reproduce sexually to produce another generation of polyps. The Scyphozoa or true jellyfish have suppressed the plant-like generation, and the free-swimming medusoid stage is most important. These animals range from tiny forms to *Cyanea*, the large arctic jellyfish, which can grow up to 2.5 metres (8.2 feet) in diameter with tentacles up to 20 metres (65 feet) long. In the Anthozoa, the medusoid generation has been completely lost, and polyps may be solitary as in sea anemones or colonial as in corals, sea whips and sea fans. Of the colonial forms, reef-building corals have a skeleton of calcium carbonate, while black corals, sea fans and whips have one made of horn.

The ctenophores or comb jellies are a small phylum of around 100 species which are exclusively marine. They may be barrel-shaped or flattened, and like some jellyfish a number possess long tentacles with sticky pads for entrapping prey. Confined to surface waters, these animals feed on fish fry and other small planktonic animals.

The bladder wrack (Fucus vesiculosus) (above) is a common sight on northern temperate shores where algae are the main primary producers. This photograph shows the reproductive bodies at the ends of the fronds, while below them can be seen the smooth, gas-filled bladders which buoy the fronds in the water when the tide comes in.

The Mediterranean jellyfish (Cotylorhiza tuberculata) (right) is a representative of the widespread and diverse group of cnidarians, which includes the corals and sea anemones. In the Scyphozoa or true jellyfish the floating medusa is the dominant life form, and capable of moving through the water by means of contractions of its umbrella-shaped body.

Biodiversity: "Worms", Arthropods and Starfish

The flatworms or Platyhelminthes include both parasitic and free-living forms which are frequently carnivorous, feeding on worms, crustaceans and molluscs. Their body form is rather curious, being flattened and leaf-like, and they creep over the bottom or sometimes swim by flapping the edge of their bodies. Another group of odd, worm-like animals, which is exclusively marine, is the Nemertea or bootlace worms which may reach six metres (20 feet) in length and are all carnivorous. They have a habit of tying themselves in knots when handled, and are fragile, breaking into shorter lengths each of which is capable of growing into a complete new worm.

The bristle worms or annelids are so called because they posses small bristles used in locomotion. They may be active swimmers, burrowers, or live a sedentary life in secreted tubes. Bristle worms are much more complex than other worm-like animals in that they have blood, a circulatory system, and segmented bodies which help with locomotion.

Crabs, lobsters and their allies

The Arthropoda or "jointed-foot" animals include the familiar terrestrial insects along with the crabs, shrimps, lobsters, barnacles and many planktonic groups in the marine environment. There are no myriapods, centipedes or millipedes in the sea, while the arachnids (spiders and mites), like the insects, have only a few marine species.

The crustaceans include animals such as crabs and lobsters whose jointed limbs provide a wider variety of locomotory adaptations and possibilities than does the worm-like body form of lower animals. The ostracods, a group of small planktonic forms, lack segmentation of the body and are enclosed in a two-part carapace or shell. Copepods or "oar-footed" crustaceans are another group of small planktonic forms, which despite their small size are important in marine food chains because they are the main consumers of diatoms, and themselves are an important food source for higher animals such as herring. Two other groups of somewhat larger size than ostracods and copepods are the amphipods or sand hoppers, and the isopods or sea slaters. Both amphipods and isopods carry their young in brood chambers rather than releasing their eggs into the sea.

The barnacles or Cirripedia do not look much like typical crustaceans as adults, although the young are free-swimming. Adult goose-necked barnacles are attached by means of a leathery stalk, and acorn or rock barnacles attach directly onto solid surfaces. These animals feed using modified limbs with long feathery attachments which waft water and food particles into the chamber within the exoskeleton.

Sea urchins, starfish and other oddities

The echinoderms are a widespread, abundant and exclusively marine group of animals, and include the sea urchins, starfishes, brittle stars, feather stars, sea cucumbers and sea lilies. They are characterized by a five-rayed symmetry and a complex water vascular system to which the tube feet are connected. Each fluid-filled tube foot has a small sucker disc at its end for attaching to a surface, and the combined action of many small tube feet serves to pull the animal along the bottom.

This group exhibits a wide variety of feeding methods and life styles, with burrowers, crawlers and even swimmers, which graze on plants, filter feed on plankton, or prey on molluscs and corals.

In addition to these more familiar groups the marine environment contains a number of minor phyla, containing few species confined to marine habitats: the Lophophorates and Bryozoa, two groups of small, encrusting animals which live in secreted, protective shells or burrows and filter feed; the tardigrades or "bear animals", small or microscopic organisms with simple limbs; the predatory chaetognaths or arrow worms, which live in the plankton, and sipunculid worms, a curious group of largely worm-like, burrowing animals which have an eversible proboscis used in feeding.

Of the echinoderms, the starfishes represented here by Henricia oculata (left) *exhibit most clearly the five-rayed symmetry typical of the group. The mouth is located at the centre of the arms, and it is possible to see the tube feet that line the underside of each arm and are used for locomotion. All echinoderms possess a skeleton made of plates of calcium carbonate which is rigid in the sea urchins but flexible in the other groups.*

The true marine worms or annelids include tube-building animals (above) *such as this featherduster worm photographed in the Red Sea.*

Horseshoe crabs (far left) *are primitive members of the very diverse group of jointed-foot animals, the arthropods. They are predators feeding on small clams, worms and other marine organisms.*

Biodiversity: Molluscs, Sharks and Bony Fish

Apart from the echinoderms, the other diverse and widespread marine group are the molluscs, which because of their beautifully coloured and intricately shaped shells are probably the best-known group of marine invertebrates. The snail-like gastropods creep along the bottom, burrow, or like *Ianthina* float in the open ocean. Their radula or strap-like tooth plate may be modified for rasping algae, or for attacking and piercing the harder skeletons of prey. In contrast, the bivalves, with shells consisting of two valves, are less active, either attaching to the bottom or burrowing in various substrates, and filter feed. The third group of molluscs includes squid, cuttlefish and octopus, which are predators, swimming, crawling and displaying advanced reproductive patterns including the production of a few, large eggs which may be brooded by the parent. The giant squid is the largest of all living invertebrates, and the largest recorded specimen came from Newfoundland and measured 17 metres (56 feet) in length including the tentacles. The scaphopods or tusk shells burrow in sandy areas or swim in the plankton, and the Amphineura or mail shells creep over rock surfaces in the intertidal zone.

The tunicates are represented in the intertidal zone by the sea squirts, which show affinity in their larval stages with higher animals, possessing a primitive notochord in place of a backbone. The larva resembles a tadpole, and when it settles it resorbs its tail, loses the notochord and turns into the sac-like adult.

The cephalochordates or lancets are a small group of eel-like animals which burrow into sandy areas in the lower intertidal and subtidal zones. Lacking jaws and a well-developed head, they filter feed using a complex gill system. The hagfishes, marine relatives of the freshwater lamprey, resemble eels but like the lancet lack jaws, feeding on dead and decaying animals by means of a funnel-shaped structure.

The sharks, skates and rays although quite diverse in body form are relatively few in number in comparison with the more successful bony fishes. Most are active swimmers, although some rest on the bottom for extended periods. Some species feed on plankton, others on molluscs, while the predatory sharks feed on other vertebrates. The well-developed teeth of these animals are continuously replaced from behind, moving forward as those in front are lost or broken.

The bony fishes are found in all marine habitats and pursue an amazing range of life styles. They owe their success to the development of an internal gas bladder, which is used in buoyancy control (see pp. 48-49), and modification to the shape and position of their fins, which fit them exquisitely for different modes of swimming. Bony fishes have adapted for feeding on almost every conceivable food source with jaws and teeth to match.

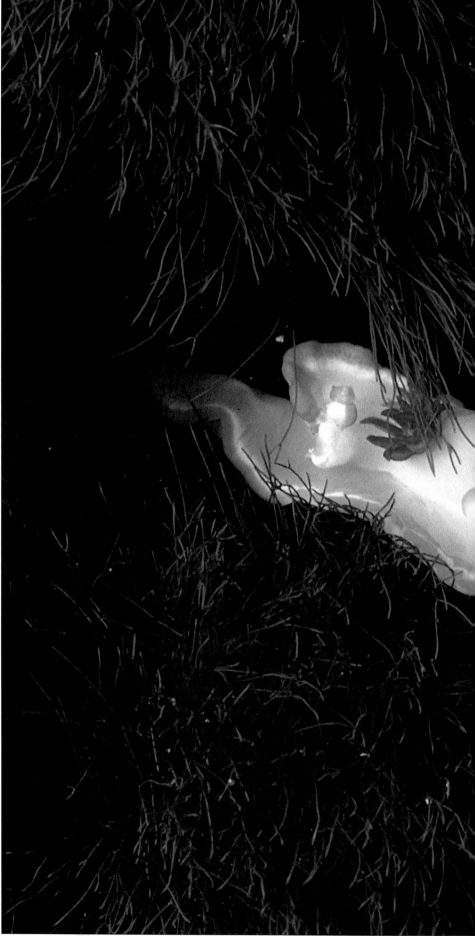

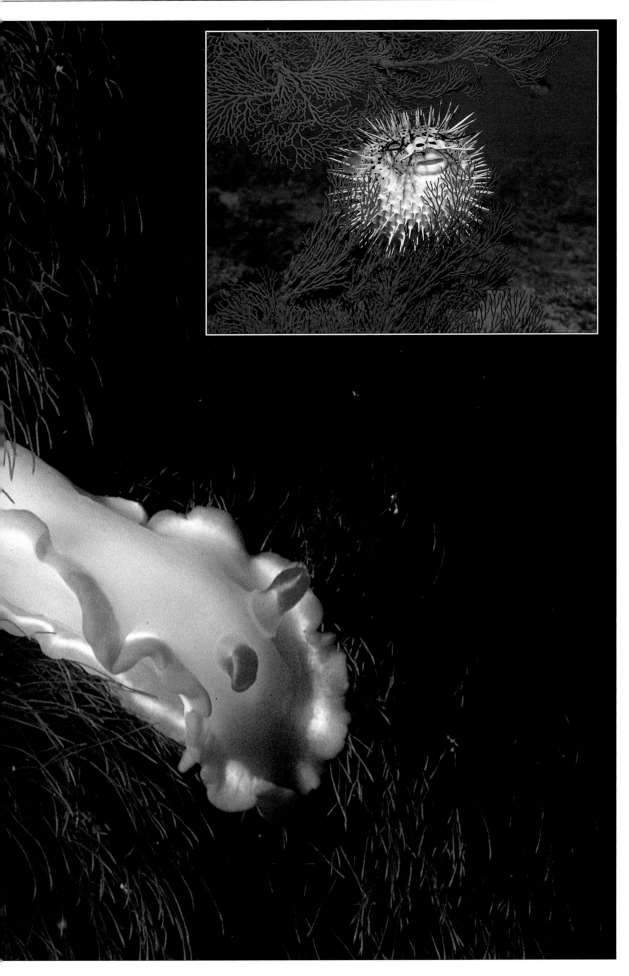

The spiny pufferfishes (inset) are members of the widespread and very diverse group of bony fishes. The outside of the animal is armed with spines, and when disturbed it swells to form a prickly ball. Pufferfishes generally swim rather slowly and the paired fins are important in maintaining their position against currents, in braking and in changing direction. The rayed fins of bony fishes are a major advance on the fleshy, lobed fins of sharks and rays, and together with the evolution of the gas bladder have contributed much to the success of these animals.

This nudibranch (Casella sp.) (main picture) or naked-gilled sea slug is a mollusc that has no shell. The red-brown tuft of tentacle-like appendages, partially hidden by the algae on which the sea slug is feeding, are the animal's external gills. Nudibranchs are among the most colourful of the molluscs, reaching their greatest diversity in tropical waters. Many of these animals are distasteful and their bright colours serve to warn potential predators from eating them.

Eagle rays (Aetobatus nurinari) (far left) have skeletons made of cartilage to reduce their weight. The long tail is armed with razor-sharp, tooth-like structures for defence, and is less important in swimming than the tails of sharks or bony fishes. Rays swim by means of enlarged pectoral fins which form "wings" along the sides of the animal's body.

Biodiversity and Distribution

In contrast to the fish, marine mammals and reptiles are much less diverse, representing as they do groups of land animals which have readapted to the sea. Even the whales and seals with their superb adaptations to swimming and diving must return to the surface to breath. The toothed, predatory species such as killer whales feed on seals, while the baleen whales feed on krill and microscopic crustaceans. In general, seals and sea lions are fish predators, though some, such as the walrus, feed on molluscs. Manatees and dugongs graze on sea grasses.

Marine reptiles include the turtles, which like seals return to land to reproduce. The saltwater crocodile, a resident of the tropical mangrove swamps of South-East Asia, northern Australia and the larger islands of the western Pacific, is strictly coastal although dispersing individuals may cross open water. The sea snakes are well adapted to a marine existence, with flattened, paddle-shaped tails for swimming. Most give birth to live young at sea. These highly venomous animals are mainly predators of fish and fish eggs.

Seabirds, although they derive their food from the sea, and in some cases such as penguins are well adapted for swimming under water, are much more tied to land and air than other marine vertebrates. Feathers do not provide good insulation in water, and when wet the animals have difficulty in flying. Oil glands are used during preening to provide a water-proofing to the feathers.

Patterns of distribution

However one interprets its meaning, the diversity of marine life is distributed about the oceans in ways that are to some extent comparable to those seen on land, but with significant differences. Marine plants, in contrast to those on land, are generally small, uni-cellular organisms whose growth and reproduction are limited by the availability of nitrogen, phosphorus and in some instances silica. Therefore in general

Manatees (Trichechis sp.) *(above) belong to the* Sirenia, *a small group of herbivorous marine mammals adapted for feeding on sea grasses in shallow tropical and subtropical waters. Their slow breeding rate makes them susceptible to over-hunting.*

Seabirds such as these puffins (Fratercula arctica) *(right), which winter at sea, return each year to land to breed on cliffs and rocky coasts. They care for their young in underground nests, bringing beakfulls of food including sand eels for their offspring.*

the open oceans contain fewer species than coastal areas, where some larger plants and algae provide a higher rate of productivity, being supplied with nutrients from the land. Patterns of diversity in the sea tend to show high numbers of species on the coastal margins and continental shelves, with progressively fewer species as one passes into the open ocean. Similarly, diversity tends to decline with depth.

Many pelagic species range widely within ocean basins, and the communities of species do not fall into the clearly defined, latitudinal zones which can be recognized on land. In contrast, the distribution of benthic communities reflects the nature of the substrate, and given the small variations in temperature at depth benthic species also show little latitudinal difference in their distribution. Coastal communities on the other hand, particularly those located in the intertidal and subtidal zones, display characteristic latitudinal patterns of distribution analogous to those on land. Thus coral reefs and mangrove swamps, typical of tropical and subtropical shores, are highly diverse communities, containing far more species than comparable rocky shores and salt marshes in temperate regions. Nevertheless, a typical mangrove community is far less diverse in terms of the number of plant species than an inland rainforest.

The full range of species diversity in the seas is not yet described, as each year more and more species are discovered. The range of genetic diversity is high in marine organisms, largely because individual species have enormous populations, which allows for the development of genetic differences on a regional and subregional scale. For example, many tuna species have recognizable, genetically different races or subpopulations. The genetic variation present in such populations may provide considerable potential in the fields of biotechnology and pharmacology.

The marine turtles (above) are well adapted to life in the sea, having modified the forelimbs as powerful flippers, which move under water in much the same way as a bird's wings move through air. The body of the animal is encased in a bony carapace, which is streamlined and covered by the horny scutes which are used to produce tortoiseshell jewellery. This photograph of a green turtle (Chelonia mydas) shows the powerful beak which replaces teeth in these animals. All living marine turtles are considered endangered or vulnerable, because both eggs and adults are harvested for food in many parts of the world.

Life Styles

From tiny animals creeping between grains of sand to the large active predators travelling over enormous distances, the diversity of life forms and life styles in marine environments is enormous. Despite this diversity, one common feature of many marine life cycles is that on hatching from the egg, the young bear little resemblance to their parents. These larval forms feed, move and live quite differently from their parents, and usually pass through a number of different stages as they grow. Through the dispersal of the larvae marine species expand their distribution.

Larval life styles

The differences between larva and adult are well illustrated by the lowly sea squirts, sac-like animals which as adults live attached to rocks feeding by filtering food from the water (see pp. 50-51). Once settled, an adult sea squirt is incapable of movement, unlike its larva which resembles a tiny tadpole. Many fish also display exotic larval forms, and when first encountered by scientists the flattened larvae of eels were considered a separate species (*Leptocephalus* sp.). In some cases the larvae of quite different species look alike: the first-stage larva of a sea urchin is indistinguishable from that of a starfish.

Most larvae spend their lives in the plankton and some feed on phytoplankton or zooplankton, growing in size over several months. They are usually small and produced in large numbers: the edible mussel *Mytilus edulis* produces up to 12 million eggs at a single spawning. If there is enough food and the ocean currents bring the mature larvae into suitable areas, then large numbers settle and mature into adults. The size of the adult population in any one area fluctuates in response to larval survival. In other species, the larvae may spend only a few days in the plankton; while others never feed, instead relying on large yolk reserves provided by the parent. In such species the main purpose of the larvae is dispersal.

Adult life styles

Following metamorphosis, the adult form and life style reflect the modes of movement, feeding and reproduction which each species adopts to fit it for particular habitats and roles within the marine community. Active swimmers and predators have limbs and bodies adapted for rapid movement, making them independent of currents (see pp. 48-49). Bottom-dwelling animals are attached or tend to move more slowly, creeping, crawling or walking along the bottom to scavenge dead materials or graze on algae and sea grasses in shallow waters. The snail-like gastropod molluscs have a muscular foot for this purpose, while many bivalves use the foot for burrowing into soft sediments. Burrowers may move through the sand or mud, "eating" the substrate (see pp. 64-65). Others construct permanent burrows, sticking their heads above the surface to catch food suspended in the water, or sweeping up food from the bottom. Yet others move water through their burrows by rhythmic body movements, the current serving to aerate the burrow and bring food to the animal.

Predators such as barracuda and squid may actively search for their prey, while others such as the angler fishes sit and wait for prey to come within reach. Slowly moving snails such as *Chicoreus* in the tropics and *Nucella* in temperate zones creep over rocky areas in search of other molluscs to eat. Once an oyster such as *Crassostrea* or a clam such as *Spondylus* has been located, *Chicoreus brunneus* drills a small hole in one valve to digest the animal

This delicate colonial sea squirt Podoclavella molucensis *(right) remains attached to the underside of rocks as an adult. It passes a water current through its body from which it strains out food particles by means of a delicate basket-like structure and strands of sticky mucus. The larvae of these animals are active swimmers in the plankton before they settle out to take up their adult life style.*

In the Sargasso Sea (above), *camouflage is used by a number of species, including the fish* Histrio histrio *and a sea anemone, to allow them to conceal their presence in the surrounding sargassum weed. This weed forms floating mats which serve as hiding places for many animals and plants, producing diverse communities, quite different from the surrounding ocean where there are no places to hide from predators.*

whole. Predatory starfish tackle the problem of closed bivalves by pulling the two valves apart, then everting their stomachs to digest their prey. Some scallops detect these starfish through chemical stimuli and "swim" away by clapping their valves together.

Avoiding being eaten leads to many different behaviour and colour patterns, with some animals being active at night to avoid daytime predators, while others are camouflaged to conceal their presence. In contrast, poisonous animals often advertise their toxicity with brilliant colours.

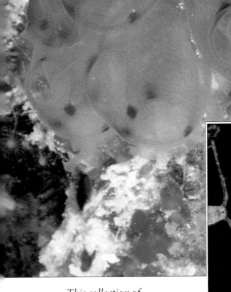

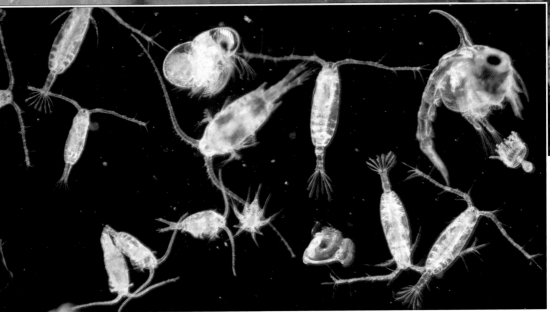

This collection of zooplankton (right) includes small crustaceans, the larvae of barnacles, crabs and bryozoans, and the medusoid stage of Obelia, *a small colonial cnidarian which spends its adult life attached to the bottom. Many marine animals have planktonic larval stages for dispersal and colonization of new areas.*

Underwater Signals

The underwater world is filled with sound, from the haunting "songs" of whales to the metallic clicks, snaps and rasping sounds of crustaceans, and the drumming, growls, grunts, snorts and hissing noises produced by various fish. Communication in the marine environment is complex and difficult, reflecting the problems of sending and receiving signals in the watery medium. Although water transmits sound much farther and five times more quickly than air, other forms of communication are more difficult. Because light is scattered and absorbed in the upper layers of the oceans, the depths are dark and visual signals are best developed by animals which live close to the surface. The bright colour patterns and displays of shallow water animals are designed to send signals to attract mates, warn off predators, defend territories or attract potential prey.

Chemical communication is well developed in marine animals, and many invertebrates have special receptors that enable them to detect potential food or predators at considerable distances. As on land, marine animals naturally exude a variety of chemicals. For example, the characteristic "smell" of a predatory starfish causes scallops on which it feeds to clap their valves together and "swim" away. But chemical signals are perhaps most important in reproduction, particularly among sedentary bottom-living species. In these animals fertilization is external and the eggs and sperm are quickly diluted in the sea. The more members of a species that release their eggs and sperm at the same time, the higher the rate of successful fertilization and hence the need for chemical signals to synchronize the process.

Detecting the signals

Because water differs in its physical properties from air, marine animals have evolved different kinds of sense organs from those of land animals. Organs similar to ears are generally not well developed. Crustaceans may "hear" through specially modified bristles on their antennae, while bony fish use their swim bladders as sounding boards for transmission of incoming signals to the brain and nervous system through a complex chain of small bones.

The production of sound signals involves other adaptations, and some fish such as the tropical drums (*Sciaenidae*) make drumming noises by vibrating the stretched swim bladder using special muscles attached to the backbone. Crabs and lobsters rasp their claws together or against their bodies, and while foraging, lobsters may keep up a continuous stream of signals to nearby individuals. On the approach of a predator, they can produce a higher frequency alarm signal whereupon the entire group moves under cover.

Fish have a line of sense organs along their flanks for detecting changes in pressure, temperature and even in some cases the chemical composition of the water surrounding them. Pressure waves from nearby individuals may serve to assist members of a school of fish to remain together, while small electrical charges built up through the contraction of muscles may indicate the presence of potential prey to a waiting predator. Many molluscs possess small, light-receptive cells in their mantles which enable them to detect the shadow of an advancing predator, and quickly close their shells to avoid predation.

Visual signals are only useful for animals with eyes and so are best developed in fish and cephalopods (squid, cuttlefish and octopus). These include brilliant colour patterns which can be changed to signal changes of "mood" or, in combination with particular

The "songs" of the humpback whale (Megaptera novaeangliae) (right) are one of the most intriguing of underwater signals. They consist of long sequences of moans, groans, roars, squeaks and chirps, combined into themes, which are then repeated in specific sequences. The humpbacks of a particular area have their own characteristic song, a kind of dialect. Only males sing, during the breeding season and occasionally on migration. Once a male has attracted a female he becomes silent. Thus, singing appears to be designed to attract a female, but why all the males in an area should sing the same song is a mystery. Many other cetaceans use sound to communicate, and with some it has been taken to quite extraordinary extremes. The loudest sound of all is produced by the blue whale (Balaenoptera musculus) – 188 decibels – which is many thousands of times louder than a jumbo jet taking off. The most far-reaching sound is produced by the fin whale (B. physalus). By using deep-water channels at around 1,500 m (4,900 ft) – the result of differences in water density, which act like a sound pipe – their low-frequency pulses can be heard as far as 800 km (500 miles) away.

As a jet of sperm is released into the water from this sponge (left), it also releases chemicals along with the sperm that act as a signal, stimulating all the other members of the species within range to spawn. By synchronizing spawning over a wide area in this way, the sponge maximizes its chances of successful fertilization.

Many deep-sea fish, including Sloane's viperfish (Chauliodus sloanei) (right), have small light-producing organs, called photophores, along their flanks and heads. These serve a variety of functions, from the attraction of prey and recognition of sex to species identification. Each species is distinguished by a different pattern of photophores, which in some cases can be switched on and off at will.

The cuttlefish (below) *can continuously alter the colour patterns in its skin, with rhythmic waves of different colours pulsing over the surface or flashing like tiny jewels. One kind of pigment cell in the skin, the iridiocytes, contains light-reflecting crystals, causing varying degrees of iridescence.*

Displays can reflect the animal's "emotions": it will flush with colour if confronted with a potential mate, when disturbed or threatened, or at the sight of food. Highly complex colour changes occur when two or more of these creatures are together, suggesting that communication is taking place.

swimming patterns, may signal to a female that a male is ready to mate. Even at depth, where sunlight does not penetrate, many species of animals have eyes or light-detecting organs because they themselves produce light which is used for signalling to other members of the same species.

Colour patterns may also signal to potential predators that an animal is poisonous or dangerous; thus the scorpion fish (*Pterois volitans*) with its brilliantly coloured red-and-white striped pectoral fins warns other animals that it possesses highly toxic spines. The angler fish (*Phrynelox scaber*) uses a specially modified, brightly coloured worm-like structure on its head to attract unsuspecting smaller fish. When the small fish attempts to eat the "worm", it is itself eaten by the angler fish which uses the signal "food" to lure its own prey within reach.

An animal's colour pattern may also provide a different kind of signal, as in the case of the blue-and-black striped cleaner wrasse (*Labroides dimidiatus*) of tropical coral reefs. These small fish establish individual territories near a suitable coral head and swim in a characteristic undulating pattern. The bright colour and peculiar swimming motion signal to all kinds of larger fish, including many predators, that this is a cleaner fish. They visit the cleaner fish, which as its name suggests cleans the visitor, removing any parasites, fungi and loose or damaged pieces of skin. While being cleaned, predatory fish remain docile, making no move to attack the cleaner which even moves in and out of its mouth with impunity. These signals of the cleaner wrasse are however copied by another small fish, *Aspidontus taeniatus*, with a similar colour pattern and swimming behaviour. When an unsuspecting fish comes towards this sabre-toothed blenny to be cleaned the blenny darts forward, bites off a scale and retreats rapidly to its refuge. The visiting fish is fooled by the colour pattern and behaviour, signals that it normally associates with the cleaner fish.

Swimming

For marine animals, the density of water provides both advantages and disadvantages: land animals need strong limbs in order to support their weight, but water helps to prevent marine organisms from sinking; on the other hand, water also provides resistance to forward movement. As a result, marine animals have evolved various mechanisms to overcome the difficulties of movement and to use the support provided by water to their advantage.

Flotation and buoyancy

For the most part, marine animals do not require "limbs" to support themselves in water. The only exceptions are a few bottom-dwelling fish whose fins have been modified to support the body. Many marine organisms possess internal mechanisms to adjust their density to that of the surrounding water, so that they neither float nor sink. Such neutral buoyancy means that the animal does not have to use up energy to hold its position in the water column. Many bony fishes can adjust their buoyancy by means of an internal bladder filled with gas. As a fish swims towards the surface, the gas expands, reducing the animal's density and forcing it to rise faster. The

fish counters this and maintains its position by absorbing gas from the bladder. When it swims downwards, increased pressure causes the bladder's volume to shrink. This increases the density of the fish and causes it to sink. By secreting more gas into the bladder the fish increases its volume, and thereby stabilizes its movement.

Many floating animals, such as molluscs and even seaweeds, have gas-filled bladders which keep them at the surface. For colonial jellyfish such as the Portuguese man-of-war (*Physalia physalis*), the bladder also serves as a sail. Sharks, which have no gas bladders, must swim continuously to avoid sinking; they also store oil to reduce their density. Small creatures such as plankton have extremely long limbs and other feathery appendages which, when expanded, increase the animal's surface area and slow the rate of sinking.

Movement and swimming

To reduce the resistance exerted by the water, active marine organisms have developed a streamlined shape. This shape presents the minimum resistance to the water, but more importantly it allows the water to flow past the animal's surface in a smooth and uninterrupted pattern. Projections from the animal's skin would slow it down, since these create resistance and set up small counter-currents.

The power for forward movement comes from muscle contractions. Perhaps the simplest form of movement in water is shown by worms, eels and sea snakes, which use the muscles on each side of the body to bend the animal into a series of curves. Water resistance to this movement results in both a forward thrust and a sideways movement, so that the animal's head moves from side to side as it swims.

Side-to-side movement wastes much of the energy used in muscle contraction. In more advanced fish, movement is restricted to the animal's tail. In advanced bony fish, the tail, or caudal fin, has lobes of equal size above and below the mid-line of the body, which, unlike a shark's tail, provides no upthrust, since these fish can maintain neutral buoyancy by means of their gas bladders. The massive flukes of the whale are used in the same way as the tails of advanced fish, except that the whale's tail is horizontal, while that of a fish is vertical.

Limbs and fins

The fins of swimming animals are used to maintain stability and to change direction. The dorsal and anal fins counter rolling movements as a fish moves through the water; the paired fins at the front of the body, known as pectorals, and the rear or pelvic fins, counter rocking movements and help to steer the animal. Many fish also use their paired fins to provide forward thrust. Animals such as turtles, whose bodies are sheathed in a rigid carapace or shell, depend entirely on their paddle-shaped forelimbs to propel them through the water.

Like starfish and sea cucumbers, sea urchins (far left) have specially adapted tube feet for locomotion. Each small tube forms part of the fluid-filled, water vascular system, and is connected to a sac-like structure inside the skeleton. When the sac contracts, fluid is forced into the foot which extends and attaches to the bottom. Muscles in the foot then contract, forcing water back into the internal sac and the foot shortens, pulling the animal along the ground.

Cuttlefish and squid often school (inset) in surface waters, swimming by gentle undulations of their fins. If attacked by predators, they are capable of jet propulsion. Water in the body cavity is expelled through a siphon situated below the tentacles, forcing the animal backwards at high speed.

Open-water sharks (main picture) are designed for swimming. Unlike many other marine organisms which can maintain their vertical position in the water without moving because of their neutral buoyancy, sharks must swim constantly or else they will sink since they are denser than water. This tendency to sink is countered by the shape of the shark's tail, which provides an upward thrust as well as the power for forward movement. As the tail moves from side to side it rises in the water, forcing the head downwards. To maintain a horizontal position, the front fins act as inclined planes, driving the head up as the animal moves through the water. The dorsal fin provides stability by reducing the tendency to roll, and the shape of body is streamlined to reduce water turbulence and resistance.

Feeding and Food Webs

The basis for all life is the energy of the Sun which is converted into chemical energy by photosynthetic plants. Herbivorous animals eat these plants and transform the energy gained from this food into their own tissues as part of their growth. They are in turn eaten by carnivorous animals, while undigested food, faeces, and dead organisms form an energy source for the decomposers, which in the marine environment are largely concentrated at the bottom of the oceans.

A major difference between these processes on land and in the sea is the size of individual plants. On land, single large plants such as trees store considerable quantities of energy, forming a food source for many smaller animals of different species. In contrast, over much of the ocean the Sun's energy is trapped by microscopic plants or phytoplankton, which are short-lived. At any one time the weight of these marine plants present in a particular area is less than that of the zooplankton which feed on them. However, the amount of energy trapped by the phytoplankton over a year is considerably more than the increase in the energy stored in the zooplankton over the same period. This results from the rapid turnover of the phytoplankton, which live for only a few days, compared with the zooplankton which grow and reproduce more slowly. The larger carnivores which eat the zooplankton are much longer-lived, and store their energy as growth in individuals over several years.

When an animal feeds, some of the energy gained is used in movement, expended as heat in the process of respiration, and some of the food is undigested and so the potential energy is passed out in the form of faeces. In this way, at each stage of the food chain less energy becomes available to the animals higher up. As a consequence, there are fewer animals near the top, and large marine organisms such as whales and predatory fish must move over considerable distances in search of food (see pp. 54-55). The number of species also decreases higher up a food chain.

Feeding strategies

Different methods of feeding reflect other aspects of the organism's life style. Active open ocean species hunt and chase smaller, living prey, while more sedentary bottom-dwelling species may sit and wait for prey to come within reach. The development of structures to capture, hold and immobilize different kinds of prey reflects both the form of the prey itself and the relative size of prey and predator. In active predators feeding on large prey well-developed teeth or sharp piercing mouthparts are needed. Where a large predator feeds on smaller prey, teeth may be unnecessary and the prey may be swallowed whole.

One mode of feeding which is widespread in the marine environment is filter feeding, where the animal uses special modifications for trapping small food particles in the water. In some sedentary, filter-feeding animals such as sponges and sea squirts water currents are set up by fine, hair-like structures, the cilia, which draw water and suspended food particles through the body cavity. Food is trapped by net-like structures and mucus in the sea squirts, while the

This unusual view (top right) *of the underside of the sea urchin* Strongylocentrotus franciscanus *shows the five teeth it uses to graze on its algal food. The teeth are supported inside the animal's skeleton by means of a framework of small structures called the* Aristotle's lantern. *Each tooth can be individually moved in and out. Surrounding the mouth there are the spines which are used to aid movement and small three-toothed structures which help to keep the animal free of settling plankton.*

water passes back out. Feather stars have long arms which are held in a cone into which mucus threads are produced forming a net. This net traps food as the water currents move through the arms, and small tube feet then move the mucus strands and trapped food towards the mouth. Barnacles have long, arm-like appendages which are moved in and out to waft food particles towards the mouth, a form of filter feeding used by many crustaceans and some fan worms.

To aid in filter feeding, a crown of tentacles surrounds the mouth of many corals and coral-like animals which may possess special stinging cells that immobilize small zooplankton. When trapped the plankton are transferred to the central mouth by the tentacles. Even larger animals such as some whales filter feed, and the special baleen plates of whales that feed on krill serve to trap their food while the water passes through. Some fish behave in a similar way, with special projections on the inside of the gills, the gill rakers, to trap plankton in the mouth before they are swallowed. Other animals such as sea cucumbers, worms and some crustaceans use modified feeding tentacles or mouthparts to sweep small food particles from the surface of the sand or mud.

Featherduster worms (above) live in tubes in soft-bottomed areas, extending their feathery arms out to filter food particles brought by water currents. When disturbed, the animals can retract rapidly inside their tubes, slowly appearing again when the danger has passed. These are true worms or annelids, related to lugworms, which burrow more actively through the substrate, and bristle worms, which crawl along the bottom.

*This grey whale (*Eschrichtius glaucus*) (left) is feeding in a kelp bed off the coast of Baja California, using its baleen plates to strain planktonic food from the water. Baleen plates replace the teeth in these whales and are made of horny material with a fringe of fine strands which act as a net, filtering out the plankton. The Californian population undertakes annual migrations of more than 9,000 km (5,600 miles) from its winter calving grounds off Baja California to its summer feeding grounds in the Bering Straits.*

Reproduction

One of the driving forces behind all forms of life is the maintenance of the population and species. Failure to reproduce successfully results in extinction, and different organisms have evolved a variety of strategies to ensure their survival. These strategies involve communication between the sexes (see pp. 46-47), mechanisms to ensure fertilization, development and metamorphosis from larva to adult, and a wide range of adaptations to ensure dispersal and colonization of suitable habitats (see pp. 54-55).

Two basic reproductive strategies characterize marine animals. Some species expend a considerable amount of energy in producing many millions of small eggs of which a few will survive to reproduce; others concentrate the same energy into fewer, larger eggs which increases the risks of egg predation, but also improves the chances of each individual larva surviving by providing it with a larger store of yolk, and making it less dependent on the plankton for food. These two strategies reflect the fact that mortality rates are generally much higher during egg and larval stages than for older individuals.

Marine organisms also have the problem of ensuring successful fertilization of eggs which are released into the open water environment. When corals spawn all the individuals do so simultaneously, often turning the water pink with clouds of eggs and sperm. Not only does this increase the chances of fertilization, but it also means that predators, although they gorge themselves, cannot eat them all.

Giant clams (*Tridacna*) combine elements from both strategies: they produce several million eggs at a single spawning, and each egg is quite large in comparison with those of many other bivalve molluscs. The swimming larval stages only last for about ten days or so, before they settle and begin to grow. This reduces the chances of their being eaten.

The production of few eggs means that the species must ensure their successful fertilization and reduce predation. Animals which have elaborate courtship rituals generally have a high rate of fertilization, and where this is combined with parental care of the eggs, or even brooding of the young, the chances of the larvae surviving are greatly increased. For example, in many bottom-dwelling fish the males construct and guard nests in which the females lay their eggs, while in seahorses and pipefishes the males have developed brood pouches in which the female deposits her eggs.

Changing sex

In an evolutionary sense, males are generally less important than females, since single males can successfully fertilize the eggs of more than one female. In some species of coral reef fish, which live together in small schools defending their territory against competing species, a single male guards a harem of females. If the male dies, then the largest female becomes a male; such sex changes in individuals are common in marine animals. For example, the giant clam *Tridacna gigas* becomes sexually mature as a male around the age of three or four years. As it grows and develops larger energy stores for reproduction, it progressively becomes both male and female, until at six to eight years of age it produces both eggs and sperm. Such hermaphrodites have an advantage over single-sexed individuals in that they do not have to seek out a member of the opposite sex to reproduce.

In some species, particularly small planktonic crustaceans, parthenogenesis (female reproduction without fertilization by a male) is common. In other organisms, asexual reproduction may be used, as in

Land crabs (Gecarcoidea natalis) *(right)* spend their adult lives away from the sea in forests and inland areas. These crabs on Christmas Island in the Indian Ocean have made their annual migration back to the shore to release their eggs into the sea. On hatching, the eggs go through a series of larval stages before returning to the shore and moving inland to adopt the adults' terrestrial way of life.

Turtles mate at sea (left) and the females move inshore to suitable beaches for breeding, where they excavate deep burrows in the sand at high tide for their eggs. The eggs are laid above the high-tide mark, and following incubation the young hatch and make the dangerous journey down the beach to the sea. During this short trip they are attacked by seabirds and crabs, and it is during the early stages of the life cycle that the highest levels of mortality occur. Turtles are long-lived animals, returning to the same breeding beaches year after year, where their eggs are harvested by coastal peoples.

The eggs of the dogfish Scyliorhinus canicula (below) contain a large yolk supply which helps in the development of the embryo. Many bottom-dwelling sharks produce eggs of this type which increase the chances of successful hatching and survival of the young. The curled tendrils at the end of each egg sac are designed to catch in seaweeds on the bottom and prevent the eggs from being swept away by currents into unsuitable areas. As the female lays the eggs, she swims close to the bottom to ensure that her eggs have as good a chance as possible of becoming ensnared.

many single-celled organisms which simply divide into two as they grow larger. Many sedentary, bottom-dwelling animals and plants reproduce asexually, thus sea grasses reproduce by small pieces of rhizome (creeping stems) becoming detached from the parent. Corals, sea whips, sea fans and anemones reproduce by budding, in which a small, new individual grows as part of the adult, eventually becoming detached as a free-living individual, or retaining connection in colonial forms.

While hermaphrodites and asexually reproducing species have the advantage of not needing a partner to reproduce, they suffer the disadvantage that the offspring are genetically identical to the parent. Such clones may be well adapted to the particular environmental conditions in which the parent is found, but genetic diversity is necessary if species are to colonize a range of different habitats. So even asexually reproducing species tend to reproduce sexually at some point during their life cycle to maintain the pool of genetic diversity needed for survival of the species.

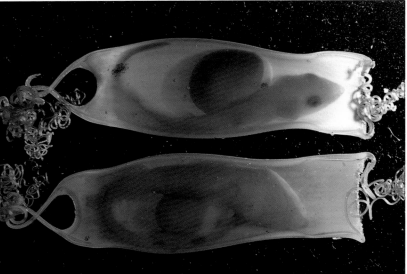

Migration and Dispersal

The movements of marine animals over long distances reflect the response to breeding patterns or to seasonal changes in the availability of food. Among marine mammals and birds, individuals gather at suitable locations to court, give birth and care for the young. These gatherings, or breeding aggregations, also occur among many species of fish, and are associated either with short migrations, as in the case of reef fish, or long-distance migrations, such as those of salmon, many eels and herring. For smaller fish and plants which live on or near the bottom in shallow waters, long-distance movements take place as eggs or larvae. Carried for tens or hundreds of kilometres by waves and currents, such movements ensure the wide dispersal of individuals.

Seasonal and breeding migrations

Many whales and larger marine species follow the annual cycles of food production in the ocean environment. These animals move into higher latitudes during the summer months, when productivity is high, and then return to warmer waters during the winter. Many larger fish and some crustaceans, such as penaeid shrimps, move closer inshore to reach suitable habitats during their annual spawning migrations. These habitats include kelp, sea grass beds and mangroves, which form ideal nurseries. After a period of growth as larvae, the young animals migrate offshore to feed in bottom sediments, where they may be harvested, returning inshore when mature to spawn.

In the case of seals, many seabirds and marine reptiles, seasonal migrations are also associated with breeding and the aggregation of individuals at suitable sites in order to lay eggs or give birth to pups. Breeding colonies of seabirds are found on cliffs, on small islands and in dune areas close to the sea. Before the female arrives, the male establishes his territory. While one parent watches over the eggs or feeds the young, the other searches for food at sea. The Manx shearwater (*Puffinus puffinus*) nests in underground burrows and forages far from land. The foraging parent may be away from the nest for long periods, but can locate its burrow – even at night – through recognition of the call of its mate. For species whose food sources are closer, the foraging parent may only be absent for a few hours.

Bull seals arrive at breeding beaches before the females and establish territories which they defend against other males. When the females arrive to breed, the bulls mate with all the females within their territory. For marine turtles, mating takes place offshore, and the females come ashore on sandy beaches to dig a nest, into which they lay their eggs. The eggs incubate beneath the sand until they hatch, whereupon the soft-shelled young turtles must return to the sea. Their journey is dangerous, because birds and other predators gather to attack them.

In contrast to turtles, saltwater crocodiles display considerably more care for their young. After she lays her eggs, the female crocodile remains nearby to guard the nest, which is usually constructed above high-water level in mangrove swamps. During their young adult life, male saltwater crocodiles range widely in estuaries and along the coast in the search of suitable areas in which to establish home ranges. They defend these ranges against other males, and occupy them for the rest of their life.

Many of the animals which aggregate for breeding disperse during the rest of the year. This dispersal reduces competition for available food supplies.

Tropical spiny lobsters such as Panulirus argus *(right) undertake seasonal migrations as part of their breeding cycle. Adults migrate to spawning grounds which are often inshore, where eggs are produced, and the larvae are then carried by currents out to sea, finally settling on the bottom. As the animals grow and reach maturity they migrate, often in long lines, marching back towards the spawning grounds – the cycle* then repeats itself. Many populations of tropical lobsters are important commercial species. They are trawled during their migrations, blast frozen and shipped to markets in the northern hemisphere. Local exploitation of such populations usually involves capturing individual lobsters in areas where they grow, and is therefore less destructive since animals are harvested outside the breeding season.

The European salmon, Salmo salar *(above), like other anadromous fish, moves from the sea into freshwater rivers to spawn. Following hatching, the young fry migrate to the sea to grow to adult size.*

*Like many seabirds, the royal albatross (*Diomedea epomorpha*) (inset) returns each year to breeding areas on land to lay eggs and rear its young. In general, seabirds lay only one or two eggs.*

Long-distance dispersal

A remarkable feature of marine animals and plants is the great distance over which the same species may be found. The life cycle of many marine organisms includes a planktonic phase. Because ocean current systems distribute these tiny creatures, the same species of sea grasses, mangroves, bottom-dwelling molluscs, burrowing worms, starfishes and many other organisms occur in both the Indian and Pacific Oceans. Depending on their tolerance of seasonal variations in water temperature, some species may be found on both sides of the Equator, from South Australia to the Japanese islands.

Such patterns of dispersal reflect not only the time many organisms spend as free-floating larvae, but also the direction of the major surface currents. Animals and plants in the bottom environment of shallow waters produce large numbers of eggs and larvae. These may be carried away by currents, and end up either in the open sea or in shallow waters. When the time comes to settle those larvae in the open ocean are unlikely to survive. However, those which end up in new areas of suitable habitat will flourish.

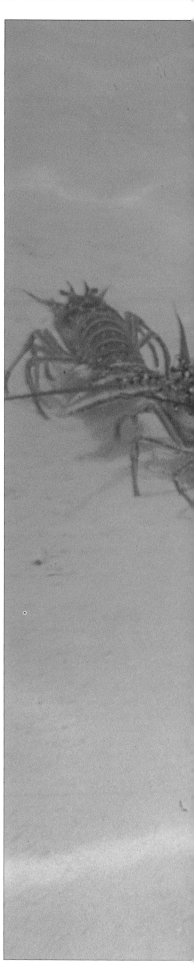

Living Together

Species of animals and plants which live together in any community develop relationships based on predation, competition and parasitism, with one species usually benefitting at the expense of another. Occasionally, more intimate relationships arise as two species evolve together, such that both benefit from the association. Close associations between quite divergent species are widespread in the marine environment: fish live in anemones, feather stars or sea cucumbers; worms, molluscs and small crustaceans live on larger marine organisms; and in some instances one organism lives in the tissues of another.

Many small animals "hitch lifts" by attaching to or living on the surface of larger, more mobile species. Many scale worms live on the bodies of sea urchins, starfish, and feather stars; while in the tropics, feather stars and starfish carry with them shrimps and even small blennies which shelter in between their arms, feeding on plankton and other food trapped there. Numerous small crabs live inside the mantle cavities of bivalve molluscs, deriving protection from the surrounding animal and feeding on the food collected by the host as it filter feeds. Some pea crabs, while feeding independently of their hosts, still gain protection as in the case of those which settle as larvae in the branches of corals that grow progressively around the crab, eventually enclosing it except for the small opening through which the crab feeds. Anemone crabs collect stinging sea anemones on their claws, with which they protect themselves against potential predators. Presumably the anemones benefit by feeding on small food particles as the crab scavenges and tears apart its food.

Whales, dolphins and turtles may carry around on their thick skins barnacles which use their hosts merely as a convenient place on which to attach and as a mode of transport, although some species have adapted to a parasitic way of life. Even sea snakes are known to carry with them stalked barnacles such as *Conchoderma*. Whole communities of fouling organisms may be found on sea snakes, including encrusting bryozoa, serpulid worms, diatoms and protozoans such as foraminifera. Many of these will grow on any floating object, but some have adapted specific mechanisms for attaching to living hosts.

Commensalism

Literally translated from its Latin origins, commensalism means "feeding at the same table", and that is what many marine organisms do. Smaller animals which live on, in or close to larger animals often feed on the scraps left from the food caught by the host. Pilot fish which accompany some sharks feed on scraps of food dropped by these large predators; remoras go one stage further, hitching a lift by attaching to the shark with a specially adapted sucker disc. Small, brightly coloured anemone fish derive protection from the host's deadly batteries of stinging cells and dart out to feed on animals which come within reach.

Symbiosis

Symbiotic relationships, in which neither of the species involved in the relationship can survive without the other, are also common between marine organisms. The most important group of symbionts are the dinoflagellates, single-celled algae which although they have a free-living, mobile stage, live for the greater part of their life cycle in the tissues of animals. Giant clams, corals, some molluscs, and even flatworms and jellyfish are known to harbour such

algae. The dinoflagellates gain nitrogen and carbon dioxide from their hosts, providing in return products of photosynthesis which enable the partner to grow, and in the case of corals and giant clams assisting in the formation of the host's skeleton (see pp. 68-69). When corals are stressed by high temperatures, an influx of freshwater, low light levels or large amounts of sediment in the water, they extrude their algae. Sustained periods of stress result in coral bleaching in which all the algae are lost, reduced growth rates and ultimately the death of the coral.

Relationships such as these must be the product of long periods of evolution, resulting ultimately in the kind of total interdependence found between the coral and its symbiotic algae *Symbiodinium adriaticum*. The range of coevolutionary relationships found in the marine environment is extensive, illustrating many stages of development, which reflect the lengths of time the two species have been associated.

A hermit crab (Eupagurus bernhardus) (above) often shares its shell with other animals, in this case a sea anemone (Calliactus parasitica). The anemone benefits from the association by feeding on particles of food missed by the crab, and in being carried from place to place so that it is not reliant on a single location for its food. The crab benefits by the presence of the anemone which deters predators from attacking. Often other animals such as worms live inside the shell with the crab. As the crab grows too large for its shell it must search out a larger, empty one into which it can move.

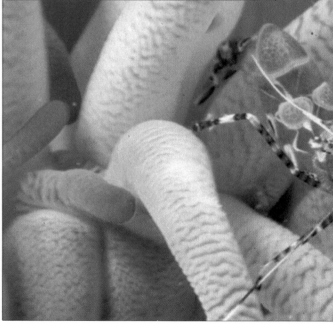

The cleaner shrimp (Periclemenes yucatanicus) (above) lives among the tentacles of the sea anemone Condylactis gigantea, eating particles of the anemone's food. The tentacles possess stinging cells, called nematocysts, which deter potential predators such as fish from attacking the delicate shrimp. Many animals live in such associations, with one or both partners gaining from the relationship.

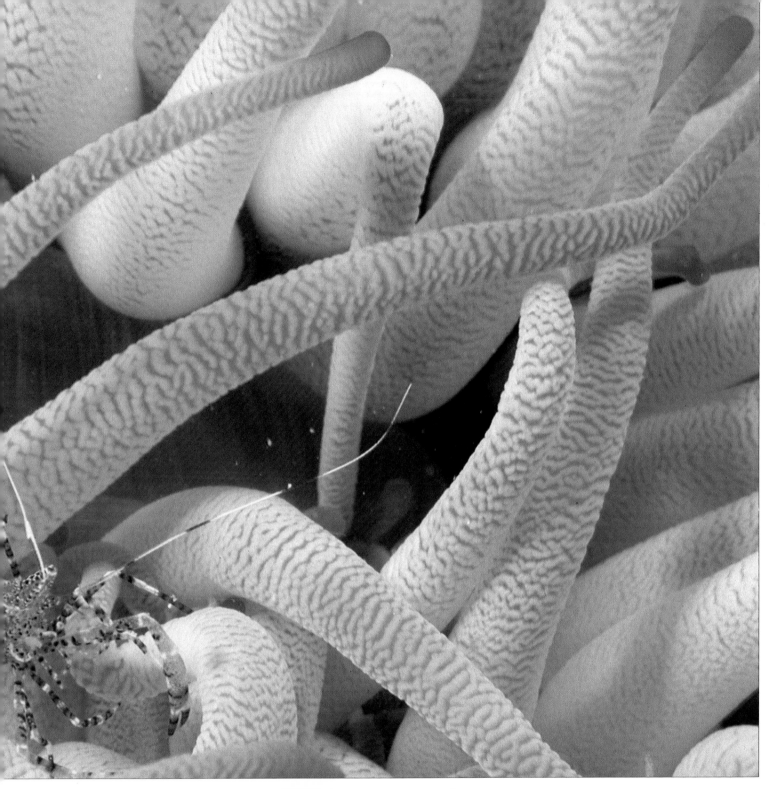

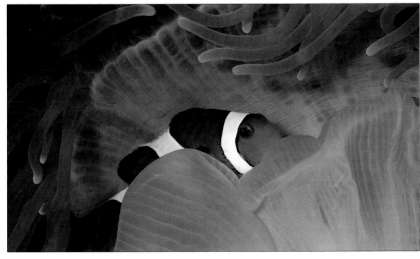

The beautiful anemone fish Amphiprion ocellaris (left), like the cleaner shrimp shown above, gains protection from predators by being closely associated with an anemone. The fish is a member of a widespread genus, which includes species that live with different kinds of anemones. The anemone gains less from the association than does the fish, although the fiercely territorial nature of the fish deters other smaller fishes from attempting to eat the anemone's tentacles. The fish receives protection from its predators, which are deterred from attacking by the stinging cells of the anemone. Several individual fish may inhabit a single anemone, and they lay their eggs on rocks nearby.

Environments for Life

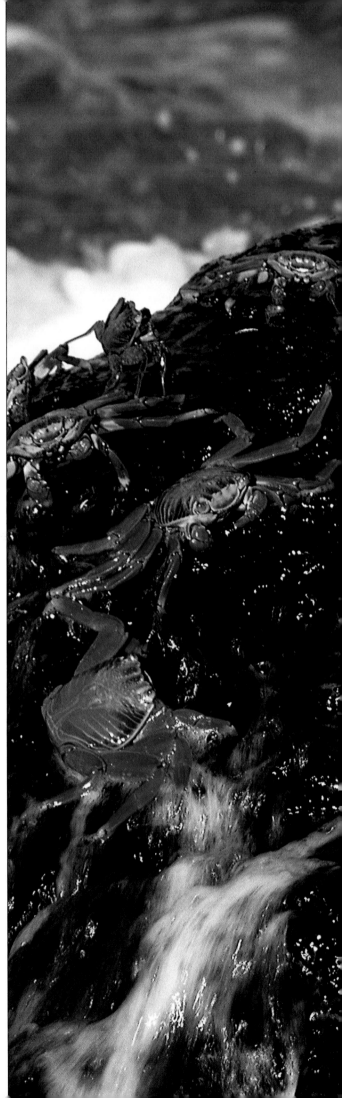

F rom the estuaries where fresh and salt water meet and the coastal regions with their bleak rocky habitats or rich mudflats, to coral reefs, the ocean depths, and unique island habitats, the range of marine ecosystems is enormously varied. Each habitat supports quite different animals and plants which interact to form an interlocked community. Species compete for space and food, eat one another, and live together in a complex web of interrelationships. This web of life is easily disturbed by human interference, and conserving habitats is the only way to sustain their living resources.

In the Galápagos, crabs (Sesarma sp.) cling to rocks to avoid being swept away.

The Land-Sea Interface

The transition zone between land and sea represents possibly one of the most difficult environments for life on the surface of the planet: a no-man's-land where for part of the day the shore becomes an extension of the relatively stable marine environment, returning at low tide to the harsh extremes of heat and cold, wind, rain and drying sun which characterize the land. Adaptations designed only to ensure survival on land or in the sea are not successful here.

The daily cycle of tides influences the coastal environment and consequently the animals and plants which inhabit these areas. The slope of the shore determines the way in which the tide advances and retreats. Where the slope is gentle, the tides advances with little wave action, whereas if the slope is steep waves break, crashing with considerable force onto the shore. The physical movement of the water itself moves pieces of the land from large rocks to small

This brightly coloured, male fiddler crab (right), seen among the breathing roots of a New Guinean mangrove, uses its enlarged claw to signal, and defend its territory from other males. Fiddler crabs emerge at low tide to feed, and while the enlarged claw is used for signalling, its other, tiny claw picks up particles of food from the ground. When the tide comes in, these animals retreat to their burrows.

particles of sand and silt; where currents are strong little deposition of material occurs. Strong wave action and large rocks are characteristic of exposed, eroding shores (see pp.62-63); while gentle wave action with sand, silt and mud bottoms is found on depositing shores (see pp. 64-65). The physical nature of the habitat determines the types of animals and plants which can survive in each area.

Daily exposure to the atmosphere means that animals with gills and other delicate structures that absorb oxygen from seawater face problems of water loss when exposed at low tide; while animals with adaptations for breathing air must constantly seek access to the surface when covered by water. Soft-bodied marine animals such as worms and snails tend to be more active when the tide is in, while animals with hard exoskeletons and protective covers for the gills such as crabs, or which trap water round the gills such as the mudskipper *Periopthalmus*, can move around when exposed to the air. The problems of drying out are particularly important for eggs and hatchlings, so many intertidal organisms which have soft, jelly-like eggs and thin-skinned hatchlings rely on planktonic life styles during the early stages of their development (see pp. 44-45).

Movement in water and on land requires quite different structural adaptations, with fins, floats and

The mudskipper (above) spends its time out of the water in search of food. It has a modified gill chamber which can be closed off full of water when the animal is on land. This prevents the delicate gill structures inside from collapsing, as they would if exposed to the air. The mudskipper's pectoral fins, with their stalk-like bases, can be used like crutches for walking on land; while for rapid skips and jumps to escape predators the animal curves its body, then suddenly straightens it with the tail acting as a fulcrum, and leaps forward. The mudskipper's eyes are prominent, and can be turned in all directions, enabling it to see both its food and approaching predators.

paddles working well in water but being useless for rapid movement on land. The shape and form of marine animals is therefore quite different from that of terrestrial animals, where strong limbs which raise the animal's body from the surface of the ground are an advantage.

Fresh and salt waters

For plants which grow and animals which live in this inhospitable environment the problems of conserving freshwater and removing salt may be important. Land plants which have invaded the edge of the land have special salt-excreting structures which remove excess salt from the sap, while land animals which have reinvaded the marine environment such as seabirds, marine mammals, turtles and snakes, have special salt-excreting organs – above the eyes in the case of seabirds, and at the base of the tongue in sea snakes.

Tidal pools (right) *serve as refuges for many marine animals at low tide. Drying out is a major problem for soft-bodied animals, so many of them move into pools as the tide retreats. During hot summer days, the temperature of the water in a pool may rise considerably, and adapting to changes in water temperature, exposure to air, wave action, and the movement of the rocks and sand, has led to a remarkable range of specializations in intertidal animals.*

Perhaps nowhere is the problem of salt regulation more important than in estuaries, where the environment is alternately subject to large influxes of freshwater at low tide and more saline conditions during high tides – the salinity ranging from less than 0.5 to 35-37 parts per thousand. Estuarine and delta areas trap freshwater close to the shore, and as a result of tidal mixing a zone of intermediate salinity is produced. Brackish water species, tolerant of salinities between about five and 15 parts per thousand, occur in these areas, overlapping with freshwater and marine species which are found in waters below and above 12 parts per thousand respectively.

Many fish avoid the problems of rapid changes in salinity by following the tides in and out of estuaries; some species however can withstand wide changes in salinity, while others may adjust more slowly during the course of migrations into and out of freshwater as part of their life cycles (see pp. 54-55).

Rocky Shores

Rocky shores are found in areas of high wave action, frequently backed by cliffs or steeply sloping land, and along sections of coast where erosion is high. The physical action of the waves and tides means that most organisms are adapted for firm attachment, while mobile, soft-bodied animals are active at high tide when there is no risk of drying out. On rocky shores the transition from land to sea is marked by clear zonation, with animals capable of withstanding long periods of exposure to air being found higher up the shore than those which prefer longer periods of immersion. Tidal range determines the width of these zones, which may be extensive in areas where the range is large and far less obvious where it is small.

At the head of rocky shores, above the extreme high-tide level, is the splash zone, which is wet by spray from waves crashing on the beach. Such zones have a varied community of lichens with some blue-green algae and hardy snails which graze when the area is damp. On tropical shores, hermit crabs such as *Clibanarlus* scavenge in this area at night, while small sand hoppers and sea slaters such as *Ligia* forage in the drift.

Passing into the intertidal zone, the variety of species increases and although some animals may be found throughout it, most display strong zonal distribution. On tropical rocky shores small snails such as *Turbo setosus* tend to occur in the upper tidal reaches, alongside *Nerita plicata* and *Nerita polita*, which are replaced lower down the shore by *Nerita chamaeleon* and other *Turbo* species. Fixed bivalves display similar zonation with the oyster *Crassostrea cucullata* occurring from the mid to lower shore, and species such as *Pedalion*, *Spondylus* and *Chama* occurring in the lower intertidal and subtidal reaches. Similar patterns of zonation are seen in temperate molluscs with species of *Littorina*.

Seaweeds grow more profusely on rocky shores than in sedimentary areas, their holdfasts securing them to the rock surface. Again different species are found in different zones, reflecting their ability to withstand desiccation at low tides. The mats of *Fucus*, characteristic of the middle and lower zones of temperate rocky shores, provide moist hiding places for many small animals when the tide is out. Below low-tide level they are replaced by kelps or oarweeds down to 12-15 metres (40-50 feet). These brown algae are generally absent from tropical rocky shores, where seaweeds are less well developed and smaller green algae dominate the intertidal community.

Zonation and distributions

On rocky shores, the height reached by a particular animal or plant in the intertidal zone is largely determined by its ability to withstand exposure to air and high temperatures while the tide is out. On shores where deep and extensive cracks in the rock surface are found, animals occur higher up a beach than in areas where the surface is smooth and moist hiding places are not available. Many snails of the upper shore have well-developed operculums, which can be used to close the opening of the shell and prevent loss of water, while the familiar limpet *Patella vulgata* of temperate zones wears a small depression in the rock surface into which its shell fits perfectly forming a watertight seal.

In the case of animals which remain fixed to the rock surfaces such as barnacles and bivalve molluscs, competition for space becomes important. Such species often produce large numbers of eggs and the vagaries of tides and environmental conditions mean

that recruitment to the population is highly variable from year to year (see pp. 76-77). In good years, when numerous larvae settle, competition for food and space limit growth and may affect zonation. For example, the barnacle *Chthalamus stellatus* is generally found in the upper shore and *Balanus balanoides* lower down. When the larvae of both species settle together the lower growth form of the latter species results in its shell undergrowing the more upright *Chthalamus*, which becomes detached from the rock and dies. But because *Balanus* cannot withstand long periods of exposure, *Chthalamus* dominates the upper shore.

Predation is an important factor on rocky shores, and predators such as starfish and crabs help to maintain species diversity by reducing competition for space and other limiting resources.

Characteristic of rocky shores is the obvious zonation (right) of animals and plants which live at a particular height above sea level according to their ability to withstand exposure at low tide. The splash zone above the high-tide mark is seen here as a band of white lichens, above the darker colour of the intertidal zone. Below the high-tide level, green seaweeds are replaced by brown seaweeds lower down the beach. As the tide retreats, animals generally move to suitable hiding places.

The edible mussel (Mytilus edulis) (above) *is a well-known animal of rocky shores which is harvested for food. The animals attach by means of strong byssus threads to rocks and cliffs in the intertidal zone, and feed by filtering small food particles from the water when the tide is in. As the tide retreats, the mussels close their shells to prevent drying out. In areas of sewage pollution, they may harbour disease organisms and cause outbreaks of* cholera and hepatitis when eaten. A single mussel can produce up to 12 million eggs at a single spawning, and the survival of eggs and planktonic larvae depends on the conditions in the open ocean. In good years, many larvae settle and the population expands; in bad years, few survive and the population declines. Also seen here are small barnacles growing on the mussel shells, and pink encrusting algae on the rock surface.

Life in Mud and Sand

To most people sandy and muddy shores appear devoid of life, presenting a barren surface when exposed at low tide; but beneath the surface these habitats teem with life. The animals range from single-celled microscopic organisms such as bacteria to larger burrowers, and the entire ecosystem depends upon organic materials brought into the habitat by the daily cycle of the tides. The size of the particles which make up a beach and intertidal zone reflects the amount of wave action (see pp. 28-29). Fine muds and silts are only deposited where gentle currents move across the surface. The daily ebb and flow of the tide stirs the surface layers, and where stronger currents are found ripple marks may develop.

To avoid this constantly shifting substrate, animals live below the surface where they construct a variety of tubes and burrows. Fan worms line their U-shaped burrows with secretions which stick the sand particles together, forming a tube through which they protrude their feathery tentacles to feed. *Arenicola*, the familiar lugworm of temperate regions, has a vertical, open tunnel at the rear, down which water is drawn for respiration and through which it defecates, leaving characteristic worm casts. At the head end is a shaft down which sand from the surface gradually falls as the worm eats it from below. At low tide, the holes and mounds on the surface provide the only clues as to the animals living beneath.

Many molluscs compact the surrounding sediments as they burrow through them using their well-developed muscular feet. Sea urchins and sand dollars remain buried in the sediment, and have specially adapted, elongate tube feet which they use to collect food particles from the surface, while others are modified as small spade-like structures to move sand particles around the burrow space.

Life on and below the surface

The animals of sandy and muddy shores can be divided into two major groups: the epifauna, active on the surface, and the infauna which spend their lives underground. The infauna is itself divided into two groups: the macrofauna, which shift or eat the substrate as they move below the surface, and the interstitial fauna whose small size enables them to squeeze between the particles. These small animals form a complex and intricate community, with bacteria being eaten by single-celled protozoans, which are in turn preyed on by rotifers and tardigrades. The diversity of the infauna varies according to the substrate, with in general the highest numbers of species being found in areas of fine mud and silt, and fewer species occurring in coarser sandy areas.

The epifauna of depositional shores is generally less numerous than that of rocky shores, and few fish species are confined to sandy and muddy areas in the temperate regions. A characteristic fish of such shores is *Ammodytes*, the sand eel, which is not an eel at all but a fish whose eel-like shape enables it to burrow in the sand. Many more species of fish are found in tropical regions, where the sea grass beds provide a moist hiding place during low tide. Numerous fish follow the tide in over mud flats, feeding on animals which themselves emerge from their burrows to feed. When the fish retreat with the tide, waders and shore birds probe the sand and mud in search of hidden worms and other invertebrates. In addition, gastropod molluscs hunt for bivalves which they attack by boring a small hole in one of the valves to reach the animal inside, and polychaete worms feed on other worms and small crustaceans.

Sand dollars (right) are flattened sea urchins which sit in the sand either horizontally and just below the surface, or as in the case of these Californian sand dollars at an angle. The edge of the body which protrudes above the surface faces oncoming currents, most likely as a food-catching device. Some members of the sand dollar family, Clepeasteroidea, such as the keyhole urchin Rotula, have holes through the skeleton from the upper to the lower surface, probably to help with burrowing.

Burrowing molluscs such as this white mussel (right) from South Africa use their powerful, muscular feet to pull themselves into the sand or mud in which they live. When covered by the tide, they extend their siphons above the surface and water is drawn down one, food filtered out, and clean water passed up through the other. This water current also serves to supply the animal with oxygen, which is in short supply below the surface of the bottom.

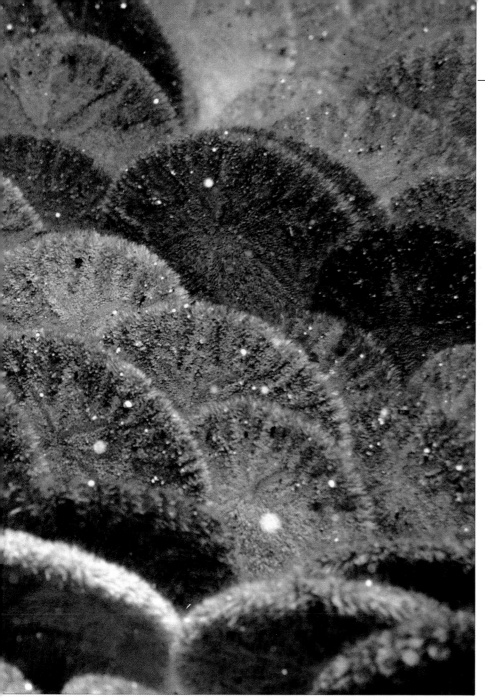

Feeding strategies among the animals of soft-bottomed habitats follow several basic patterns. Sea cucumbers, such as the edible *Holothuria atra* of tropical shores, sit on or just below the surface of sandy lagoons ingesting the entire substrate, digesting out the organic matter, and passing out fine sand. This mode of feeding is also practised by many worms, as is filter feeding using modified tentacles to trap food particles suspended in the water. The surface of the habitat is a rich source of dead and decaying organic matter which is sifted, sorted and eaten by a wide variety of worms, sea cucumbers, crabs, shrimps, and brittle stars. These animals pick up materials or suck the surface of individual particles to remove digestible material.

Oystercatchers (Haematopus ostralegus) (left) are a common sight on the muddy and sandy shores of estuaries in northern Europe. In such habitats, the inflow of freshwater adds to the problems of living. Estuaries contain not only a mixture of marine and freshwater species, but also estuarine species specially adapted to the estuarine environment. This results in high species diversity in these areas. Frequently, large areas of mud flats and eel grass are exposed at low tide, forming important feeding grounds for many birds, both resident and migratory. Since mud and sand are deposited in these environments, they are suitable for land reclamation for agriculture. Worldwide, such habitats are under threat from increasing human interference and modification.

The large sea cucumber Thelenota ananas (above) is one of the most valuable commercial species of bêche-de-mer or trepang – the names given to the dried, and sometimes smoked, body walls of sea cucumbers that are popular in China. Found in the tropical waters of the Indo-West Pacific, it prefers sandy lagoon areas where it lies on the bottom. Thelenota feeds on small particles of organic matter, using enlarged tube feet which surround the mouth to pick up particles of food and sand. It moves slowly, using normal tube feet on its ventral surface, similar to those of sea urchins and starfish to which, despite its appearance, it is closely related. Sea cucumbers are not restricted to shallow lagoons, being found from shallow coastal waters to deeper, offshore waters.

Mangroves and Sea Grasses

Characteristic of muddy estuarine shores in the tropics and subtropics, mangroves with their dark, closed canopy and tangled mass of roots appear to be impenetrable and uninviting, but on closer inspection reveal a remarkable diversity of plants and animals. Fish and crustaceans feed on the bacteria-rich mud, insects feed on the mangrove leaves, and geckos eat the insects. Snails such as *Litorina scabra* graze the film of algae which grows on the leaves and trunks of mangrove trees.

In contrast, sea grass meadows grow in more sandy areas, and by stabilizing the mobile sediments they make the habitat suitable for a wide variety of burrowing organisms, including calianassid shrimps, worms and bivalve molluscs.

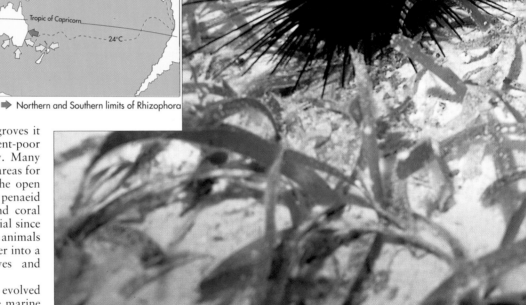

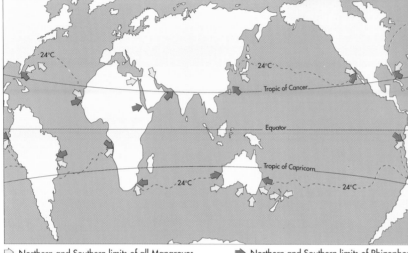

▷ Northern and Southern limits of all Mangroves   ▶ Northern and Southern limits of Rhizophora

As the sea washes in and out of the mangroves it transfers nutrients from the soil to the nutrient-poor coastal waters, increasing their productivity. Many mangroves and sea grass beds act as nursery areas for fish and crustaceans from coral reefs and the open ocean, including commercially exploited penaeid prawns. Separating mangrove, sea grass and coral reef ecosystems is therefore somewhat artificial since the boundaries have little meaning for the animals living there. These habitats are linked together into a super-ecosystem with animals, dead leaves and organic nutrients being cycled between them.

Both sea grasses and mangroves have evolved through a series of separate invasions of the marine environment by species from different families of land plants. Thus although they have evolved similar physiological and structural mechanisms to cope with living and reproducing in a tidal environment and remaining upright in soft sediments, they show quite different leaf, flower and seed shapes, reflecting their various terrestrial ancestries. The flowers of both mangrove trees and sea grasses are rather inconspicuous, and although most are wind pollinated, several mangrove species are pollinated by insects.

Obtaining oxygen

Just a centimetre (0.4 inch) or so below the substrate surface in sea grass beds and mangrove swamps the substrate is black and oxygen levels are low. Bacteria that use sulphur rather than oxygen to produce energy thrive in this environment, and when stirred the mud produces a strong smell of hydrogen sulphide. As a consequence, most burrowing animals have developed ways of ventilating their burrows, producing currents of water by rhythmic movements of their bodies ensuring that a plentiful supply of oxygen-rich water is brought down into the burrow from above.

Some mangrove trees such as *Avicennia*, *Brughiera* and *Lumnitzera* have overcome the problem of low oxygen levels around their roots by having specially adapted breathing roots called pneumatophores, which rise above the surface of the mud and are covered with lenticels or breathing pores. *Rhizophora* and *Avicennia* have lenticels on their aerial roots, others on surface roots and yet others on their trunks and supporting prop roots, all used for breathing.

Despite their height, most mangroves have relatively shallow root systems, and to increase their stability in the wave-swept environment many species of *Rhizophora* and *Ceriops* have extensive prop or stilt root systems. In contrast, the roots of sea grasses hardly penetrate the sand but spread out in complex networks of underground stems just beneath the surface where there is more oxygen.

Long-spined sea urchins, such as these Diadema *(above) photographed in a Caribbean sea grass bed, are common inhabitants of coral reef lagoons worldwide. Despite the protective spines, these animals are eaten by fish which break off the spines one by one, before turning the urchin over and attacking the unprotected lower surface.*

Although mangroves are confined to the tropics and subtropics (above left), sea grasses occur in the Mediterranean and temperate regions, forming nursery areas for fish and feeding grounds for marine turtles.

The archer fish (Toxotes jaculator) (above right) feeds on insects and other animals which crawl on the surface of leaves and branches overhanging the water in mangroves and estuaries. A jet of water is forced out of the mouth knocking the prey into the water where it is swallowed by the fish.

These isolated mangrove clumps (top right) are firmly rooted in the shifting sand and mud by means of prop and stilt roots. The roots form a tangled mass, trapping sediments around the base of the tree. In this way, mangroves protect coastlines by preventing erosion.

One characteristic feature of mangrove swamps is their zonation, with the so-called "pioneer" species of *Avicennia* and *Rhizophora* growing in the seaward zones, backed by *Brughiera* which grows in the less saline and more sheltered inland areas. The zonation of mangroves differs greatly according to the type of coast. In areas where large rivers discharge freshwater and sediments into the coastal waters, mangroves may be extensive, passing several hundred kilometres inland with creeks and river channels lined by species such as *Sonneratia* and *Nypa fruticans*. Where freshwater inputs are small, seasonal salt flats may develop on the inland side of mangroves and such areas are colonized by salt-tolerant species including *Ceriops* and *Heritiera*.

Vivipary – a condition in which the seeds germinate while still attached to the parent plant – is common in mangroves and sea grasses worldwide, and found in some desert and freshwater plants. In some mangrove species, such as *Brughiera*, *Ceriops* and *Rhizophora*, the seedlings do not root beneath the parent plant, but instead are carried away by the water until their small roots become attached to the mud. It would appear that vivipary benefits mangrove species by allowing the seedlings to develop away from the soil which, with its low oxygen concentration, high salt and sulphide content, and high acidity, is not suited to seedling development.

Human pressures

Traditionally, mangrove swamps have been used as sources of thatching, building materials and fuelwood; of edible fish and crustaceans; as land for rice and root crop production; and as areas for the farming of fish and shrimps. *Nypa* sap is even used in some areas in the production of alcohol. However, in general mangrove communities are viewed as nonproductive areas. The current rate of clearance for mariculture, for fuelwood and land reclamation poses a threat to these habitats throughout the tropics.

Coral Reefs

Coral reefs have been aptly compared to tropical rainforests because, like rainforests, they are centres of diversity. The richest reefs of the Indo-West Pacific (see pp. 146-151) are home to more than 2,000 species of fish, 5,000 species of molluscs, 700 species of corals and countless other forms of crabs, sea urchins, brittle stars, sea cucumbers and worms of different groups. This great profusion of life occurs in the nutrient-poor coastal waters of the tropics and, as in rainforests, most of the nutrients of the system are locked in the bodies of the organisms themselves.

Reefs are formed from the limestone skeletons of dead corals cemented together by the action of coralline algae. The surface of a reef below low tide level is covered by a living crust of corals, tiny communal animals related to the sea anemones of temperate waters. Reef-building or hermatypic corals thrive in warm waters where the temperature stays between 22° and 28°C (72-82°F). They are absent from western continental coastlines where colder temperatures are found in zones of upwelling, and from areas where large rivers pour freshwater and sediments into the sea. Corals cannot tolerate suspended sediments which smother the delicate coral animals or polyps and prevent light penetrating to their surface. Reef-building corals are rarely found at depths below 70 metres (230 feet), and they grow best just a few metres from the surface of the ocean where there is plenty of light and oxygen.

The reef builders

Each individual polyp is a cup-shaped creature sitting in its own coral shelter. Growing in colonies, the individually secreted skeletons are stuck together forming massive coral blocks, plates or tree-like structures. Growth is rapid; it has been estimated that individual colonies can grow between 8 and 25 millimetres (0.3-1 inch) a year. Not all corals are colonial and the individuals of some species such as *Fungia* grow very large – up to 30 centimetres (12 inches).

This extraordinary rate of growth is believed to reflect the intimate relationship that exists between the polyp and single-celled algae called dinoflagellates (*Symbiodinium adriaticum*) which live inside it. The plant-like dinoflagellates need light to photosynthesize, using carbon dioxide produced in the coral's tissues and excreting nitrogenous materials which the coral uses for growth. The algae also increase the rate of coral skeleton formation.

The shape of a coral colony depends on the temperature, the amount of wave action, and the nutrient and light levels, all of which vary in different parts of a reef system. In lagoons, sheltered behind fringing or barrier reefs, where water temperatures are high, and wave action is low, massive boulder-like colonies of *Porites* grow from the sandy bottom to the low water level, expanding outwards as the colony grows. The surface of such colonies dies where it is exposed to the air at low tide, and variations in height from the centre of the colony to the outside record annual variations in mean sea level over the life of the colony (around 60 or more years). In sheltered areas behind the reef flat, delicate, branched forms such as *Stylophora* may be found, while the wave-washed outer edge of the reef is characterized by robust "brain" corals without branches which could be damaged by the waves. Growing from the reef face in deeper, darker and calmer waters are sea fans, black corals and large plate-like forms of *Acropora*. The latter grow horizontally, presenting a large surface area upwards to catch as much light as possible.

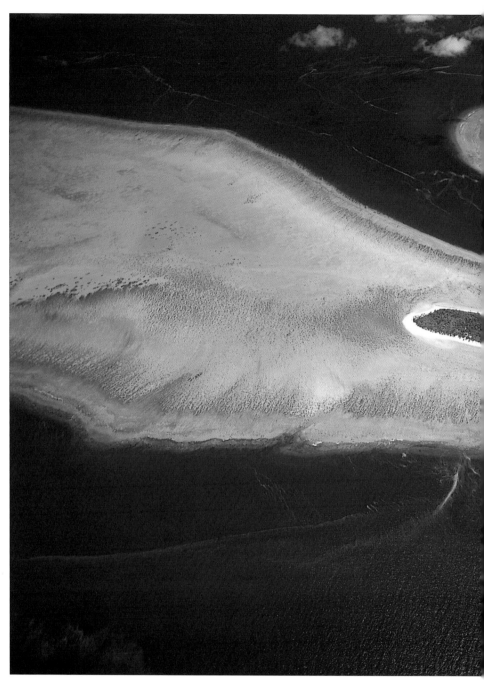

The reef stucture

In the tropics, there are three major classes of reef structure: fringing reefs which grow as platforms from the shores of continents or islands; barrier reefs which are found offshore and are separated from the coast by deep lagoons; and atolls, circular reef structures occurring in the open ocean. Charles Darwin was one of the first scientists to suggest that since corals grow best in shallow waters, atolls were formed originally as fringing reefs surrounding volcanic islands. As the islands sank or the sea rose, the reefs grew upwards until only the coral remained as a circular or oval structure, sometimes capped with a sandy islet known as a *motu* in the Pacific and a cay in the Caribbean. Drilling on Enewetak Atoll in the Pacific, nearly a century after Darwin proposed his theory, revealed that the coral limestone was 1,283 metres (4,208 feet) thick, covering a sunken volcanic cone. The oldest reef structures at the base of the limestone were around 60 million years old.

Heron Island and Wistoria reef (above) on the Great Barrier Reef off the north-east coast of Australia are separated by a deep-water channel linking the lagoon and the open ocean. In this part of the reef, shallow lagoons are common, the result of small areas being enclosed by raised sections of coral. Sand derived from the weathering of coral skeletons and those of other animals leads to the formation of sandy cays, such as Heron Island itself, and covers the floor of the lagoons.

Once dead, a reef may take many decades to recover (above) and such reefs are characterized by a low diversity of fish and other animals. Whole areas of coral may be killed by predators such as crown-of-thorns starfish (Acanthaster plancii) or by high water temperatures which cause bleaching.

In deeper waters (below) on this Fijian reef, corals take on growth forms different from the wave-dominated environments near the surface. Delicate structures flourish, such as the plate-like Acropora growing at a depth of 28 m (90 ft), shaped to catch as much of the light filtering down from above as possible.

Similarly, Darwin argued that barrier reefs were once fringing reefs growing along a sinking coastline. As the coast sank, the reef continued to grow outward and upward, with corals closer to the shore growing less well because food and oxygen were more plentiful at the seaward edge. Thus shallow lagoons were formed between the reef edge and the coast, becoming deeper as the coasts continued to sink. The best-known barrier reef, the Great Barrier Reef, lies off the east coast of Australia and extends for 2,000 kilometres (1,250 miles) covering about 200,000 square kilometres (80,000 square miles). To the north and west of this lies the less well known but more diverse Papua Barrier Reef, which extends for about 560 kilometres (350 miles), to within five kilometres (three miles) off the southern tip of mainland New Guinea. It is remarkable that these structures, formed as the result of the intimate relationship between tiny, anemone-like creatures and single-celled algae, are visible from the Moon.

Reef Communities

How such rich and diverse communities as those found on coral reefs grow in nutrient-poor, tropical waters has for a long time presented scientists with a puzzle that is only now beginning to be unravelled. The lack of nutrients in tropical waters reflects the efficiency with which reefs remove the available nutrients from the surrounding water, and the high diversity reflects the efficiency with which the nutrients, once taken from the sea, are cycled and recycled through the complex food chains which characterize these ecosystems.

Nutrients enter a reef system dissolved in the water and as particles of organic material from neighbouring land, or in the form of planktonic food from the open ocean. Because the water is warm and the sunlight intense, growth on a reef occurs throughout the year in contrast to colder, higher latitudes where it is seasonal. The primary producers in the system include the algae contained in the cells of the corals themselves (see pp. 68-69) together with a vast array of microscopic plankton, large seaweeds and sea grasses and smaller filamentous and encrusting algae which grow in profusion on dead corals and in sandy areas. The filamentous algae and seaweeds are grazed by a variety of fish and larger invertebrates, such as sea urchins and molluscs, while the plankton are filtered from the water by delicate feather stars, fan worms and the coral polyps themselves.

Once trapped within the system, nutrients are cycled through complex and highly specialized food chains, allowing different animals, many with bizarre lifestyles, to coexist by using different sources of food. One such specialized food source is the mucus with which reef systems abound. Corals produce mucus as a means of protection when stressed by freshwater (for example, after a strong rain storm) or large amounts of sediment. In addition, many filter feeding organisms produce mucus strands in which to trap floating food particles. The mucus strands which break free float through the lagoon waters, gradually

Although one of the top predators on the reef, the moray eel (above) acts non-aggressively towards the blue-and-black striped cleaner wrasse (Labroides dimidiatus), in response to the wrasse's characteristic swimming motion and colour pattern. It allows the fish to come close and remove any parasites or dead skin that it can find, even permitting it to clean inside its mouth.

sinking to the bottom, where they are consumed by large populations of bacteria, which are themselves harvested by a variety of detrital feeding animals.

Detritus, consisting of the faeces, dead organisms and particles brought in from the neighbouring land, is filtered, sifted, sorted and eaten by large sea cucumbers which plough the sandy surface of lagoons, eating the sand and digesting edible particles. Filter-feeding worms and feather stars take particles from the water, and small crabs brush the food from the surface of individual sand particles with their delicate mouthparts. Once they have entered the system, nutrients are trapped, cycled and recycled through the organisms of the reef, which act as a vast storehouse of different kinds of food.

Since much of the primary production on reefs actually occurs in the corals themselves, they form the basis for an important food chain. Starfishes evert their stomachs over living corals, digesting away the polyps; molluscs with sucking mouthparts delicately extract individual polyps from their skeletons; while parrotfish crunch the coral whole.

Structural diversity

The staggering diversity of life found in coral reef communities is not due only to the high rate of production and the complexity of food chains and food sources. The wide range of growth forms among the corals themselves, and the differences in environmental factors in different parts of a reef, also contribute to diversity, producing a variety of living conditions which suit many different kinds of organism.

Delicate soft-bodied animals such as tunicates grow attached to the underside of coral blocks, out of the way of damaging waves and predators. Brittle stars crawl in the coral debris, extending their long and flexible arms to pick food particles from the reef surface. Feather stars prefer sheltered, deeper water, producing mucus strands to trap passing food and themselves forming homes for small shrimps and crabs which nestle among their arms. Sponges grow in turbid areas, where light is low, or in sandy lagoon bottoms which are unsuitable for corals.

Coral colonies also offer hiding places for a myriad of different animals which use them for protection. Small angel fish shelter among the branches to escape a passing predator; pea crabs sit on the coral branches allowing the coral to grow around them, only keeping a small opening free through which they feed; clams and other bivalves burrow into massive corals where they live in chambers which they enlarge as they grow by rotating their shells to wear away the surrounding coral skeleton; fan worms secrete calcareous tubes through the coral and boring sponges dissolve their way through passages in the inner recesses of the skeleton itself.

Among the larger crevices of a reef system may be found lurking the large predators: hungry octopuses always on the lookout for molluscs, or moray eels (*Gymnothorax* sp.) waiting for some unsuspecting fish to venture near. The voracious moray eels are themselves food for sea snakes of the genus *Laticauda*. These characteristic black-and-white sea kraits prowl the reef surface, investigating likely holes in search of eels, which they kill by means of a highly toxic venom.

A coral reef is a world of vivid colour, with animal colour patterns and movements serving as signals to other members of the same species or to potential predators, or camouflaging potential prey against their favourite backgrounds.

The beautiful and delicate shapes of soft corals and sea fans (left) dominate this view of an Indonesian reef. They are found in deeper, sheltered water away from the damaging effects of waves. Also present are several different feather stars, some of them a yellowish brown colour, which attach to the reef and other animals, and use their long arms to filter food from the water. It is in the Indo-West Pacific that the greatest diversity and abundance of feather stars occur. Unlike the corals, they are capable of swimming by waving their arms up and down and so can move away from areas where the current is too strong or there is a shortage of food.

The individual polyps (above) of a coral colony have the appearance of a sea anemone with a ring of tentacles around a central mouth. The tentacles are armed with batteries of stinging cells or nematocysts, giving them a knobbly texture. These stinging cells are used to paralyse the small plankton on which these animals feed.

The strong, beak-like mouthparts of the parrotfish (Scarus sp.) (top) are adapted for crunching coral. It bites off the tips of coral colonies, grinding them with specially modified plate-like teeth in the floor and roof of its mouth. The entire mixture is ingested and the coral skeleton excreted as a fine sand which adds to the sand in lagoon and shallow-water areas.

The Open Oceans

Although 70 per cent of the world's surface is covered by ocean, biological productivity is not uniform throughout this vast area. As much as 90 per cent of the world's fish comes from coastal waters, while the open oceans are the equivalent of deserts on land, with low densities of microscopic plants, zooplankton and larger animals. This is because the nutrients required by the microscopic phytoplankton are most abundant at depth; but below 150-300 metres (490-980 feet), where nutrients are plentiful, light, the other essential requirement for plant growth, does not penetrate. Only where nitrogen, phosphorus and other trace elements are brought to the surface in zones of upwelling do the plankton have abundant nutrients and production is high. More than 50 per cent of the fisheries production in the entire Pacific Ocean comes from the Peruvian zone of upwelling.

In coastal areas, nutrient runoff from the land supports larger plants, such as seaweeds and sea grasses, which are grazed by herbivores, which in turn are consumed by carnivorous fishes and humans. In the open ocean, large plants are generally absent and all primary production is carried out by microscopic phytoplankton. These tiny organisms are too small and too widely dispersed to feed larger organisms directly, so small zooplankton graze on them.

The zooplankton is diverse, including the larvae of many larger species and of coastal organisms which disperse over long distances as members of the plankton. In addition, a wide variety of small copepods and other tiny crustaceans spend their lives as members of the plankton community. These small herbivores are in turn eaten by carnivorous zooplankton such as the arrow worm *Sagitta* and other larger crustaceans; small fish feed on the zooplankton which are then eaten by larger fish.

Since the tiny phytoplankton only live for a few days, while the zooplankton may live for several weeks and the fish for several years, the biomass or living weight of phytoplankton is usually less than that of zooplankton. In contrast, the biomass of plants in any terrestrial habitat is often much greater than that of herbivores.

The need to move

Since the numbers of food organisms in any one area are never high, open ocean species such as tuna must range over long distances in search of sufficient food. Although there are variations between the species, in general tuna show marked annual cycles of movement over many hundreds and in some cases thousands of kilometres. These species may also migrate on a daily basis, as for example in the vicinity of islands where they follow downstream currents, feeding on smaller fishes during the day, resting on the seaward side of the island overnight. Other top predators such as sea birds and some marine mammals also travel long distances following their prey.

Unlike the tuna and other actively swimming fishes, squid and large crustaceans (which form the nekton), microscopic plants and animals all depend

The open oceans (right) *are the watery equivalents of deserts. The growth of the phytoplankton is limited by the availability of nutrients such as nitrogen, phosphorus and silica. These occur in high concentrations only at depth, below the level to which light penetrates. Since light is* necessary for photosynthesis, most primary production occurs close to the surface in areas where for one reason or another higher concentrations of nutrients are to be found. In temperate regions, peaks of production occur in the summer when water temperatures are higher.

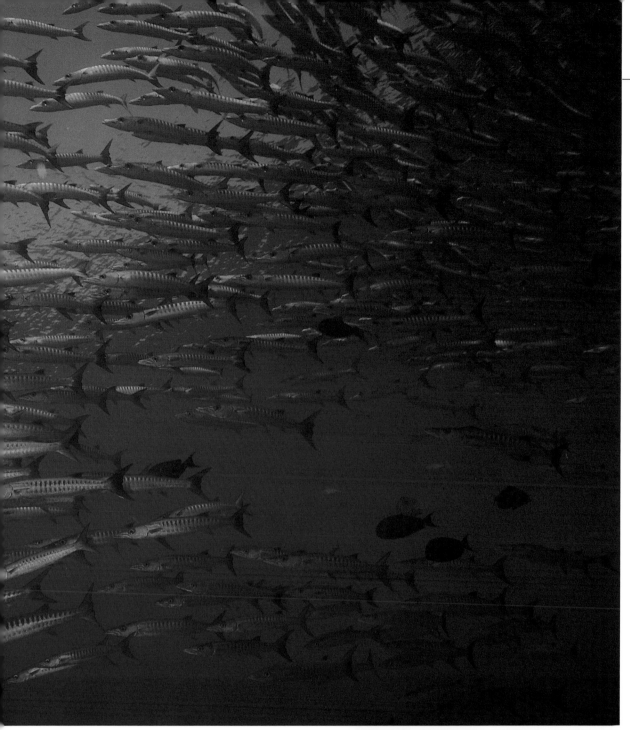

upon currents for long-distance movements. Small
zooplankton may actively migrate up and down in
the water column, rising to the surface to feed at
night and sinking during the day to take advantage of
faster-moving, deeper currents. By doing this they
are able to move is search of areas where food is
abundant. Just as the zooplankton migrate so do the
members of the nekton which prey on them.

While much of the production in surface waters is
consumed by the organisms living there, some of it in
the form of corpses and faeces falls slowly towards
the ocean depths. As it sinks, bacteria commence the
process of decomposition, releasing nutrients back
into the water, and themselves forming food for other
animals. This "faecal rain" and its associated bacteria
support the food chains further down.

Water currents, temperature, sunlight and nutrients all vary from area to area, hence the pattern of
plant and animal distribution is also variable. Where
warm and cold currents meet, an ocean front may
develop where masses of plankton and smaller fish
are to be found, forming a rich food source for larger
predators such as billfish.

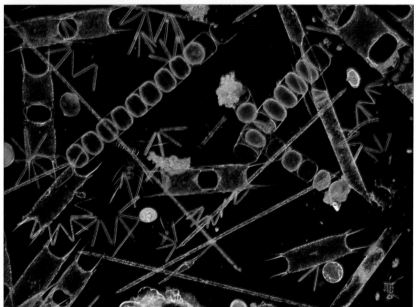

The Ocean Depths

Beneath the sunlit surface waters of the oceans lie the ocean depths, vast expanses of soft sediments where no light penetrates, and where the depths of water result in pressures equivalent to several hundred atmospheres. Water temperatures are generally low, salinities high, and the environment is fairly stable, showing no seasonal variations. The only source of food is the "faecal rain", the bodies of decomposing organisms and faeces falling from the surface waters. Despite their apparently inhospitable character, the ocean depths support a variety of animals.

The fishes

Passing from the surface to the ocean depths one finds quite different fish communities. The surface waters down to about 150 metres (500 feet) are dominated by swift, predatory fishes such as tunas and swordfishes, together with swarms of smaller forms such as the lantern fishes (Myctophidae). Between 150 and 500 metres (500 and 1,650 feet) there are many kinds of small silvery fishes with large eyes adapted to the dim light conditions. Below this occur the bathypelagic fishes, widemouths (Stomiatidae), angler fishes of the suborder Caratioidei (mostly black in colour and with small eyes), and finally the true abyssal fishes such as the grenadiers (Macrouridae) which live on or near the bottom.

On the continental margin, the diversity of bottom-dwelling (benthic) fishes is much higher than in the abyssal depths. During surveys carried out by scientists on H.M.S. *Challenger*, 40 sampling sites at depths of between 180 and 900 metres (600 and 2,950 feet) yielded 150 individual fish from 47 different species, while 25 sites at depths of 4,500 metres (14,750 feet) yielded only 24 individuals of just six species. Pelagic fishes that inhabit the water column are generally more diverse than these benthic communities, but even here diversity changes with depths. Deep-sea fish, those which live below about 250 metres (800 feet) are ten times more diverse than those living in the upper ocean waters, and as many as 2,000 species may be found below that depth compared with only 200 above it. Most of these species have wide geographic distributions, being found in several if not all of the world's ocean basins.

Colour and vision

Living in the dark or very low light intensity poses problems for the use of vision. In deep-sea fishes the pupil and lens of the eye may be as much as three-quarters of the width of the eyeball, allowing more light to enter the eye. What little light is present is then focused by the enlarged lens onto a sensitive retina, which possesses more sensory cells than fishes living in brightly lit conditions. Below about 910 metres (3,000 feet) fishes generally have small or degenerate eyes, in some cases none at all, and the animals rely more on chemical communication.

In the absence of light the characteristic spots, bands and colour patterns of shallow-water fishes cannot be seen and are therefore absent. Between 100 and 500 metres (350 and 1,650 feet), where some light still penetrates, fishes are generally of a silvery hue, although some dark brown or velvety black colours are also found. The silvery coloration acts as a mirror, reflecting the same light as the surroundings, thus making the animal invisible to potential predators. Many fishes at these depths show counter-shading, with the dorsal surface being darker than the ventral. When viewed from above, the dark tones blend with the darker waters below; while seen from below, the silvery reflection matches the light from above. Below 500 metres (1,650 feet), where there is little or no light, prevailing colours are brown, black or violet-black, generally quite dull.

Living in the depths

Animals found in the mid-waters and abyssal depths of the oceans often have reduced skeletons, muscles and other body tissues, reflecting the low availability of food. Between 1,000 and 2,000 metres (3,280 and 6,660 feet) many fish lack swim bladders, maintaining neutral buoyancy by other adaptations.

Many oceanic fishes have proportionally large heads and very wide mouths, enabling them to swallow the occasional large prey item: the great swallower *(Chiasmoden niger)* can consume prey almost the same size as itself. In some fish such as the guipers *Eupharynx pelecanoides* and *Saccopharynx ampullaceus* the head is huge while the rest of the body

Deep-sea angler fish such as Linophyrne polpogon (right) rarely grow to more than 8 cm (3 in) in length, but because they cannot afford to pass up the opportunity of eating every possible item of prey that is attracted to their lunimescent lure they have very elastic stomachs. The stomach of one Linophyrne *specimen was found to contain a deep-sea eel, two bristle mouths, five shrimps and a hatchet fish. In some deep-sea species the light is produced by bacteria, while that from the chin barbel of* Linophyrne *is produced chemically, controlled by the presence of oxygen in the animal's blood.*

may be reduced to a long, almost whip-like tail.

Problems of low food availability have led to widely dispersed populations in abyssal species. Problems of communicating with potential mates have been uniquely solved by the deep-sea angler fishes. In one species, *Ceratias holboelli*, spawning takes place in deep water during the summer, and the eggs float to the surface when the young hatch. At around eight millimetres (0.3 inch) in length, the small larvae sink to a depth of around 1,000 metres (3,280 feet) and the males, with their long slender bodies, attach themselves to the females. Ultimately the skin surrounding the male's mouth becomes fused with that of the female, except for two small holes through which the water current needed for respiration is drawn. The blood supply of the two becomes linked, and the male lives out its existence dependant on the female for all its nourishment, functioning as little more than an attached testis.

Deep-sea hydrothermal vents, such as this one off the Galapagos Islands (left), are home to their own specialized faunas. A variety of animals including crabs and other crustaceans, molluscs, and metre-long tube worms aggregate around these vents. At this depth the lack of light means that photosynthesis is not possible, so the primary producers are not the phytoplankton that are found elsewhere, but instead bacteria that derive their energy from the reduction of sulphur present in the hot vent waters. Some of these bacteria form symbiotic relationships with other organisms, such as tube worms and molluscs, supplying a large proprotion of their energy requirements, while others are free living.

Islands: Ocean Oases

Islands form hotspots of diversity and production in the sparsely inhabited and relatively uniform environments of the world's oceans. Rising from the ocean depths, they provide a solid foothold for shallow-water organisms that need somewhere to attach in the sunlit waters of the upper ocean. The sediments washed from an island into the sea support high productivity, nourishing the algae which form the basis of shallow-water food chains. Living on the coastal fringe of an island is not without its problems; long distances may separate an island from the nearest land, forming a barrier to dispersal and making colonization a difficult and chancy process.

Islands are of two basic types, and their animal and plant communities reflect the geological history of each type. Continental islands, once joined to larger neighbouring land masses, generally possess a selection of the species found in the more widely distributed mainland coastal communities. In contrast, oceanic islands have never been joined to continents, so their animals and plants have arrived across the open ocean. But the vagaries of long-distance travel introduce an element of chance, and not all the characteristic organisms one finds on the mainland are found on nearby islands. An island down current from a rich coastal community is likely to support a more diverse biological community than one lying a similar distance up current.

Finding a foothold

For animals and plants living in shallow coastal waters the open ocean is an unsuitable habitat for adult life. Such species are able to survive away from land and to cross many hundreds of kilometres during their larval life as plankton. When the time comes to settle in the shallow waters of the intertidal and subtidal zones, larvae which do not reach a suitable environment in time die. Those which reach islands may survive to establish new populations, but once established there are problems in maintaining these populations, because adverse winds and currents may sweep young larvae away from the island. While this helps further dispersal, it also reduces the numbers of larvae which settle on the home shore to continue the existing population. Life therefore becomes a compromise between the demands of long-distance travel, where a longer larval life is an advantage, and the need to restock the existing population, for which a shorter larval life is preferable. Many marine species found around oceanic islands use circulating eddy currents to ensure that their larvae are kept inshore.

The more isolated an island is from neighbouring land the more likely it is to have an impoverished marine fauna and flora. In parts of the world where large numbers of islands are found close to one another, they form "stepping stones" for colonization, with each successive island acting as a centre for dispersal to islands further away. In areas such as

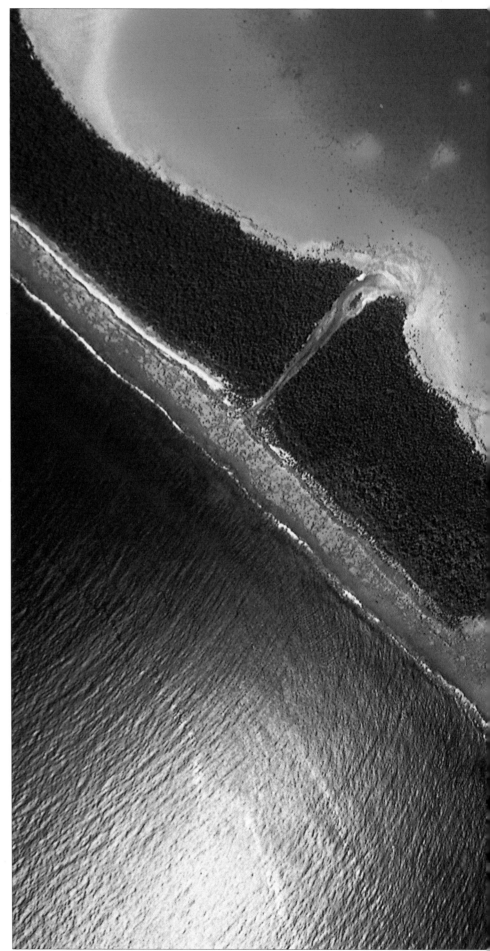

From the air (right) *the fragile nature of an atoll island, perched on top of coral reefs enclosing a shallow lagoon, is revealed. The difference between the deep, dark blue waters on the outside and the shallow, pale blue of the lagoon emphasizes the contrast between island environments and the vast expanse of the surrounding open ocean.*

Coral growth is vigorous around the outside of the reef where oxygen and food organisms, such as plankton, are in plentiful supply. The calm waters of the lagoon are not completely enclosed because breaks in the surrounding coral allow for the exchange of water with the ocean. Small, isolated patches of coral can also be seen inside the lagoon.

South-East Asia, many islands lie between the rich Indian and Pacific Oceans, and the community of marine organisms is extremely diverse. The way in which marine species are distributed on islands therefore depends on the past history of the island in question and its surroundings.

In the tropical Pacific, distributions reflect both the major current systems and the geological history of the islands and surrounding seas. Species diversity decreases from west to east across the Pacific, reflecting the importance of the Indo-West Pacific as a centre of marine biodiversity and the direction of major currents. Oceanic islands have existed on the Pacific plate for at least 100 million years as volcanoes rose above the ocean surface before gradually sinking as they moved away from the areas of submarine volcanic activity. The earliest fossil shallow-water communities of molluscs, sea urchins and fishes show affinities with Caribbean and eastern Pacific species. Later communities show increasing degrees of affinity with the faunas of the western Pacific as the Caribbean connection was lost through continental drift and sea floor spreading which closed the Isthmus of Panama.

Between 50 and 60 per cent of the shallow-water species of Polynesia have colonized from the western Pacific region over the last 40-50 million years. The remainder represent older elements of the fauna more closely related to Caribbean species. These older species eventually evolved into new species found only around the islands of the Pacific plate. Consequently, the faunas of Hawaii, Fiji and Polynesia are more similar to one another than they are to those of the Marshall Islands and Micronesia.

Bora Bora (above) in the Pacific is an old volcanic island which is gradually sinking. Since it is located in the tropics, the island is surrounded by coral reefs which, if they continue to grow as the island sinks, will ultimately form an atoll. The high productivity of these reefs is in part due to the influx of nutrients they receive as a result of erosion and nutrient runoff from the high, steep-sided island. The island also acts as a focus for cloud formation, increasing the rainfall which in turn increases the nutrient runoff into the sea.

Harvesting the Seas

For centuries the oceans have appeared as an endless store of resources for humans to harvest. Their immensity has led to their use as dumping grounds for many types of unwanted materials, from solid and liquid waste, industrial and domestic effluent, to radioactive material. Burgeoning human populations using advanced technologies are placing pressures on the oceans that they can no longer withstand, resulting in the degradation and destruction of unique communities and habitats in many parts of the world. A few species have been hunted to extinction, while many animal populations have been reduced to perilously low levels. Human impacts on the oceans can no longer be ignored, and must be controlled to ensure maintenance of the health of the marine environment and the future of the resources upon which we depend.

North Sea oil rigs extract one of the richest of the ocean's resources.

The Conquest of the Oceans

The exploration and use of the sea has required immense ingenuity and adaptability on the part of humans. To harvest living marine resources, technologies have evolved from simple hooks and nets to large trawls and 30-kilometre (19-mile) long drift nets. Vessels have changed with time from small, surface, hand or wind-powered craft to huge supertankers, factory mother ships and nuclear-powered submarines. Similarly, navigational skills have evolved from using knowledge of the position of the stars, Sun and Moon to satellite guidance systems.

Ocean transport

Moving from place to place and transporting heavy loads by water is far easier than by land. It is likely that man's mastery of water began with the development of canoes and rafts for use on sheltered inland waters. As trade links were gradually established with other coastal communities, larger and more stable craft were required. In the Pacific, such developments included the addition of outriggers, either single or on each side of the main hull, and construction of large double-hulled canoes. The Pacific double-hulled canoes inspired the development of modern catamarans and trimarans.

As vessels became larger, keels and rudders were needed to increase stability and reduce the effort needed to steer the vessel. The development of sails decreased the need for large crews, allowing extra cargo to be carried. The design of the sails and the number and arrangement of supporting masts and booms varies enormously from place to place, reflecting different hull designs, and the different wind and sea conditions under which they were used.

Navigation

Early trading and fishing vessels remained within sight of land, so that their crews could know where they were. Development of navigation skills would have freed early sailors from the tyranny of remaining close to shore, where the ever-present risks from reefs or onshore winds could spell disaster.

An extract (right) *from a mid-16th century map by Diego Homen forms part of an atlas created for Philip II of Spain. Maps made in the 1500s were a great improvement on those of the previous century because they incorporated the new knowledge gained by Renaissance mariners who had rounded the Cape of Good Hope and crossed the Indian Ocean. Maps appeared which showed a far more realistic representation of the size of Africa, Asia and the Indian Ocean, which early maps had shown as a landlocked sea.*

An Athenian cup (below) *made in about 540 BC shows an ancient Greek warship (trireme). The steersman occupied a position in the stern where he could control the steering oars. The trireme was equipped with a bronze spike on the prow which could be used to ram enemy ships. Maritime supremacy was crucial to the ancient Athenians, who controlled a large maritime empire stretching across the Aegean. Ancient Athenian manuscripts refer to the need for all seamen (regardless of status) to "learn the language of the sea" and to acquire the skills of an oarsman.*

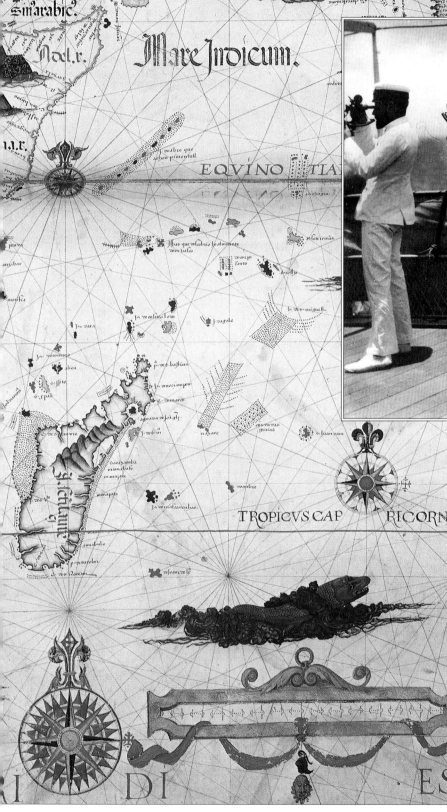

The sextant (below) enables latitude to be measured relatively precisely. The instrument consists of a mirror which reflects an image of the Sun or star onto a silvered glass screen, through which the observer can see the horizon. By moving the sliding arm and changing the angle between the mirror and the silvered screen, the image can be brought to rest on the horizon and the angle between the Sun and the horizon determined. Once this angle was known, and the correct time of day read from the ship's chronometer, the latitude of the ship's position could be accurately calculated by the navigator.

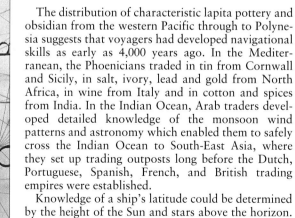

The distribution of characteristic lapita pottery and obsidian from the western Pacific through to Polynesia suggests that voyagers had developed navigational skills as early as 4,000 years ago. In the Mediterranean, the Phoenicians traded in tin from Cornwall and Sicily, in salt, ivory, lead and gold from North Africa, in wine from Italy and in cotton and spices from India. In the Indian Ocean, Arab traders developed detailed knowledge of the monsoon wind patterns and astronomy which enabled them to safely cross the Indian Ocean to South-East Asia, where they set up trading outposts long before the Dutch, Portuguese, Spanish, French, and British trading empires were established.

Knowledge of a ship's latitude could be determined by the height of the Sun and stars above the horizon. In the *Odyssey,* Homer records how the Great Bear just touched the horizon when seen from the Nile Delta, but stood a little less than a hand's breadth above it when seen from mainland Greece.

It was not until the first accurate ship's chronometer was developed in 1773 that longitude could also be determined with any accuracy. By knowing the time at the port of departure and comparing it with the time on board ship gauged from the Sun, a ship's position could be accurately determined east or west of the home port. Today, no part of the vast ocean expanse remains untouched by man.

Traditional Fishing

Traditional and artisanal fisheries are widespread among coastal peoples who use many different techniques to harvest a wide variety of species. Ten per cent of the world's catch is from these fisheries, which provide between 40 and 100 per cent of animal protein in the diets of people in tropical developing countries. Artisanal fishing differs from industrial fishing in that the vessels used are often small, not motorized, and are operated by single fishermen or small crews. The catch is consumed close to the port of landing.

In many fishing communities women and children have the task of collecting shellfish, sea urchins, crabs and even worms along the shoreline, while the men concentrate on catching fin fish in deeper waters. Although artisanal fishing is labour intensive, the average time spent fishing is small; as little as 3-7 hours per week in the Pacific provides about 70 per cent of the animal protein in the diet. Where fish are only available seasonally as in the case of salmon in British Columbia, whole communities move to spawning grounds to catch, fillet, dry or smoke fish as a winter food.

Equipment and techniques

Collecting by hand does not usually involve the use of any tools other than a net or bag in which to place the catch. Sometimes mangrove or derris poisons are used, without affecting the edibility of the fish. Hand-held nets with frames, or circular throw nets with weighted edges are used to catch small fish and crustaceans. Larger nets are set from boats or from a beach as encirclement traps. In the past, the nets were woven from vegetable fibre, but this has now been replaced by synthetic fibre in even the most remote fishing communities.

Traps are often used in shallow water and vary in size from the thorn-lined traps of South-East Asia for single fish, to crab and lobster pots designed to catch many individuals of a particular species. Extensive permanent tidal traps, consisting of stone or wooden structures, are designed to catch different kinds of fish as they move offshore with the falling tide.

A fisherman from the Tuamotu Islands in Polynesia (top) empties a catch of parrot-fish from a tidal trap on a reef flat. Fish swim into and along the fence to funnel-shaped sections, ending in a trap.

A Madagascan fisherman's catch (above) shimmers in the sun. The range of line fishing techniques using baited hooks is extensive.

A spear fisherman (right) from the Caroline Islands in the Pacific displays the night's catch. These reef fish and spiny lobsters were caught at night with the aid of a torch. Spear fishing in shallow water requires considerable skill since refraction at the water surface makes the fish appear further away but closer to the surface than it really is.

Fishermen also stretch nets across the mouths of creeks or deep water channels at high tide, trapping the fish when the tide goes out.

Fishing with hand-held spears or bows and arrows is widespread throughout the tropics. This method is most effective in clear, shallow water, where the fisherman can see the fish. In deeper water, lines are more popular, used either with baited hooks, lures or gorges (which twist and lodge themselves in the fish's throat). The fisherman chooses the bait with care, taking the preference of the prey into account. Small fish or pieces of fish, worms and shellfish are used. Artificial bait can be made from shells, feathers, wood and even spiders' webs. In Micronesia, a lure made from a small piece of wood wrapped in spider's web is attached to a kite flown by the fisherman. The web traps air bubbles, making the lure look like a small, silvery fish.

Traditional or artisanal fisheries depend heavily on skill and knowledge handed down from generation to generation. This includes information on lifestyle and habits of the prey, migration and reproductive patterns, feeding and spawning grounds, and preferred food. Fishermen also need to know about tides and currents in the fishing grounds. Such detailed local knowledge may be vital in determining where to fish at different times of the day or night, at different phases of the moon, or seasons of the year. Pacific fishermen have long known that during spawning many reef fishes gather together, become docile and are easily caught. Western scientists were unaware of this until the 1980s, even though the ancient Greeks observed this behaviour in Mediterranean mullet about 1,900 years ago.

Detailed traditional knowledge, although vital to the survival of fishing communities in the past, is rapidly disappearing. Modern innovations such as nylon nets, outboard engines, and Western European technology reduce the level of skill required to exploit marine resources. Unfortunately, the use of such technology often results in over-exploitation, and traditional conservation mechanisms are frequently lost along with the traditional knowledge, making management of artisanal fisheries for sustainable development difficult.

A Thai fishing vessel unloads its catch into baskets on the quay (above). Artisanal net fisheries such as this result in substantial catches, which are usually marketed and consumed close to the port at which they are landed.

Commercial Fishing

Commercial or large-scale fishing provides more than 90 per cent of the world's supply of living marine products. About 75 per cent of this catch is used for food, and is either marketed fresh or treated for storage by freezing, canning, drying, curing or smoking. The rest is used in the production of fish oils and fish meal used in animal foods and fertilizers. Fish and shellfish provide between five and ten per cent of the world's food supply, and from 10 to 20 per cent of the world's protein.

Commercial fishing methods

A wide range of boats, nets and other equipment are used in commercial fishing. Nets include trawl, seine and gill nets, as well as long lines with multiple hooks. In shallow coastal waters, otter trawls catch demersal (bottom-dwelling) species. In deeper waters and the open ocean, trawls catch pelagic species, which dwell in the upper layers of the ocean.

Purse seine nets are used to encircle large schools of fish, such as sardines and tuna, in surface waters. Unlike trawl and seine nets, gill nets are static and drift with the currents. They are suspended vertically in areas where fish are known to move. Fish swim into the net and are trapped by their gills when they try to back away.

Fishing fleets which concentrate on demersal coastal species sell their catches either fresh or chilled on ice, close to market centres. Those which concentrate on pelagic species, and operate at considerable distances from shore, are often organized around a factory "mother ship". A fleet of small catcher vessels transfer their catches to the central mother ship for mechanical gutting, filleting, freezing and even oil extraction.

The detection of fish schools forms an important aspect of modern commercial fishing. Echo sounders are used to detect subsurface schools. Tuna fleets even employ helicopters to search for surface schools of their target species.

Major fish species

Half of the world's commercial fish catch is made up of two groups of fish, pelagic and demersal. Among the pelagic species, herrings, sardines and anchovies are the most important. They are exploited both for human consumption and for the production of oil and fish meal. In contrast, the demersal catch, which also includes crustaceans such as shrimps and prawns, is dominated by cod, hake and haddock, and is used almost exclusively for human consumption. In 1986, the catch of these three species amounted to around ten million tonnes, or about ten per cent of the total world harvest.

The cod forms the basis of the North Atlantic fisheries. It is caught by bottom trawls, seines and by hook and line. The average weight of commercially caught cod is around 4.5 kilograms (10 pounds). In the Pacific and Indian oceans, the pelagic fisheries include tuna. Surface species are caught by means of purse seine nets or by "pole and line" fishing. For deeper swimming species, such as the yellowfin tuna, long lines are used. The use of purse seine nets often results in the accidental trapping and death of dolphins and other animals.

Unlike artisanal fisheries, commercial fisheries concentrate on only one or a few species. The processing of fish for human consumption relies on equipment designed to handle fish of uniform size and similar cooking qualities. Despite the resistance to change of commercial world markets, new products are being

Commercial fishing (above) is based upon highly mechanized methods, involving large fishing fleets and very efficient nets. These Norwegian fishing boats are hauling in a huge school of herring using seine nets. Unlike the world's artisanal fishermen, who gather and catch a huge variety of fish for local consumption, industrial fishermen take a relatively small range of species, and often operate far from their home ports. Of the world's estimated 20,000 or so species of fish, less than 300 are of commercial interest.

Tuna, here being landed by a Spanish ship (left), are a particularly important species for commercial fisheries. More than 2 million tonnes were caught worldwide during 1988.

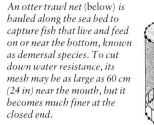

An otter trawl net (below) is hauled along the sea bed to capture fish that live and feed on or near the bottom, known as demersal species. To cut down water resistance, its mesh may be as large as 60 cm (24 in) near the mouth, but it becomes much finer at the closed end.

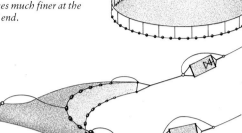

Purse seine nets (above) are used to encircle whole shoals of fish at one time. They are used to take fish which swim and feed near the surface of the water. The net is drawn out into a large circle, the two ends are joined, the bottom drawn in and the captured fish taken in towards the boat.

sought as existing stocks become depleted. For example, the oceans around Antarctica now support a growing krill fishery.

In some cases, whole fleets have moved to new fishing grounds, in response either to declining profits or to the closure of traditional fishing grounds due to the enforcement by many countries of new 200-mile Exclusive Economic Zones. Development of the "orange roughie" fishery off New Zealand took place following the decline of cod fishing in the North Sea. This also involved the development of new types of trawl for use at depths of up to 2,000 metres (6,500 feet).

Commercial fisheries cannot keep pace with the growing world demand for fish and fish products. It has been estimated that around 90-95 per cent of the world's available fish stocks are already being exploited at maximum levels. To meet growing demand, new technologies will need to be developed to exploit such under-utilized resources as mesopelagic squid stocks. These cephalopods inhabit the intermediate depths of the oceans, between 100 and 1,000 metres (330-3,300 feet). Expansion and improvement of mariculture methods would also provide a way of meeting the increasing demand for fish. Already, mariculture provides around four per cent of total marine production.

Southern cod (above) are now caught by deep-sea trawlers off the coast of New Zealand. These ships, like many of their type, can spend several weeks at sea. Refrigerated holds allow them to store large amounts of fish.

There has been a general trend towards increased fish catches in recent years, as shown by the diagram (right), although catches have not increased for all species. These figures are produced by the United Nations Food and Agriculture Organization, and are used as a basis for monitoring the state of fisheries worldwide. Because many scientists believe that we are now approaching the maximum sustainable catch for marine fish, monitoring is of crucial importance to determine acceptable levels of catch, thus helping to conserve stocks that might otherwise be overfished and depleted.

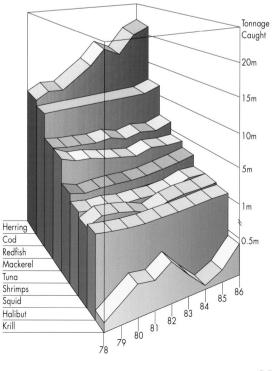

Whaling

The blue whale (*Balaenoptera musculus*) is one of the largest animals that has ever lived. It can reach up to 30 metres (100 feet) in length and weigh as much as an estimated 170 tonnes. At the end of the last century the Antarctic blue whale population may have numbered 250,000; today, only a few hundred may be left. The North Atlantic right whale (*Balaena glacialis*) has been brought to the edge of extinction through hunting and it is not known whether some of the most depleted whale populations such as this will ever recover.

Traditional whale hunting had little impact on populations, because hunters concentrated on smaller species inshore, and used the entire whale carcass for food and oil. In Fiji, the teeth (*tabua*) of the sperm whale (*Physeter macrocephalus*) were used as ceremonial items by chiefs and other important people.

Large-scale commercial exploitation of whales began around 250 years ago. Catches increased rapidly following the introduction of the explosive harpoon head, invented in 1864 by Svend Foyn. This allowed more whales to be caught, because carcasses could now be inflated with air and left to float. Initially, whale oil furnished both lamp fuel and lubricants. Sperm whale oil was used in the cosmetics, candle and tanning industries. Other whale oils were used in the production of glycerine, margarine and soap. Some meat was processed for pet food, but most of the whale carcass was discarded after the oil had been extracted. However, in Japan whale meat has always been prized as food. Other whale products included ambergris for perfumes, tendons for racket strings, baleen (flexible plates used to filter food) for stiffening corsets, ivory (from toothed whales) and medicines from organs such as the pituitary gland.

Whale populations are especially vulnerable to over-hunting because their breeding cycles are so long. Females are pregnant for between 11 and 16 months, and female blue whales only start to breed at about five years of age. Historically, commercial whaling exploited one species or area to exhaustion before turning to another species or more distant hunting grounds. The last great whaling area to be exploited was Antarctica. In 1925, around 5,000 blue whales were taken in this area, but this rose sharply to 30,000 by 1930. As blue whales became scarce, whalers turned to fin whales (*Balaenoptera physalus*), then in the 1960s to sei (*B. borealis*) and minke whales (*B. acutorostrata*). Originally these populations were estimated at around 250,000 blue, 500,000 each of fin and minke, and around 100,000 humpback (*Megaptera novaeangliae*) and sei whales. Antarctic populations are now estimated to be as low as 500 blue whales, 2,000 fin whales, a few thousand each of humpback and sei whales and less than 100,000 minke whales.

Whaling by agreement

The rise of the petroleum industry in the early 20th century steadily reduced the demand for sperm oil, but there continued to be a market for other whale products. Ironically, the main factor behind the first effective international agreement on whaling was a desire to keep whale oil prices high by limiting production. This came into force in 1935 and included protection for right whales, to be followed by protection for the grey whale (*Eschrichtius robustus*) and the setting of minimum body sizes for blue, fin, humpback and sperm whales.

In 1946, the International Whaling Commission (IWC), an organization open to all nations, was

In recent years, the plight of the great whales has become the focus of public concern and direct action (above) by conservation groups such as Greenpeace. Activists from this group have on a number of occasions placed themselves in the path of whaling boats in an attempt to draw the attention of the world's media to the bloody nature of the whaling industry and the very real possibility of whale extinctions.

With a radio beacon stuck into the side of one of its victims (right), the catcher ship can immediately start searching for new prey, leaving the factory ship to home in on the beacon and pick up the carcasses. Modern technology has made whaling an extremely efficient operation. The age of modern whaling is considered to have begun with the introduction of a number of innovations in the middle of the 19th century. Hand-held harpoons were succeeded by guns which fired harpoons containing an explosive charge. Steamers replaced the rowboats that were formerly sent out from the "mother ship" to catch the whales. Until then, only the slower species, such as right, sperm and humpback whales, could be caught. The use of faster boats brought blue, fin and sei whales within the reach of the whalers. Factory ships, developed towards the end of the 19th century, enabled the whole job of processing the dead whale to be carried out at sea. This meant longer hunting trips with even bigger catches.

TRADITIONAL WHALING

In the Faeroe Islands, which are situated in the North Atlantic approximately halfway between Iceland and the Shetland Islands, pilot whales (*Globicephala melaena*) – called *grindehual* by the islanders – are driven ashore in large numbers as part of an annual hunt. Pilot whales swim in large herds, sometimes several hundred strong. When a herd is spotted offshore, the islanders set off in boats to get on the seaward side of the herd. The whales are then driven in to shore by splashing and throwing stones into the water. Pilot whales are very gregarious, so the herd tends to stay together even as it is trapped. The hunt has been described as a combination of "sport, tradition and a way of obtaining cheap food". Various conservation groups have expressed concern about the effects of traditional hunting, but the annual kill by indigenous peoples is small.

established. It retained all existing protection and set quotas for whaling in the Antarctic, although these were far too high. Because the IWC was dominated by the whaling nations, commercial interests were often put above the need to conserve rapidly diminishing stocks. Although during the 1960s the IWC gave complete protection to humpback and blue whales and set catch limits for sperm, fin, sei and Bryde's whales (*Balaenoptera. edeni*), there was growing concern outside the IWC that this was not sufficient.

This concern was mainly due to the fact that the IWC did not have the power to completely control its member nations' activities. In 1972, the United Nations called for a ten-year moratorium on whaling, and the IWC responded by placing more emphasis on the scientific basis for determining quotas.

The IWC's membership grew as non-whaling nations joined it, and with their influence a moratorium on commercial whaling was finally agreed that came into operation in 1986. Even so, some whaling continued. In addition to aboriginal subsistence whaling, Japan, Iceland and Norway took a certain number of whales for "scientific purposes", which was allowed under the moratorium, although Iceland has since stopped. In 1990 Norway asked the IWC for a quota of Atlantic minke whales, claiming that numbers were now high enough to sustain hunting – a claim that is disputed by other members of the IWC.

There is a great deal of public opposition to whaling, although some nations believe that certain whale stocks have now recovered to a point where they can be sustainably exploited. Whaling nations may eventually break away from the IWC and set up their own rules and regulations, which would be bound to permit more whaling than takes place at present.

At an Icelandic whaling station, workers cut up the carcass of a fin whale (inset). The large chunks of blubber will be boiled down to produce oil and other products. Blubber varies in thickness from up to 50 cm (20 in) in the case of right whales, to only around 15 cm (6 in) for rorqual whales (whales in the family Balaenopteridae, which also includes the humpback, blue, fin, sei and minke whales). Apart from insulation, it increases the buoyancy of the whale because it is lighter than water.

Farming the Sea

Mariculture, the farming of fish, shellfish, molluscs and plants in saltwater, probably began several centuries ago in South-East Asia. Today, East Asia produces about two-thirds of all world aquaculture output (both fresh- and saltwater). In some countries, up to 60 per cent of dietary protein comes from farmed marine organisms. In 1987, world production from aquaculture exceeded three million tonnes, around four per cent of total marine production. Production grows annually as more and more species are brought into cultivation.

The origins of mariculture may lie in the tropics, where people traditionally blocked off mangrove swamps and estuaries to trap young fish and crustaceans. These were allowed to grow before they were harvested. In time, permanent ponds were constructed, which were then stocked with young fish caught in the wild. Elsewhere, the harvesting of wild molluscs encouraged the development of systems to ensure steady supplies.

Mariculture: techniques and species

Most farming of fish, shellfish and some crustaceans relies on specialized centres for the production of mollusc spat (larvae) or fry (young fish) which are sent to "grow-out" farms. At present, not all farms possess the skills and equipment needed to produce their own juveniles. In some cases, the capture of wild juveniles continues. Farming methods include ponds, rafts and floating enclosures, as well as fixed pens or beds in tidal areas. Large-scale commercial farms provide food in pellet form, but smaller farms in the tropics may rely on the natural production of algae and other nutrients in the ponds. The addition of fertilizers encourages the growth of algae.

The range of organisms farmed in mariculture includes such species as the popular milkfish (*Chanos chanos*) of South-East Asia, as well as salmon in the temperate regions. Norway is the world's largest producer of sea-farmed salmon, with an estimated yield in 1990 of 150,000 tonnes. Some ten per cent of Norway's workforce is employed on fish farms, and the country supplies about 80 per cent of the world's salmon production. Salmon farming is also of growing importance in Chile, the Faeroe Islands and New Zealand. The yellowtail (*Seriola quinqueradiata*) represents another important sea-farmed fish, and yielded over 160,000 tonnes in 1987.

Over 30 different species of seaweeds are grown in farms, of which sea mustard (*Undaria* spp.) and kelp (*Laminaria* spp.) are the most important. Korea and China each produce more than 250,000 tonnes of seaweed annually. Dried seaweeds are used as food for farmed fish and crustaceans. Seaweeds are sources of alginates, used in industry as gelling, clarifying and thickening agents. Agar, a gelatinous substance derived from seaweed, is used in health care as a growth medium for bacteria.

The high price of crustaceans on the world market makes them an attractive mariculture prospect for some tropical developing countries. In many instances,

Oysters are cultivated both as food and for their pearls. These black pearl oysters in Tahiti (right) are suspended in the ocean from which they filter plankton. Culturing starts with the collection of oyster larvae – spats or "seeds" – by stringing oyster or scallop shells onto a wire hung in the water. The "seeds" settle on these and are grown until ready for harvesting. Pearl oysters are "seeded" by inserting a small bead of shell from a freshwater clam between the oyster's shell and its living tissue. The oyster then builds up layers of pearl around this core.

culture relies on the capture of wild, spawned juveniles and so cannot sustain itself. Prawns (*Penaeus* spp.) are grown in areas of high salinity, such as mangroves converted for pond culture.

Environmental problems

Perhaps the most important problem caused by mariculture is the conversion of mangrove swamps into ponds to raise prawns. Ecuador's total prawn production rose from 4,700 tonnes in 1979 to 35,600 tonnes in 1983. However, this also led to the removal of one-third of the country's mangroves. This destruction of natural habitats leads to the decline of wild populations, resulting in fewer juveniles with which to stock mariculture ponds. In Louisiana and the Mississippi basin of North America, the exploitation of freshwater mussels to provide shell fragments for "seeding" pearl oysters has led to a significant decline in the number of these animals.

However, destruction of coastal habitats is not the only problem created by mariculture. The build-up of faecal matter beneath the cages of mariculture facilities encourages the growth of algae, which depletes the oxygen supply in the water. Oyster culture has been demonstrated to reduce the phytoplankton food stock by 75-90 per cent. The unrestricted use of antibiotics and other chemicals and the siting of mollusc farms near sewage outfalls pose potential health risks to humans.

The introduction of cultured marine organisms can also result in the accidental transmission of diseases and pests. In 1928, the American oyster drill (*Urosalpinx cinerea*) was introduced to England in this way and became a serious predator of oyster populations. International agreements now regulate the movement of molluscs and shellfish from country to country in an attempt to restrict the spread of disease and other pest-related problems.

Algae, or seaweed, shown under cultivation (left) on Sabu Island, Indonesia, forms an important mariculture crop. The annual world yield of farmed seaweed is greater than that of any farmed species of fish or shellfish. Algae play an important role in the cuisine of many Asian countries, notably Japan. Extracts from algae are also used in the production of beer, iodine and cosmetics. Algae can be cultivated in several ways, including the use of rafts. Here, algae are being harvested from rock pools. Small pieces are tied to a rock with raffia. They are then placed in the pool and allowed to grow until large enough to be harvested.

MILKFISH FARMING

The milkfish is a popular mariculture species in some parts of South-East Asia. The adult milkfish spend most of their lives at sea, but return to shallow coastal waters to spawn. The milkfish fry are collected in shallow water by fishermen using nets. They are then transferred to brackish, warm water ponds, known as *tambak* in Indonesia. The first pond acts as a "nursery" where the fry feed and grow. Later the fish are transferred to larger, deeper ponds and part of the crop may be harvested for food at each growth stage. The toothless younger fish feed on the blooms of blue-green algae which develop in the water. Larger fish graze on the mat of algae which grows on the bottom of the ponds. Animals such as crabs, which might compete for food with the young fish, are removed from the ponds by hand. In some systems, the addition of natural or artificial fertilizers encourages the growth of algae. The adult milkfish are harvested when they reach a size of 300-450 grams (0.7-0.9 pound).

Minerals from the Sea

The oceans are a vast storehouse of valuable non-living resources. These range from oil, gas, metals and building materials to salt and even fresh water. The mineral and energy resources of the oceans could be more important than those of the continents, but the expense and difficulty of exploitation has limited the degree to which they have been developed so far. The exploitation of minerals from the sea bed is an increasing possibility as technologies advance and the more readily exploited mineral reserves on land become exhausted.

Minerals from the surface of the sea bed

Two types of mineral resources are found on the deep-sea bottom: metallic muds and polymetallic nodules (sometimes known as manganese nodules, although they contain a mixture of metals). Poly-metallic nodules are found individually, or clumped as pavements, in all of the world's oceans. The nodules are made up of mineral salts which crystallize from sea water, and contain valuable metals such as manganese, iron, cobalt, chrome, vanadium, radium and titanium. Forty billion tonnes of manganese could be extracted from the nodules of the Pacific alone, representing over 40 times the estimated continental reserve. Metallic muds and brines are found in the Red Sea, part of the East African rift valley system, and around oceanic ridges. These coloured muds are often hot or of extremely high salinity. Among the useful minerals that can be extracted are zinc, copper, iron, manganese and lead. Rarer minerals include cassiterite from South-East Asia, diamonds from South Africa and gold from Alaska. The continental shelf is also a source of sand, gravel and pebbles of mineral and biogenic origin (from coral, for example).

Hydrocarbons from beneath the sea bed

The continental shelves contain a significant proportion of the world's supplies of hydrocarbons. Submarine reserves of oil and gas represent at least a third of the estimated total world reserves. Of these reserves, 85 per cent are found within 320 kilometres (200 miles) of the coastline. The high commercial value of these resources has been sufficient to spur significant investment in the development of offshore exploration technologies, and about 20 per cent of the natural gas and 25 per cent of the oil produced annually are now obtained from continental shelves. The extraction of coal from beneath the sea bed is usually a continuation of land-based mining activities. More than 100 sites have been discovered around the world where galleries extend for more than 20 kilometres (12.5 miles) under the sea bed, and undersea sources now meet two per cent of world production.

Alternative energy extraction

The kinetic energy of waves, currents and tides, and the temperature variation with depth, represents a source of power that could potentially be tapped. Although the technologies required to make this

Under the bed of the North Sea lie large reserves of oil and natural gas, but oil-drilling platforms (right) like this Norwegian rig must be able to withstand the region's heavy seas and frequent storms. Development of North Sea oil and gas began in the 1960s, following the discovery of a large gas field off the coast of the Netherlands. Although the search for oil and gas has led to important technological advances, development of these resources has also led to increasing pollution of the marine environment. Norway and Great Britain own most of the major oil and gas deposits.

Large evaporation pans, like these in Thailand (right), *are used in warmer climates to extract salt from sea water. Sea water contains large quantities of dissolved minerals, the most important and abundant of which is sodium chloride. More than one-third of the world's supply is obtained through evaporation. Other minerals extracted from sea water include magnesium, and much of the world's supply of bromine. Sea water is also used to produce fresh water.*

After machines have removed the sand cover, workers clean the bedrock by hand (below) *to remove diamond-bearing gravels along the Namibian coast. Diamond mining accounts for 31 per cent of Namibia's export income. The country also boasts rich placer deposits in the sea around the Orange River Delta. These diamonds were probably carried by the river from sources far inland.*

energy available to man are complex and expensive, there have been some successful developments. Tidal energy has been extracted since 1966 at the mouth of the river Rance in France, and the power output from this site is now 550 MkW per hour. At present there are only three tidal barrages operating around the world, although there are a number of river mouths with a long tidal reach suitable for the production of tidal energy. Wave energy is currently used only in powering automatic buoys used for navigation and research purposes.

Ocean thermal energy conversion (OTEC), which exploits the temperature difference between water at different depths by the use of heat exchangers, has proved successful at a number of experimental sites and might be developed for commercial use on a small scale. Renewable ocean thermal energy continues to be an area of active research and development, but at present its exploitation does not offer an economic alternative to non-renewable forms of energy except in a few limited areas.

These manganese nodules (above), *also known as polymetallic nodules, are found on the bottom of the Pacific Ocean, at a depth of 4,876m (16,000ft). The potato-shaped nodules contain a range of minerals, and are found on the floor of the deep ocean. In terms of commercially valuable mineral content, some of the most promising areas for possible future exploitation lie in the north-eastern equatorial* Pacific, *and in the central Indian Ocean. Although composition of the nodules varies, the main element present is manganese. However, commercial interest centres on their copper, nickel and cobalt content. They may also contain iron, silicon, aluminium, sodium and calcium. Manganese nodules form through the crystallization of minerals and salts from sea water and the pore waters of the sea bed.*

Environmental Stress

Dramatic events such as major oil spills in Alaska or the Persian Gulf, the detonation of nuclear devices on Mururoa Atoll in the Pacific, mass mortalities of seals in the North Sea and corals in the Caribbean, and the appearance of harmful algal blooms in the Mediterranean may make headlines in the world press. However, these events are merely symptomatic of more widespread and less obvious pressures facing the marine environment and its resources. The underlying cause of many of the problems of marine and coastal areas is the increased demands placed on them by expanding populations. The rapid growth of coastal settlements, the expansion of recreational areas and the concentration of industrial development in coastal areas all result in an accelerated rate of environmental degradation and habitat loss along the world's coastlines.

The population explosion

Around 65 per cent of cities with populations above 2.5 million inhabitants are coastal. Several of those are at, or below, present sea level. By the year 2050, the world's population is expected to increase from its present level of five billion to nearly 12 billion. Around 60 per cent will live within 60 kilometres (40 miles) of the coast and perhaps as many as three-quarters will inhabit tropical developing countries. Many of the world's largest delta systems are also the sites for major cities, since the rivers themselves serve as a means of communication inland and the cities are linked by maritime trade routes to other international centres. Deltas, their associated wetlands and, in particular, marsh, swamp and mangrove ecosystems, are threatened worldwide.

Population increases along the coast reflect both changes in the distribution of human populations and the absolute increase in human numbers. In many countries, problems of "urban drift" are also problems of "coastal drift", since most urban settlements are themselves coastal. Increases in population numbers result in direct pressure on coastal land and marine resources with reclamation of wetland areas, increased waste discharge to coastal waters, increased exploitation rates of living marine resources, and an increase in inshore areas used for mariculture.

In some cases, the causes of coastal marine ecosystem degradation are less obvious, but may include poor land-use activities at a considerable distance from the coast. For example, depletion of upland forest in Madagascar, the use of marginal lands for grazing or subsistence in Africa, mining in Latin America, South-East Asia and the Pacific, and construction activities worldwide all increase soil erosion and hence increase sediment inputs into inshore waters. Such sediments may smother sensitive habitats and biological communities such as coral reefs and sea grass beds, silt up harbours or contaminate shellfish when the sediments carry high loads of heavy metals.

Altering the environment

Dam construction for freshwater management or hydro-power generation reduces sediment and freshwater inputs to coastal floodplains and deltas. This causes nutrient starvation, accelerated erosion and remobilization of coastal sediments, interrupts fish migrations, alters the salinity in coastal waters, and changes the boundaries between fresh and saline water plant communities. On small tropical islands, the lack of suitable building and construction materials means that populations must rely on coral reefs to supply construction blocks and sand.

Local people sell items gleaned from a coral reef near Mombasa, Kenya (left). Raiding coral reefs for tourist souvenirs is a burgeoning industry, despite attempts that have been made in many areas to restrict this form of harmful exploitation. In addition to shells collected for sale to tourists, the reef itself may be irreparably damaged by the collection of coral heads, which are bleached and sold as curios. In addition the collection of marine fishes for the international aquarium trade involves chemicals that not only stress the fish but also harm nearby organisms.

Mangrove forests like this Australian example in Queensland (left) are often cleared for industrial development – in this case for oil storage. In other parts of Australia, mangroves have been cleared for housing. In South-East Asia they have been chopped down to make woodchips; over 1,200 sq km (463 sq miles) – 40 per cent of the total – have been destroyed for this purpose in the Malaysian state of Sabah. Other causes of mangrove destruction include clearance for salt ponds and fish farms.

Seasonal influxes of tourists (below) place further direct pressure on the marine and coastal environment. To meet the demands for accommodation, coastal construction of hotels and resorts occurs in already densely populated areas. Construction activities increase sediment runoff into coastal waters, damaging sensitive habitats.

In some instances, the use of coastal habitats for one purpose may directly affect its use and productivity for the same purpose. The removal of tropical mangroves to construct mariculture ponds for the culture of penaeid prawns, for example, results in loss of the very habitats needed by the juveniles that are captured to stock pens. This not only causes declines in the wild populations, and hence commercial catches, but also a decline in the availability of juveniles in the wild, which are used for stocking culture ponds in many areas.

Conflicts of use

It is interesting to note that many of the present human uses of coastal and inshore areas are themselves in conflict. For example, raw sewage is often discharged in the vicinity of bathing beaches, and undersea cables or pipes may disrupt trawl fishing grounds. Resolving such conflicts of use poses a major problem for coastal zone managers worldwide. The problems of conservation and protection of the marine environment and its unique fauna and flora must be addressed within the framework of continued human use of the sea.

Diminishing Resources

The plight of the great whales and fur seals, whose populations declined in numbers as a consequence of commercial exploitation, is well known. Less well known is the decline in status of many commercial fish and shellfish stocks worldwide, and the local and global extinction of species of marine mammals, birds and molluscs. The expanding human populations of coastal areas increase demand for marine products, placing wild populations under increasing pressure through habitat destruction and incidental death of animals in fishing gear.

The populations of many fish and other marine resource species undergo natural fluctuations in numbers. Under suitable conditions for larval survival, populations undergo explosive increases, reaching numbers several tens or hundreds of times as large as previous generations. Natural fluctuations in numbers often follow long-term cycles and involve mechanisms which are unclear. The catches of Far Eastern, Californian and Chilean sardines, for example, have fluctuated in numbers simultaneously over the last 90 years, suggesting that some Pacific-wide environmental factor may be affecting these populations. Distinguishing between natural and anthropogenic changes is difficult, making the task of regulating catches very much a matter of inspired guesswork. Ideally, exploitation should not exceed the maximum sustainable yield of a particular species, that is the numbers taken for human use should not exceed the natural rate of replacement. In practice, many fisheries have exceeded these limits, with consequent decline in individual size and abundance of the exploited populations. This is due to difficulties in determining what the optimum yield actually is, in setting limits to fisheries' catches, and in enforcing limits once they are agreed.

The impact of fishing

Fishing results in two sorts of change to the population being caught: decrease in the average size of individuals; and decline in abundance of the "target species". Many species of marine organisms grow continuously throughout life – the older an individual is, the larger it becomes. Because fishing gear is generally designed to catch individuals of larger sizes, one consequence of fishing is the reduction in the numbers of older individuals and hence a decline in the average size of the population. Decline in size of the individuals in a catch is the first sign of overfishing.

Such declines in size of individuals are found not only in commercial fisheries but also in artisanal and in some traditional fisheries where catch rates are high. A good example of decline, recovery and subsequent decline in the size of individuals is found in a population of lobsters on the South Island of New Zealand. Archaeologists examining the remains of these animals from Maori middens found that the average size declined over the several hundred years the site was occupied. Following the Maori wars and the abandonment of the site, the population recovered, reaching larger average size than during the late stages of the Maori occupation. Subsequently, the size declined again under renewed exploitation following the establishment of a commercial fishery in the 19th century.

For populations of animals which have low rates of reproduction, producing only a few individuals during each spawning, or where the growth to maturity takes a long time, the chances of decline in abundance of the animals are increased. In extreme cases, the population may be reduced to such low numbers

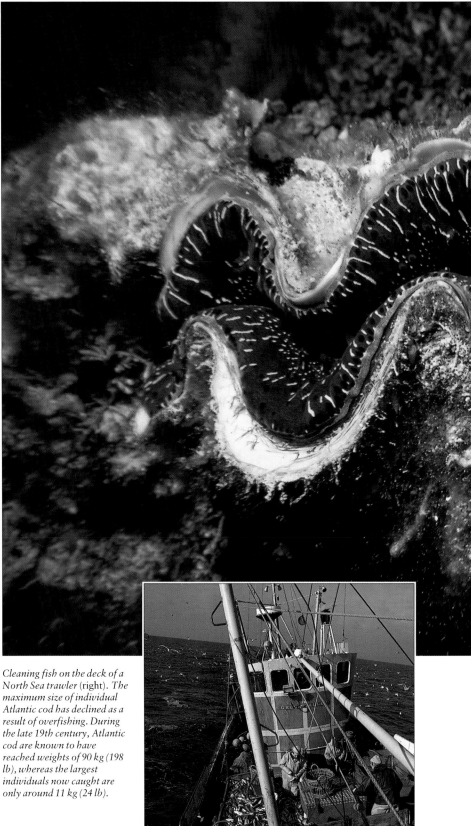

Cleaning fish on the deck of a North Sea trawler (right). The maximum size of individual Atlantic cod has declined as a result of overfishing. During the late 19th century, Atlantic cod are known to have reached weights of 90 kg (198 lb), whereas the largest individuals now caught are only around 11 kg (24 lb).

A reef clam (Tridacna maxima) (left) *from the Great Barrier Reef in Australia. All giant clams are considered to be vulnerable or endangered and are protected under the Convention on International Trade in Endangered Species. Unlike its larger relatives,* Tridacna gigas *and* Tridacna derassa, *this clam is not commercially exploited, but is eaten by indigenous peoples throughout the Asian Pacific region. Commercial exploitation and poaching has led to declines and local extinctions of the larger species in various places throughout their range. Smaller species such as* Tridacna squamosa *and* Hippopus porcellanus *are collected for their shells, which are sold throughout South-East Asia.*

Dolphins accidentally captured in tuna purse seine nets (below) will eventually die by suffocation. Large numbers of marine mammals and seabirds are ensnared in this way. One fishing trip by a fleet of 32 Japanese ships using drift nets is reported to have resulted in the deaths of over 50,000 sharks, over 1,000 small cetaceans, 52 fur seals and 22 turtles, in the process of taking a catch of 3 million squid. These large drift nets not only affect non-target species but also threaten the continued survival of the very species being sought.

that it cannot recover and the species becomes extinct. Steller's sea cow, *Hydrodamalis stelleri*, became extinct only 27 years after its discovery in 1742, and the great auk was hunted out of existence in 1844. In Fiji, the local extinction of the horseshoe clam, *Hippopus hippopus*, around 1,000 years ago, occurred as a consequence of exploitation by coastal Fijian populations, and the subsequent disappearance of the giant clam, *Tridacna gigas*, followed European exploitation this century. Luckily, these species survive in other Melanesian and South-East Asian islands, unlike the great auk and sea cow.

In the past, small numbers of people, using less efficient technologies, limited the extent to which such societies could remove resources. When traditional communities increase in numbers, the resulting increase in demand can and does result in over-exploitation of marine resources. Local depletion of turtle stocks and of dugong, and decline in productivity of coral reef fisheries, are all symptomatic of the overuse of stocks by subsistence populations.

Marine Pollution

Refuse dumped in coastal waters (above) includes plastics, which take many years to decay. Such refuse may drift for thousands of kilometres, often fouling beaches and habitats a long way from the source. Other marine pollutants include agricultural and industrial chemicals such as fertilizers, pesticides, heavy metals and acids, many of which are toxic or change the chemistry of the sea.

The vast extent of the oceans has led people to view them as potential dumping grounds with an endless capacity to absorb waste products. However, evidence from around the world now points to severe damage to the marine environment as a result of the discharge and dumping of sewage, toxic mining wastes, industrial effluent and solid wastes, including litter. The leaching of pesticides, fertilizers and other chemicals from land-based activities such as agriculture causes even more damage. It is estimated that as much as 40 per cent of all marine pollutants stem from land-based sources.

Sewage

The discharge of sewage directly into coastal waters contaminates shellfish and bathing waters with faecal coliform bacteria, and poses a health risk to both swimmers and people dependent on marine resources for food. In recent years, outbreaks of cholera, typhoid and viral hepatitis in Latin America, the Mediterranean and South-East Asia have all been traced to contaminated seafood.

Sewage contains substantial quantities of nitrogen and phosphorus, nutrients which are in short supply in coastal waters. As a result, the discharge of sewage increases primary production – the growth of tiny marine organisms which depend on light and nutrients in the water for their growth. This may increase fish catches – an effect seen in the Mediterranean – but can also result in the formation of extensive blooms of algae. These form a thick scum on the surface of the water. When the algae die and sink to the bottom of the sea, they may increase the rate of decomposition by bacteria which can lead to the deoxygenation of bottom waters, resulting in the death of benthic organisms.

Industrial wastes often contain a mixture of chemicals, such as lubricating oils, heavy metals including cadmium, zinc and copper, bleaching agents, and

strong acids and alkalis. Even in low concentrations, some of these chemicals are extremely toxic to marine organisms. Many chemical contaminants take a long time to break down or become inert. Some chemicals, such as polychlorinated biphenyls (PCBs), continue to cycle in marine organisms even in areas where their use and manufacture have long been discontinued.

Indirect contamination of the marine environment also occurs as a consequence of land-based activities, such as agriculture and industry. The unregulated discharge of effluent into streams and rivers ultimately increases the pollution load of coastal waters. Fertilizers, insecticides and herbicides enter marine waters through river discharge. Agricultural sprays release aerosols into the atmosphere, which then enter the sea through rainfall.

The disposal at sea of solid wastes, including litter, is another major problem. Plastics do not degrade easily and float for long distances. Today, discarded plastic can be found as far afield as isolated Pacific islands or remote beaches in Somalia, while accidental loss of nylon fishing nets presents a hazard to many marine species.

Off the coast of Australia, a small motor vessel dumps jarosite waste into the sea (above). The offshore dumping of mining waste presents localized pollution problems. Direct discharge of mine wastes into rivers and watercourses results in pollution of coastal waters and the smothering of benthic communities.

Major oil spills, such as the 1991 incident in the Persian Gulf (above), result in severe local damage to habitats and to wildlife. Oiled seabirds, such as the guillemot in this picture, usually do not survive contamination. The Exxon Valdez oil spill in Alaska in 1989 is estimated to have led to the deaths of 36,000 seabirds, 3,000 sea otters and 150 sea eagles. The full extent of the damage to habitats and wildlife in the Gulf will take some time to assess.

CONTROLLING MARINE POLLUTION

There is a strong need for international action to control marine contamination and pollution. Pollution is now the subject of numerous regional and international agreements. Conventions regulating the discharge of oil from ships, and the development of emergency response systems to oil pollution accidents have contributed to the apparent decline in ship-based sources of oil pollution over the last two decades. The moratorium on dumping of radioactive wastes at sea under the London Dumping Convention also represents another response to concerns about the risks posed by such disposal. Some regions have concluded agreements which ban dumping or discharge of particular types of wastes. For example, the Latin American region bans the dumping of any radioactive waste at sea. In the Mediterranean and Red Sea, all discharge of oily wastes from ships is also banned.

Oil slicks

Major accidents, such as the *Exxon Valdez* oil spill in Alaska in 1989, result in catastrophic damage to coastal habitats from the smothering and toxic effects of oil. Despite such disasters, marine pollution caused by oil from shipping is estimated to have declined since the early 1970s, as a consequence of international agreements and the control of ship-based discharges. In contrast, oil pollution from land-based sources is estimated to have significantly increased over the same period.

Many problems of marine pollution are localized, and often associated with particular economic activities. The discharge of mine wastes can smother coastal communities, as in Thailand, where tin mining has disrupted coastal sediments. Offshore oil platforms affect sensitive bottom-dwelling communities through the discharge of drilling mud, which is often contaminated by oil, while fish mariculture in enclosed bays or inlets can lead to the eutrophication (depletion of oxygen) of bottom waters. As the pressures for space in coastal and near-shore areas increase, so will the frequency and intensity of localized pollution problems.

The appearance of massive blooms of algae along Italy's Adriatic coast prompted this protest (above left). Algal blooms may appear in areas where nutrients from human sewage or agricultural fertilizers build up in enclosed or calm waters. Unpleasant in appearance, the blooms often contain toxic algae. When filtered out of the water by molluscs, the toxic residues can make these food resources poisonous to humans. In recent years such outbreaks of shellfish poisoning have increased in frequency.

The Atlas

The differences between terrestrial regions are well known. Less well known are the features that distinguish the Atlantic from the Pacific oceans, or the coasts of South America from those of Southern Africa. Regardless of this, the various regions of the world's oceans are all affected by human activities, with pollution and harvesting of resources being common to all seas and oceans. The various marine resources, as well as the extent of human impacts on them, are examined region by region, illustrating how stresses on the marine environment threaten the very existence of some habitats and species.

There is a long and varied tradition of fishing off the Malabar Coast, India.

The Global Ocean

Dividing seven-tenths of the Earth's surface into distinct areas which can be mapped and discussed separately is not easy. For example, a division which works well for physical oceanography will not work well for migratory species or regional pollution issues. The divisions used in this atlas have been made on the basis of reasonably separate, recognizable areas which share common problems and ocean systems. These groupings of countries usually have some form of joint approach to conservation and management of the marine environment, and the areas are similar to those of the Regional Seas Programme of the United Nations Environment Programme (UNEP). The maps do not indicate any expression of opinion concerning the legal status of any state, territory, city or area, nor the delimitations of its boundaries or frontiers. The maps focus on coasts, because ocean environmental problems are largely concentrated in coastal and inshore areas, where the highest densities of people and human activity are located.

Symbols used on the maps

Pollution of coastal and inshore areas is shown in a qualitative way based on three major divisions: domestic effluent (including sewage), which generally reflects population density and concentration; oil pollution around production and trans-shipment sites, and chemical runoff from sources such as agriculture; and pollution from mining and industrial sources. Mining pollution results from disposal of wastes from ore processing plants and the mines themselves, while industrial pollution includes a variety of different types of waste. The size of each pollution symbol gives an idea of the amount of marine pollution at the site, but the relative importance of the three types of discharge is not indicated. This is because data on the levels and quantities of pollutants entering the sea are not available for most areas of the world.

Ocean dump sites used for disposal of low-level radioactive wastes during the 1960s and 1970s are also indicated. The sites shown are only those which have been officially reported and are no longer operational, following the moratorium on ocean dumping of radioactive wastes agreed to by the signatory states of the London Dumping Convention.

In some areas, tourism is a major source of coastal environmental problems, both in terms of the number of visitors and in terms of coastal modifications to provide tourist facilities. In areas where the entire coastline is used for tourism, sites have not been individually mapped, but the existence of problems is indicated in the text.

Threatened species have been mapped using the IUCN Red Data Book, and a full list appears on page 194. The maps show species that are threatened locally as well as those that are threatened in more than one ocean. However, some species are difficult to map because they are dispersed globally. For example, blue, fin and humpback whales may be found in many ocean regions, but they are not shown on all maps because this could imply that their numbers are greater than they actually are. Instead, their major migration routes are mapped.

Important coastal ecosystems such as mangroves, coral reefs, kelp and sea grass beds are shown on the regional maps. Each regional map contains an overview box which summarizes fisheries, environments, development status, and legal conventions of that region.

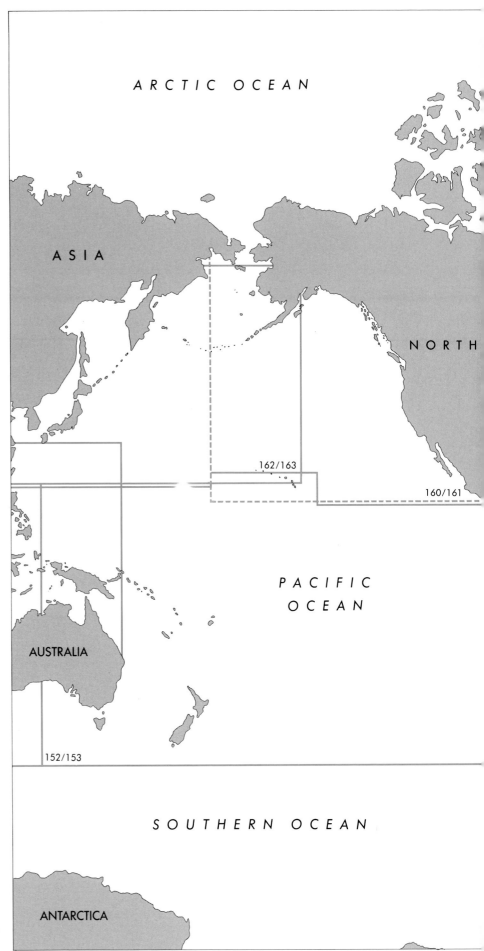

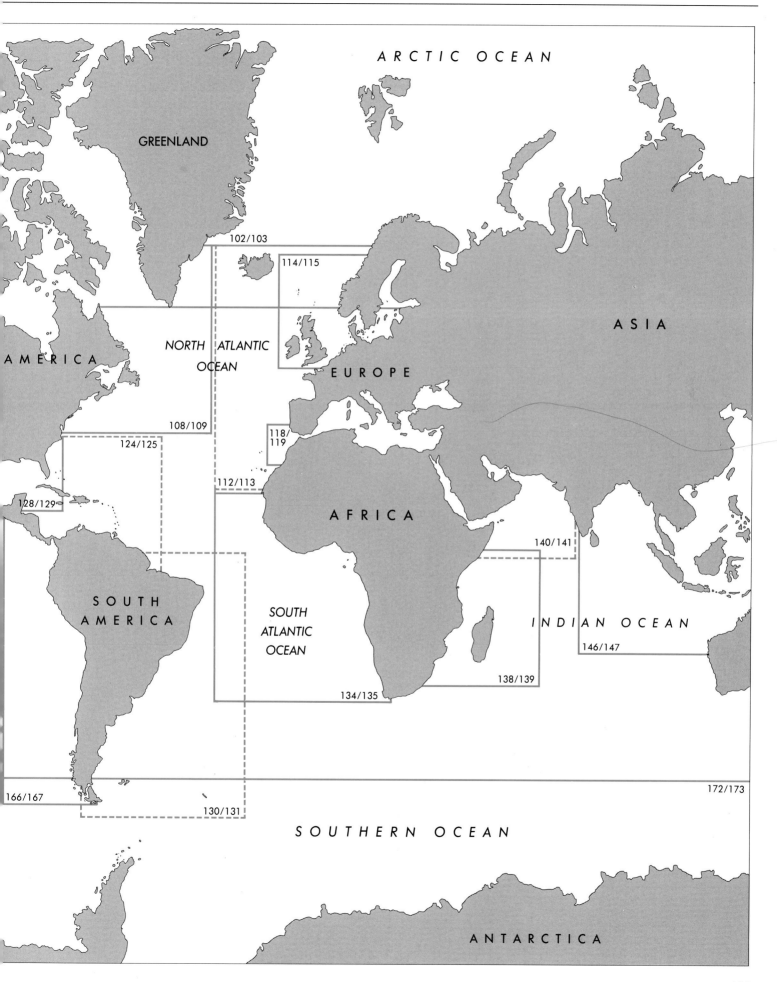

ARCTIC OCEAN

GREENLAND

102/103

114/115

ASIA

AMERICA

NORTH ATLANTIC
OCEAN

EUROPE

108/109

118/
119

124/125

112/113

128/129

AFRICA

140/141

SOUTH
AMERICA

INDIAN OCEAN

SOUTH
ATLANTIC
OCEAN

146/147

138/139

166/167

172/173

134/135

130/131

SOUTHERN OCEAN

ANTARCTICA

Arctic Ocean

The Arctic Ocean is the smallest of the world's oceans. It is encircled by Eurasia, Greenland and North America. Its average depth is about 1,000 metres (3,300 feet), though in places it does reach about six times this. There are four major basins separated by three oceanic ridges of which the largest, the Lomonosov Ridge, extends for 1,750 kilometres (1,100 miles).

Water enters and leaves the Arctic Ocean through the gap between Svalbard and Greenland. A deep-water current near Svalbard accounts for nearly 80 per cent of the incoming water, which is balanced by a less saline outflow on the surface. Two per cent of the water leaving the ocean is in the form of icebergs. The ocean itself is covered by a layer of sea ice which in late winter extends to up to 15 million square kilometres (six million square miles). In summer, it shrinks to about half this size.

Animals and people in the Arctic

Many marine animals in the Arctic migrate as the sea ice advances and retreats with the seasons. Most live near the edge of the ice. It provides hauling-out areas for such animals as polar bears, seals and walruses. Numerous species are found all round the North Pole, but are often divided into several distinct stocks or subspecies. Many bird species are seasonal and also undergo long migrations.

Human populations have existed around the Arctic Ocean for thousands of years. A distinction is often made between the Nordic populations, whose life style is based on the herding of reindeer, and the North American, Siberian and Greenland populations who subsist by hunting marine mammals.

The Arctic attracted commercial hunting expeditions from the 16th century onwards. They came from the Basque region of northern Spain and based themselves in Svalbard. Although commercial hunting has now been stopped, subsistence hunting remains important to indigenous peoples.

The small number of indigenous people and the scarcity of major resources (except petroleum) mean that human pressure is relatively low. Oil was discovered on the Arctic coast of Alaska in 1968. Nine years later the 1,270-kilometre (800-mile) Trans Alaska pipeline came into operation, carrying crude oil south from Prudhoe Bay on Alaska's Arctic coast. Although the direct environmental impact of drilling is very localized, indirectly the traditional life of the Inuit has been disrupted in many ways. In the Soviet Arctic there is potential for both gas and oil drilling which is as yet unexploited.

The Arctic is strategic to the USSR, Canada and the United States, and is governed by international maritime law. But there are initiatives by circumpolar people to deal with common issues, and the idea of a Regional Convention, similar to the one for the Mediterranean Sea, has been proposed to guide the future management of the region.

Despite the low levels of industrial activity, air pollution is transported northwards from industrial regions. The airborne contaminants consist of particles and gases such as sulphur dioxide which form aerosols, scattering light and reducing visibility. Levels of some contaminants are comparable to those over urban areas. The haze has been extensively researched, but 60 per cent of the material remains unidentified. It has the potential to alter the heat balance of the Arctic region, though it cannot yet be ascertained whether the net effect would be an increase or a decrease in temperature.

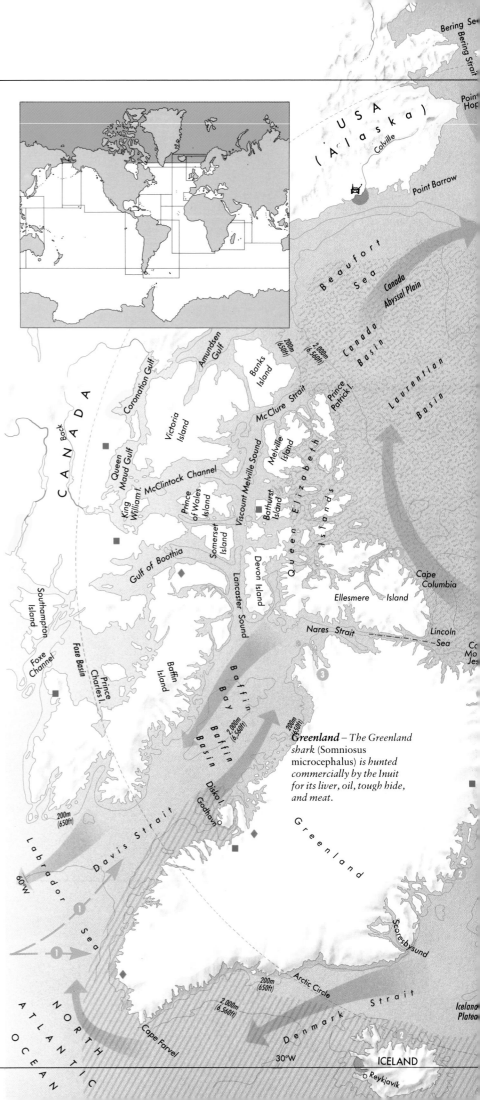

Greenland – *The Greenland shark (Somniosus microcephalus) is hunted commercially by the Inuit for its liver, oil, tough hide, and meat.*

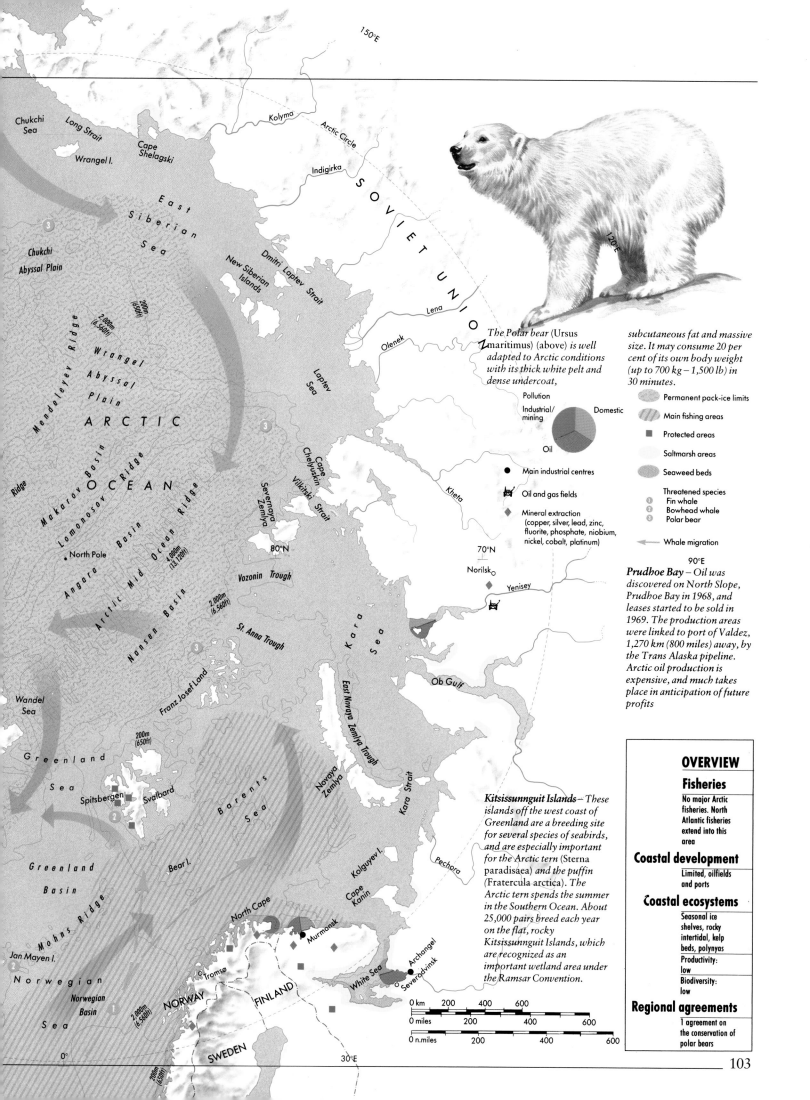

Chukchi Sea

Long Strait

Cape Shelagski

Wrangel I.

Kolyma

Arctic Circle

Indigirka

150°E

S O V I E T   U N I O N

120°E

East Siberian Sea

Chukchi Abyssal Plain

3

Dmitri Laptev Strait

New Siberian Islands

Lena

Olenek

Laptev Sea

Mendeleyev Ridge

Wrangel Abyssal Plain

2,000m (6,560ft)

200m (650ft)

A R C T I C

Makarov Basin

O C E A N

Lomonosov Ridge

Severnaya Zemlya

Cape Chelyuskin

Vilkitski Strait

Kheta

3

Ridge

Angara Basin

Arctic Mid Ocean Ridge

4,000m (13,120ft)

North Pole

Vozonin Trough

80°N

Nansen Basin

2,000m (6,560ft)

St. Anna Trough

Franz Josef Land

3

Kara Sea

70°N

Norilsk

Yenisey

Wandel Sea

East Novaya Zemlya Trough

Ob Gulf

Greenland Sea

200m (650ft)

Spitsbergen

Svalbard

2

Novaya Zemlya

Barents Sea

Kara Strait

Greenland Basin

Bear I.

Kolguyev I.

Pechora

Mohns Ridge

Cape Kanin

Jan Mayen I.

1

North Cape

Murmansk

Norwegian Sea

Norwegian Basin

Tromsø

NORWAY

Archangel

Severodvinsk

2,000m (6,560ft)

White Sea

FINLAND

SWEDEN

0°

200m (650ft)

30°E

The Polar bear (Ursus maritimus) (above) is well adapted to Arctic conditions with its thick white pelt and dense undercoat, subcutaneous fat and massive size. It may consume 20 per cent of its own body weight (up to 700 kg – 1,500 lb) in 30 minutes.

Pollution

Industrial/ mining

Domestic

Oil

● Main industrial centres

Oil and gas fields

◆ Mineral extraction (copper, silver, lead, zinc, fluorite, phosphate, niobium, nickel, cobalt, platinum)

Permanent pack-ice limits

Main fishing areas

■ Protected areas

Saltmarsh areas

Seaweed beds

Threatened species
① Fin whale
② Bowhead whale
③ Polar bear

→ Whale migration

90°E

***Prudhoe Bay** – Oil was discovered on North Slope, Prudhoe Bay in 1968, and leases started to be sold in 1969. The production areas were linked to port of Valdez, 1,270 km (800 miles) away, by the Trans Alaska pipeline. Arctic oil production is expensive, and much takes place in anticipation of future profits*

***Kitsissunnguit Islands** – These islands off the west coast of Greenland are a breeding site for several species of seabirds, and are especially important for the Arctic tern (Sterna paradisaea) and the puffin (Fratercula arctica). The Arctic tern spends the summer in the Southern Ocean. About 25,000 pairs breed each year on the flat, rocky Kitsissunnguit Islands, which are recognized as an important wetland area under the Ramsar Convention.*

0 km	200	400	600
0 miles	200	400	600
0 n.miles	200	400	600

OVERVIEW

Fisheries

No major Arctic fisheries. North Atlantic fisheries extend into this area

Coastal development

Limited, oilfields and ports

Coastal ecosystems

Seasonal ice shelves, rocky intertidal, kelp beds, polynyas

Productivity: low

Biodiversity: low

Regional agreements

1 agreement on the conservation of polar bears

103

Life in the Arctic Ocean

Mammals dominate the Arctic marine ecosystem. They include seals, walrus, whales and polar bears. Although there is little wildlife at the centre of the Arctic Basin, around the edge, where the sea ice advances and retreats with the seasons and winds and currents bring up nutrients from the depths, an abundance of marine animals and plants flourish during the summer. Polynyas (small areas of open water in the ice) are used by birds and mammals as feeding grounds and by the peoples of the Arctic. The polynyas only open in warm weather, and many animals die if they fail to appear.

The base of the food chain

The primary productivity (the rate at which plants and algae convert sunlight into food) of the plankton at the base of the Arctic food chain is only about one tenth of that found in temperate regions. It is limited by low light levels as a result of the presence of sea ice, the long dark winters, and the low angle at which the sun shines on the region even in summer. Spring brings an increase in the light level, which triggers an explosion of photosynthetic algae, mainly diatoms, that live on the underside of the sea ice and in open water. The ice algae start to grow in February and by the end of March have formed a yellow-brown layer within the bottom 30 centimetres (12 inches) of ice. They are directly grazed by the Arctic cod (*Boreogadus saida*), the only fish which is found in the central Arctic Basin. Around the edge of the Basin, other plankton-feeding fish are found, including the Arctic char (*Salvelinus alpinus*) and the capelin (*Mallotus villosus*). Kelp is found in a few isolated coastal areas, but it is photosynthetically active only in the summer. The fauna associated with the kelp are active all year round, and are eaten by migratory fish in summer. In addition, a significant supply of detritus enters the ocean from the Pacific. It is consumed by bacteria and tiny shrimp-like amphiopods and isopods. These animals survive all year round by avoiding areas of deep-sea ice in winter.

The walrus (Odobenus rosmarus) (right) lives mainly on moving pack ice over shallow continental shelf areas, and often gathers in herds of several thousand individuals. It feeds on the sea bed, using touch to locate food in the sediment at a depth of 10-50 m (33-165 ft). The walrus uses its tusks to open its preferred food, clams. The walrus is preyed on by killer whales, polar bears, and traditionally by humans – hunting by indigenous people continues in most parts of the animal's range, and population fluctuations have caused hardship in the Bering-Chukchi region.

The polar bear (Ursus maritimus) (below) spends the brief Arctic summers on drifting ice and migrates southwards in winter. Young bears may be killed by wolves in places where the ranges of the two species overlap, but the major predator is man. The International Agreement on Conservation of Polar Bears was ratified in 1976 by the five countries in whose territories the bear is found. It is protected in Alaska under the US Marine Mammal Act 1972 – only indigenous people may hunt, then only for personal consumption.

The Arctic tern (Sterna paradisaea) (below) has excellent camouflage against the mossy ground cover of the Arctic regions. Although it breeds in the Arctic, the tern undertakes one of the greatest migrations of any living creature when it flies 15,000 km (9,300 miles) to its summer feeding grounds in the Antarctic. The tern takes an indirect route to take full advantage of prevailing winds.

Links in the food chain

Arctic food webs contain relatively few "intermediate" species – those which feed on the plankton and are in turn consumed by top predators. In the Barents Sea, for example, the community living below the ice includes three species of amphipod believed to form a link, along with Arctic cod, of energy transfer from primary producers to seabirds and mammals. There are few species of diving birds because of the small number of fish species for them to feed upon. The seals of the Arctic feed on a diet which consists mostly of fish. The exceptions are the walrus (*Odobenus rosmarus*) and the bearded seal (*Erignathus barbatus*) which feed on bottom-dwelling molluscs and crustaceans. These two species are the main food of the polar bear (*Ursus maritimus*).

Mammals, including man, are top predators in the Arctic food chain. Whale species include the minke whale (*Balaenoptera acutorostrata*), a baleen whale which feeds on fish, squid and shrimp, and the orca or killer whale (*Orcinus orca*), a toothed whale which feeds on seals. The orca may also take the calves of the plankton-feeding baleen whales. Only the beluga whale (*Delphinapterus leucas*) and the narwhal (*Monodon monoceros*) are true Arctic species. The rest, including the bowhead (*Balaena mysticetus*), bottlenose (*Hyperoodon ampullatus*) and blue (*Balaenoptera musculus*) whales, are migratory species that use the edges of the Arctic Ocean only during the summer months to feed and breed.

Adapting to the cold

The animals of the Arctic are suited to the extreme climatic conditions by a number of physiological and behavioural adaptions. Physiological adaptations in mammals include the thick layer of insulating blubber, which acts as a food reserve in times of hardship, a high body mass and a low surface area. The blubber is built up by seals and whales during their summer feeding period. Constant foraging when conditions are favourable and the rapid development of young are adaptations that help individuals to meet their high energy requirements. The excellent insulating qualities of feathers enable birds to survive and even overwinter in the Arctic; however, a high proportion of the Arctic birds migrate southwards in the summer.

Arctic Peoples

The people who live on the shores of the Earth's most northerly sea have developed a close relationship with the fish, birds and mammals of the Arctic. Most Arctic peoples live between 60° and 72°N, but in north-west Greenland, the Inuit are found as far as 79°N. The average temperature during winter in coastal regions is –34°C (–29°F), so survival depends on a high degree of adaptation to the harsh environment, and efficient use of its resources. Although they once led a nomadic existence, many Arctic peoples have now settled. The igloo is probably the best-known form of housing used by the Inuit, but they also use subterranean houses which have earth walls, and driftwood or occasionally whalebone frames. Raised sleeping benches enable them to keep warm during the long, cold nights of winter. The introduction of modern technology has led to dramatic changes in the traditional lifestyle, and many Arctic people now live in prefabricated houses.

The western Arctic peoples of North America, Greenland and Siberia have developed in relative isolation over the centuries. They are distinguished by their location and to some extent by life style. Their existence depends heavily on the exploitation of the various species which live in the Arctic waters, especially fish and marine mammals. The elephant seal (*Mirounga angustirostris*) has been an essential resource. Its skin is used for boats, clothing and fishing lines; its blood provides dyes; transparent membranes from the intestines can be used for windows, and oil and meat for fuel and food. The Inuit also fish for crustacea, in particular the king crab (*Paralithodes camtschatia*), the legs of which may reach up to one metre (three feet) in length.

In contrast, the Eurasian peoples of the Arctic have been influenced by other cultures over a longer period. They show a greater diversity of culture, with 19 distinct languages. Some of these groups do not exploit ocean resources directly, but live by herding reindeer, hunting and fishing. They include the Lapps of northern Europe, the Nganasan and the Nentsy. Groups which use the sea directly include the Chukchi of Siberia, the Inuit and the Aleut.

Traditional and modern lifestyles

Traditional clothing was made from two layers of animal skin with long fur in between to trap air, which acts as insulation. This provides excellent protection against water, wind and cold. A hooded *parka* jacket, trousers and boots, with drawstrings at the wrists, ankles and around the face, was worn by both men and women. Seams were carefully waterproofed. Snow goggles made from pieces of leather with narrow eye slits were also used.

The traditional tools of the Arctic peoples include the toggle-headed harpoon (its detachable head becomes embedded in the prey); a bow made of wood and bone, bound and strung with sinew; and an *atatyl*, which is used for throwing spears. *Kayaks* (canoes) made from skin stretched over bone frames were used for fishing and hunting expeditions.

Today, most Arctic peoples combine traditional and modern materials to make clothing, tools and buildings. Materials obtained from seals and other mammals are still important, especially for clothing, but the harpoon used for hunting seals has now largely been replaced by a high-velocity rifle, and transport has been revolutionized by the introduction of the motorized snowmobile. Some Arctic peoples have given up their traditional life style completely, in exchange for work at oil installations.

Inuit hunters (right) *return home in their kayaks after a day's hunting. Their white clothing and canoes provide camouflage against the background of ice floes, allowing them to approach and harpoon seals without being seen.*

Dog sleds (left) *were an important form of transport for many Arctic peoples during the winter months. The life style of these Arctic people involved travelling great distances to take advantage of seasonally available stocks of fish and marine mammals.*

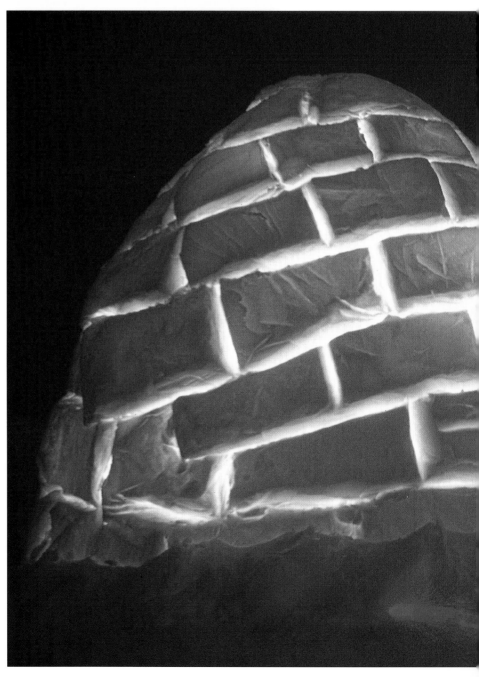

Although traditional materials have been replaced, local handicrafts are still valued and there is a strong movement among many groups to preserve their cultural heritage. The rights of Arctic peoples to continue to lead their unique life styles, which includes traditional harvesting of Arctic animals on a sustainable basis, is being recognized as integral to the future of the whole Arctic region.

The position of the Inuit in the Arctic food web was traditionally limited by technology and by management systems which recognize the dependence of man on the region's wildlife, and therefore the need to conserve resources. The traditional management systems are unwritten but often complex, involving taboos, beliefs and cultural measures such as sharing among kin. This form of self-regulation has often come into conflict with systems imposed from outside which involve cumbersome and bureaucratic licensing and permit arrangements. There is now a growing movement to resolve the issue by comanagement systems.

The traditional igloo (left), photographed at night, shows the spiral construction which makes the dome self-supporting. Igloos can only be constructed where the snow is sufficiently compact to allow blocks to be cut out. Where snow is too powdery, a quinzee *is constructed by piling together a large mound of snow, allowing it to settle, and burrowing in to hollow out the inside.*

Salmon (below) are an important seasonally available food source for many people who live on the Arctic fringes. During spawning runs the fish are speared, netted and trapped and dried or salted for use as a winter food reserve. These fish are eaten by sled dogs as well as by humans. Exploiting the runs of fish may involve whole communities in the catching and processing.

North-West Atlantic

The North Atlantic Ocean extends from tropical to chilly, ice-bound Arctic waters. Most of the world's major industrial countries lie on its shores. As a result, it is one of the world's busiest shipping areas. The North-West region of the Atlantic takes in the coastal waters of the eastern United States and those of Canada.

From its origins in the Caribbean Sea, the Gulf Stream carries warm water north from the tropics and then eastward to Europe. The broad continental shelf of the North-West Atlantic supports one of the richest fisheries in the world. It is narrower near Delaware and Chesapeake Bays which, with the Gulf of Maine, are exceptionally productive because of their extensive salt marsh systems.

Great glaciers shaped the coastal landscape of the North-West Atlantic region. The coasts of Maine and the Canadian provinces of Nova Scotia and New-foundland are rugged, with numerous small rocky islands. Narrow estuaries lined by salt marshes are characteristic as far south as the New York Bight, and mark the furthest limit of glaciation during the last Ice Age, which ended around 10,000 years ago. Cape Hatteras is the southern limit of cold temperate fauna and the northern limit of tropical fauna. Some scientists regard the transition zone between Cape Cod and Cape Hatteras as a separate region, but there are few endemic species.

Animals and plants

In the coastal plain area, extensive salt marshes have developed behind the barrier beaches of Long Island, New Jersey and North Carolina. These areas provide an important wildlife habitat. Salt marshes act as feeding and overwintering grounds for many species of wildfowl and shore birds. However, marshes are increasingly threatened by industrial pollution, dredging, land reclamation, drainage and river control.

The cord grass *Spartina altiflora* is the dominant plant in salt marshes from Florida to the Bay of Fundy. Other primary producers include the phytoplankton (single-celled algae), which bloom in the nutrient-rich waters of estuaries and support consumers. The eelgrass (*Zostera marina*) grows below the tide limit. Its roots help to stabilize bottom sediments, and it is important as a fish nursery. The dominant alga over much of the coastline is the knotted wrack (*Acopyllum nodosom*), which occurs as far as 40°S and as far north as the Arctic Circle. In some areas, up to 80 per cent of the standing crop is harvested, principally for its alginate derivatives.

The Gulf of Maine is an important feeding area for many marine mammals, including the northern right whale (*Eubalaena glacialis*), which is believed to be the most endangered of the large whales.

Fisheries

The current annual fishery is around three million tonnes – close to 75 per cent of the estimated sustainable yield. Fishing is central to coastal communities in Nova Scotia, Newfoundland, and the Gulf of Maine. The most productive fishing grounds are the Grand Banks. Cod, flounder, haddock, pollock and the scallops are harvested on Georges Bank. Four thousand lobster boats operate in the Gulf of Maine. Farther south, striped bass, bluefish, mackerel, menhaden, clams and crabs are caught. Important mariculture species include salmon, trout, mussels, oysters and clams. Mariculture expanded through the 1980s and is expected to continue, but degradation of water quality may be a limiting factor.

The beluga (Delphinapterus leucas) (above) is a close relative of the narwhal. Both belong to the Monodontidae family of toothed whales. The adult beluga reaches a length of 3-5 m (10-15 ft). The beluga inhabits northern coastal waters around North America, Greenland and the northern Soviet Union. It feeds on schooling fish, crustaceans, worms and molluscs. In winter, beluga migrate south in herds of hundreds. In summer, they return to their rich feeding grounds in the Arctic Ocean.

Portland, Maine – *In 1988, an unexpected bloom of the toxic alga* Gymnodinium nagasakiense *around Portland, Maine, killed many bottom-dwelling organisms, including lobsters and clams. Shellfish harvests are also affected by faecal pathogens, which force the closure of contaminated areas. The discovery of contamination in mussels led to the closure of about 1,460 sq km (560 sq miles) of harvesting areas in Canada in 1988.*

Chesapeake Bay – *The largest estuary in the United States is that of the Susquehanna River. There is a gradual increase in salinity from the inland waters of Maryland to the coastal waters of Virginia. Extensive shellfish beds and fish spawning grounds have been the basis of important commercial fisheries in the region. More than 8 million people live within the watershed of the bay, a figure which is expected to increase by a further 2-4 million by the year 2000. Many parts of this unique bay are now polluted, and resources have declined.*

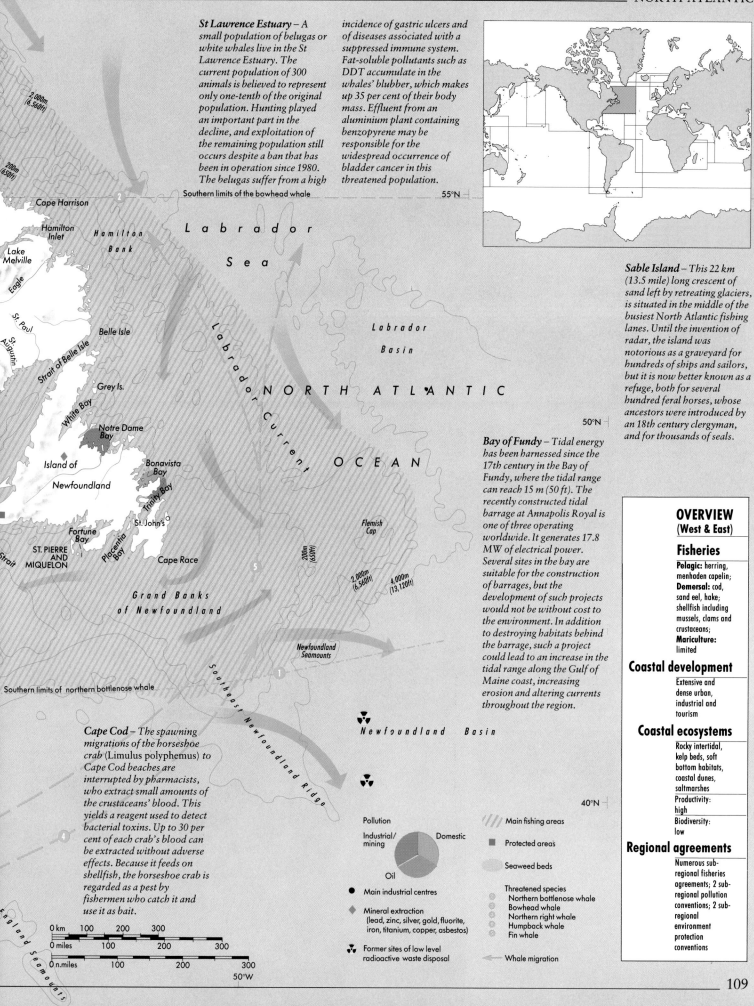

St Lawrence Estuary – A small population of belugas or white whales live in the St Lawrence Estuary. The current population of 300 animals is believed to represent only one-tenth of the original population. Hunting played an important part in the decline, and exploitation of the remaining population still occurs despite a ban that has been in operation since 1980. The belugas suffer from a high

incidence of gastric ulcers and of diseases associated with a suppressed immune system. Fat-soluble pollutants such as DDT accumulate in the whales' blubber, which makes up 35 per cent of their body mass. Effluent from an aluminium plant containing benzopyrene may be responsible for the widespread occurrence of bladder cancer in this threatened population.

Southern limits of the bowhead whale   55°N

Sable Island – This 22 km (13.5 mile) long crescent of sand left by retreating glaciers, is situated in the middle of the busiest North Atlantic fishing lanes. Until the invention of radar, the island was notorious as a graveyard for hundreds of ships and sailors, but it is now better known as a refuge, both for several hundred feral horses, whose ancestors were introduced by an 18th century clergyman, and for thousands of seals.

Bay of Fundy – Tidal energy has been harnessed since the 17th century in the Bay of Fundy, where the tidal range can reach 15 m (50 ft). The recently constructed tidal barrage at Annapolis Royal is one of three operating worldwide. It generates 17.8 MW of electrical power. Several sites in the bay are suitable for the construction of barrages, but the development of such projects would not be without cost to the environment. In addition to destroying habitats behind the barrage, such a project could lead to an increase in the tidal range along the Gulf of Maine coast, increasing erosion and altering currents throughout the region.

Cape Cod – The spawning migrations of the horseshoe crab (Limulus polyphemus) to Cape Cod beaches are interrupted by pharmacists, who extract small amounts of the crustaceans' blood. This yields a reagent used to detect bacterial toxins. Up to 30 per cent of each crab's blood can be extracted without adverse effects. Because it feeds on shellfish, the horseshoe crab is regarded as a pest by fishermen who catch it and use it as bait.

Southern limits of northern bottlenose whale

Map labels

Labrador Sea
Cape Harrison
Hamilton Inlet
Hamilton Bank
Lake Melville
Eagle
St. Paul
St. Augustin
Strait of Belle Isle
Belle Isle
Grey Is.
White Bay
Notre Dame Bay
Island of Newfoundland
Bonavista Bay
Trinity Bay
St. John's
Fortune Bay
Placentia Bay
ST. PIERRE AND MIQUELON
Strait
Cape Race
Grand Banks of Newfoundland
Labrador Current
Labrador Basin
NORTH ATLANTIC OCEAN
Flemish Cap
200m (650ft)
2,000m (6,560ft)
4,000m (13,120ft)
Newfoundland Seamounts
Southeast Newfoundland Ridge
Newfoundland Basin
England Seamounts
50°N
50°W
40°N

2,000m (6,560ft)
200m (650ft)

Legend

Pollution

Industrial/mining — Domestic — Oil

● Main industrial centres

◆ Mineral extraction (lead, zinc, silver, gold, fluorite, iron, titanium, copper, asbestos)

☢ Former sites of low level radioactive waste disposal

/// Main fishing areas

■ Protected areas

Seaweed beds

Threatened species
- Northern bottlenose whale
- Bowhead whale
- Northern right whale
- Humpback whale
- Fin whale

← Whale migration

Scale

0 km — 100 — 200 — 300
0 miles — 100 — 200 — 300
0 n.miles — 100 — 200 — 300

OVERVIEW (West & East)

Fisheries

Pelagic: herring, menhaden capelin;
Demersal: cod, sand eel, hake; shellfish including mussels, clams and crustaceans;
Mariculture: limited

Coastal development

Extensive and dense urban, industrial and tourism

Coastal ecosystems

Rocky intertidal, kelp beds, soft bottom habitats, coastal dunes, saltmarshes

Productivity: high

Biodiversity: low

Regional agreements

Numerous sub-regional fisheries agreements; 2 sub-regional pollution conventions; 2 sub-regional environment protection conventions

Environmental Degradation

Tourism and fishing are vital to coastal economies in this region and are dependent on high-quality coastal environments, which have come under increasing pressure in recent years. The North-West Atlantic seaboard includes the broad, sandy beaches of Massachusetts and New Jersey, and nature reserves such as Maine's Acadia National Park, all of which represent popular tourist destinations. Every year, several million tourists visit the coasts of Nova Scotia, Newfoundland, and the Gulf of Maine, and areas such as Cape Cod and Long island are favourite choices for second homes. City dwellers are attracted both by the beautiful coastal landscape and by the quality of life to be found there.

Sources of pollution

One of the most visible forms of pollution is non-biodegradable wastes, such as plastics, which litter the beaches, and pose a hazard to fishermen and tourists as well as to wildlife. In 1988, medical wastes washed ashore around New York and New Jersey causing the closure of beaches, and the loss of billions of dollars to the tourist industry.

Organic pollution of coastal waters results from sewage discharges as well as from mariculture and industry. Offshore dumping and the discharge of industrial and domestic wastes from metropolitan centres such as New York and Boston have created severe but localized degradation in estuaries and coastal waters. Fish processing plants and pulp and paper mills produce effluent with a high biochemical oxygen demand (BOD). The rapid increase in the numbers of bacteria in water feeding on the effluent reduces dissolved oxygen levels in rivers, estuaries and coastal water, and contributes to excessive algal blooms and toxic algal tides.

The gradual build-up of pollutants also presents a significant environmental threat. Sources of toxic contamination include pesticides from agricultural runoff, tributyl tin (TBT) used in wood preservatives and marine anti-fouling paints, polycyclic aromatic hydrocarbons (PAHs) from the combustion of fossil fuels, and various heavy metals. Significant quantities of these materials have been measured in coastal sediments and in marine organisms such as mussels. Affected organisms suffer reduced resistance to other stresses, and impaired reproduction which may affect the population in the long term. Flounder have been found to be suffering from fin erosion and lesions – conditions which could be caused by the presence of these contaminants.

Overfishing in the North-West Atlantic has reduced numbers of certain species to a level where the fishery may no longer be viable. Efforts are now under way to regulate stocks through the selection of only larger fish.

Many foreign fishing fleets operate in the waters of the North-West Atlantic. As a result of overfishing, fish species on the Georges Bank are unlikely to recover their original diversity. Fishing activities also damage non-target species through entanglement. An estimated 35 per cent of deaths of the endangered northern right whale occur in this way.

A fisherman in Nova Scotia (right) prepares a load of herring as feed for tuna raised in pens in St Margaret's Bay. Herring and cod form the basis of the rich fisheries of the North-West Atlantic, which centre on Georges Bank and the Grand Banks. In recent years, overfishing by commercial fishing fleets has reduced fish stocks.

A yacht skims past the summer houses (far left, inset) *which line the shore of Long Island Sound, an arm of the Atlantic bounded by Long Island and the coasts of Connecticut and New York. Tourism is an important industry in the North-West Atlantic region, and Maine, Massachusetts and New Jersey are major vacation areas. Tourists and summer visitors demand an environment free of obvious pollution. However, the development of tourism itself threatens coastal environments, destroying wildlife habitats such as salt marshes, estuaries and beaches.*

Workers from the US Army Corps of Engineers scoop up floating debris from the waters of New York Harbour (below), *but more serious pollution occurs below the surface. Large metropolitan areas such as New York and Boston generate huge amounts of sewage and other waste, much of which is dumped offshore.*

North-East Atlantic

The North-East Atlantic includes the busy coastal waters around western Europe, a wide continental shelf surrounding the British Isles, and the North Sea. Linked to the North Sea is the shallow basin of the Baltic Sea. The warm Gulf Stream, or North Atlantic Drift, ensures that the waters of the region remain ice-free all year round.

The temperate waters support a rich coastal fishery. Annual catches averaged nearly 3 million tonnes from 1985 to 1987. The sustainable yield of the region may be as high as 4.3 million tonnes per year. The most important species for the region's fisheries is the herring (*Clupea harengus*). This valuable species was initially caught using drift nets, but the fishery became more intensive with the use of trawls.

From the 1960s onward, the use of purse seine nets led to overfishing, and eventual stock collapse. In 1976 a complete ban was imposed on herring fishing, a measure that has stimulated some recovery.

Stocks of many other commercial species such as mackerel, haddock, whiting, saithe and Norway pout, are still in decline. Sand eel stocks are on the increase, but the shrimp fishery faces the possibility of overfishing. Since 1983, North Sea fisheries have been regulated by the European Community's quota system, based on total allowable catches. The Community encourages a reduction in fishing fleets, in an effort to make the number of boats compatible with sustainable yields.

Mariculture is also a significant area of activity. Salmon pens are a common feature of many Scottish sea lochs and Norwegian fjords. Oysters have been cultivated for centuries in the sheltered bays along the coast of Brittany. In 1987, French production of the Pacific cupped oyster (*Crassostrea gigas*) exceeded 125,000 tonnes, and Spain produced more than 240,000 tonnes of the blue mussel (*Mytilus edulis*). Seaweed is also harvested for a wide range of industrial and domestic uses.

Marine life

Fish species support large populations of seabirds and seals. Important breeding populations in the region include the fulmar, gannet, shag, great skua, lesser and great black-backed gulls and razorbill. Northern populations of birds from Arctic Canada and Siberia may overwinter in the North Sea, while other populations migrate southward.

Waterfowl habitats include numerous river deltas and the Waddenzee, a shallow portion of the North Sea surrounded by the West Frisian Islands and the coasts of the Netherlands, Germany and Denmark. River deltas in the United Kingdom alone support around 1.5 million wading birds, or about 40 per cent of the European total.

Three species of seal are found in the North-East Atlantic region. The most numerous is the grey seal (*Halichoerus grypus*), whose numbers have increased since the 1940s. An estimated 92,000 live around the British Isles; however, numbers in the Baltic are declining. In 1988, the harbour seal (*Phoca vitulina*) was severely affected by the sudden appearance of a disease which caused nearly 18,000 deaths, from a stock of 45,000 around the British Isles, North Sea, Waddenzee and the Baltic. The ringed seal (*Phoca hispida botnica*) is found in the northern and eastern parts of Baltic. Its population has declined from more than 100,00 at the start of the 20th century to around 7,000 today. One possible cause of the seal's decline may be the increased level of pollution from organic compounds containing chlorine.

Irish Sea – The nuclear fuel reprocessing plant at Sellafield, England, is responsible for making the Irish Sea one of the most radioactive seas in the world, in spite of the fact that it is not an official dump site.

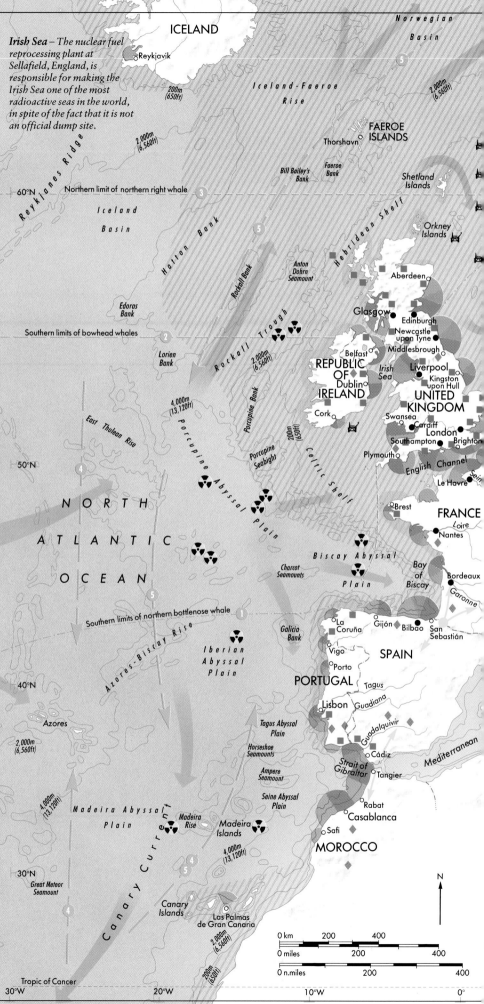

Waddenzee – The Waddenzee covers an area of around 10,000 sq km (3,900 sq miles) along the coasts of Germany and the Netherlands. The salt marshes along the margins of this shallow sea support a varied population of plants and animals. These areas are particularly important to birds, and up to 3 million waders, geese, ducks, gulls and terns may be counted in the region in mid-winter. Large proportions of species such as the barnacle goose (Branta leucopsis), oystercatcher (Haematopus ostralegus), *and* dunlin (Calidris alpina) *depend on the region as a place to overwinter, breed, moult or feed. Some 4,850 sq km (1,900 sq miles) of the Waddenzee enjoys protection as a nature reserve. In addition to mussel culture, the Waddenzee also supports local shrimp and cockle fisheries.*

Anholt Island – The first indicator of the seal disease which swept the North Sea in 1988 was a marked increase in the number of aborted harbour seal (Phoca vitulina) pups on the tiny island of Anholt in the Kattegat. Over the following months the disease spread to almost all of the seal populations in European waters, killing an estimated 18,000 harbour seals from a total population of around 45,000. The deaths were caused by a bacterial influenza known to be a lethal secondary infection to viral diseases which suppress the immuno-response system. The source of the disease and the reasons for its exceptionally rapid spread are unknown, although environmental factors such as changing nutrient balances and changes in seal population dynamics may have aggravated the epidemic.

Orkney and Shetland Islands – These northerly outposts of the British Isles are important breeding grounds for the puffin, one of the few endemic birds of the North Atlantic region. It nests in burrows 1-2 m (3-7 ft) in length, located in turfy soil on rocky slopes facing the sea, or in crevices in cliffs, an option which may lead to competition with the black guillemot or razorbill. The principal component of its diet is fish, which is obtained from coastal waters.

Portsall, France – The Amoco Cadiz oil tanker spilt 1.3 million barrels of light crude oil when it broke up in high winds in March 1976. The oil was rapidly emulsified in water to form a mousse, much of which washed onto Brittany beaches and oyster beds. Oil remained on the beaches for years, killing invertebrates such as sea urchins and clams, as well as an estimated 20,000 migrating birds.

The diminutive puffin (Fratercula arctica) (top right) is a member of the auk family. It inhabits coastal waters in the Arctic Ocean and the North Atlantic. The animal stands around 30 cm (12 in) in height. Puffins are expert swimmers and divers. During June and July, they come to land in order to breed. The gannet (Sula bassana) (bottom right) is the largest of the north european seabirds, with a wingspan of almost 2m (3.3ft). Gannets are noisy and aggressive birds. Their crowded colonies are characterized by constant squabbles.

Legend

Pollution

Industrial/mining — Domestic — Oil

☢ Former sites of low level radioactive waste disposal

Main fishing areas

■ Protected areas

Seaweed beds

● Main industrial centres

⛏ Oil and gas fields

◆ Mineral extraction (copper, lead, zinc, silver, gold, titanium, iron, tin, tungsten, chromium, nickel, uranium, manganese, sulphur, phosphate, cobalt, potash, barytes, fluorite, mercury)

Threatened species
1 Northern bottlenose whale
2 Bowhead whale
3 Northern right whale
4 Humpback whale
5 Fin whale

← Whale migration

Critical locations on soaring bird migration routes

North Sea

With such a heavy concentration of population and industry along its coasts, the environment of the North-East Atlantic and the North Sea faces grave threats to its health. The region suffers both from the exploitation of its resources and from land-based activities. Deep-sea fishing affects the North-East Atlantic ecosystem directly and indirectly. A variety of trawling equipment is used to harvest bottom-dwelling flatfishes, such as plaice and sole. The heavier trawls can damage the environment of the sea floor and its associated benthos. This affects the tiny organisms that are important food sources for the flatfish, as well as for bottom feeders such as cod and haddock. Long after they have been discarded, nylon and plastic fishing nets continue to drift and to catch fish and other animals. Seabirds and fishermen compete for fish, so overfishing causes seabird populations to decline.

Increasing numbers of diseases and unusual physical characteristics have been evident in North Sea fish since the late 19th century. These problems include tumours, fin rot, skeletal deformations, and ulcers. Disease and deformity are most marked in fish caught in the German Bight (or Helgoland Bight), along the Danish coast, and on the Dogger Bank area off the east coast of the United Kingdom. Natural forces like tides and currents influence patterns of disease, but the physical stress caused by pollution may make the situation worse.

Oil and the North Sea

The North Sea receives a constant input of oil from both transportation losses and discharges from production platforms during normal operations. The effects of such chronic pollution are difficult to assess. Oil drilling produces large amounts of waste cuttings that are contaminated by oil. As these materials settle, the sea bottom is subject to prolonged exposure. This can damage the fertility of the bottom environment for a radius of 500 metres (1,640 feet) around the platform, and have serious effects for up to 2.5 kilometres (1.5 miles). Plankton are exposed to hydrocarbons by the discharge of contaminated water used in the production process. Some fish caught near oil platforms show signs of stress, and high levels of hydrocarbons occur in some shellfish. Birds which spend most of their lives at sea, such as guillemots and puffins, also suffer from exposure to the effects of oil.

Accidents which lead to acute pollution are rare, but may have a highly visible impact on wildlife. In July 1988, the explosion which ripped apart the Piper Alpha oil platform led also to the release of oil from 36 neighbouring wells. Although the oil dispersed and sank, damage to four electrical transformers on the platform released dangerous PCBs (polychlorinated biphenyls). When PCBs burn at low temperature, highly toxic dioxins are produced, so it is possible that organisms near the platform were exposed.

Organic pollution results from the discharge of animal wastes, human sewage and chemical runoff from agriculture. Such pollution contributes to toxic algal blooms, which have become more common in recent years. Other major sources of pollution in the North Sea include dumped industrial waste, dredged materials, sewage sludge, ash from power stations, and wastes incinerated at sea. In 1988, the Second Ministerial North Sea Conference resolved to reduce by 50 per cent between 1985 and 1995 the inputs of toxic substances from rivers, including those substances which cause eutrophication.

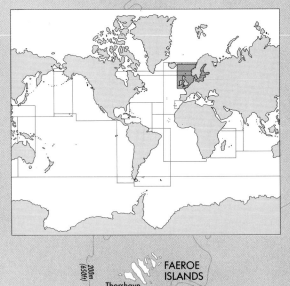

North Sea – Oil production is heaviest in the Shetland Basin, where water depth is up to 200 m (660 ft). Gas production developed in the 1970s in the Southern Bight, where water depths are under 50 m (165 ft). By 1989 there were 149 platforms operating in the North Sea, of which 92 were British, 36 Dutch, and the remainder Norwegian, Danish and German. Some 8,000 km (5,000 miles) of transportation pipelines have been installed. The investment to date has exceeded US$75 billion, and 50,000 people earn a direct living from this industry. So far 20 per cent of estimated reserves have been exploited, and annual production is greater than 150 million tonnes.

Scotland – Farming of the Atlantic salmon (Salmo salar) is practised in Scottish sea lochs and Norwegian fjords. The salmon eggs are incubated in trays, and one year old smolts are gradually acclimatized to natural conditions over a period of 3 weeks, before being put in the sea in net cages suspended from a flotation collar. Natural water movement oxygenates the water and removes wastes.

Rotterdam – More than 250 million tonnes of cargo pass through Rotterdam each year, making it the world's busiest port. Some 45 per cent of the cargo is oil and petroleum products, but solid and liquid chemicals are also important. About 23 million cu m (30 million cu yds) of contaminated silt are dredged each year, of which 40 per cent is considered too dangerous to be dumped in the North Sea. Upstream polluters are the major cause of the problem.

Baltic Sea – This sea is severely polluted as a consequence of coastal populations, agriculture and industries. DDT and PCB levels are believed to be responsible for reproductive problems in seals, and the decline of the white-tailed sea eagle (Haliaeetus albicilla). Metallic wastes from smelting industries may be responsible for deformities in fish, and effluent from kraft pulp and paper mills have destroyed seaweed communities.

Waddenzee management – The Waddenzee coast of the Netherlands has been physically altered by the construction of dykes, from the 13th century onwards. Embankments continue to be reinforced and extended. The threat of sea level rise as a result of climate change is an additional factor to be considered by physical planners. Sand dredging from channels occurs in Netherlands waters, the sand being used for dykes, road construction and infill. About 8-20 million cu m (10.5-26 million cu yds) of sand enters the Waddenzee each year from the North Sea – probably through coastal and seabed erosion. Dredging could enhance erosion in this sensitive region and a removal limit of 4.5 million cu m (5.9 million cu yds) per year was set in 1978. The natural environment of the Waddenzee is also affected by land reclamation for agriculture beyond the dikes, gas and oil exploitation, freshwater extraction from dune areas, recreation, military activity and pollution from the rivers Scheldt, Meuse, Rhine, Ems, Weser and Elbe.

Legend

- ⚒ Major oil and gas production
- ⋯ Oil and gas pipelines
- ● Industrial centres
- 🚢 Tanker terminal
- ⚑ Petroleum refineries
- ░ Sand and gravel dredging areas
- ☢ Former sites of low level radioactive waste disposal
- ○ Burning areas for incinerator ships
- ▒ Saltmarsh areas

Scale

0 km	100	200
0 miles	100	200
0 n.miles	100	200

North Atlantic Basin

The North Atlantic is divided into two basins by the Mid-Atlantic Ridge, an undersea mountain range. The ridge was formed by the upwelling of volcanic material from beneath the Earth's crust, and in some places, such as Iceland and the Azores, it juts above the ocean surface.

The waters around Greenland and Svalbard are major sources of bottom water – the cold, dense water which flows along the ocean floor. North Atlantic bottom water comes from the meeting of cold water from the Arctic Ocean with warmer water from the Gulf Stream. Cold winds chill the mixed water, which then sinks to the bottom. These areas are extremely rich in nutrients and are important feeding grounds for fish, marine mammals and seabirds.

The Gulf Stream

The surface currents of the North Atlantic are dominated by the North Atlantic Gyre, a roughly circular system driven in the south by North-East Trade Winds between 10° and 30° N, and in the north by the Westerlies between 40° and 60° N. The most important part of the North Atlantic Gyre is the Gulf Stream. This fast-flowing current of warm water is formed by the junction of the Antilles and Florida Currents at the Florida Straits. From here it flows north-eastward along the coast of the United States at about five knots. Around Long Island, it turns eastward across the Atlantic Ocean, and becomes known as the North Atlantic Current.

Off the Grand Banks of Newfoundland the Gulf Stream forms meanders, which break off as Gulf Stream rings. These flow anticlockwise to the south of the stream and clockwise to the north, reaching a diameter of some 300 kilometres (190 miles), and may circulate for up to two years.

Sargasso Sea

In the south-west of the North Atlantic region lies the Sargasso Sea, an area of warm, clear water bounded by a clockwise current system, of which the Gulf Stream forms the western branch. The most famous feature of the Sargasso Sea is its drifting, wind-blown seaweed *Sargassum natans* which floats in the water, supported by numerous small air bladders. Sailing vessels often have to negotiate areas of the weed, which could stretch for considerable distances. The seaweed supports a range of creatures more commonly found on shorelines or in inshore waters, and includes some unique species.

The Sargasso Sea is also the spawning ground for the European eel (*Anguilla anguilla*) and the American eel (*Anguilla rostrata*). Both species inhabit coastal waters and rivers, but migrate to the Sargasso Sea to reproduce. During the autumn the European eel crosses the Atlantic in as little as 80 days reaching the Sargasso Sea in February. Spawning occurs as deep as 1,200 metres (3,940 feet). After they are born, the young eels, known as elvers, take about two and a half years to reach the European coast. The American eel takes only one year to complete its migration from the Sargasso to the North American continent.

Like the eels, the Atlantic salmon (*Salmo salar*) migrates for long distances. The salmon is native to rivers on both sides of the Atlantic, but spends much of its life near the rich feeding grounds off Greenland, Norway and the Faeroe Islands. Atlantic salmon return as many as three times to their home rivers to spawn. Young fish spend several years in rivers before they enter the Atlantic, and many do not survive the journey to the ocean. Large-scale commercial

The port of Rotterdam (right) is the largest seaport in Europe, and the focal point for the European Community's seaborne trade. Located on the North Sea at the mouths of the rivers Rhine and Maas, the port handles around 250 million tonnes of cargo every year. Its Europoort facility is the world's leading port for bulk goods, such as iron ore and grain, but above all for petroleum and chemicals. Rotterdam is the terminus for barge traffic from the Rhine, which carries pollution from as far upstream as Switzerland.

A team of Greenpeace activists (above) protest against the arrival of the Soviet nuclear-powered icebreaker Vaygach *in the harbour of Tromsø, Norway. Used to carry tourists to the Arctic Ocean, the movements of vessels like the* Vaygach *focus attention on the health of the marine environment of the North Atlantic region. Ocean dumping of domestic and industrial wastes, weapons and even radioactive materials is a problem on both sides of the Atlantic. Many non-governmental organizations like Greenpeace help to increase public awareness of marine environmental problems.*

fishing, particularly off the Greenland coast, has severely depleted the numbers of Atlantic salmon.

The North Atlantic is also home to some of the most threatened species of marine mammals, including the bowhead whale (*Balaena mysticetus*), the humpback whale (*Megaptera novaeangliae*) and the northern right whale (*Eubalaena glacialis*). Only a few hundred bowhead whales remain, mainly around Svalbard and in the Hudson Bay-Davis Strait area. The humpback whale, endangered worldwide, undertakes long migrations through the North Atlantic from its polar feeding grounds to breeding areas in warmer waters. The northern right whale has been hunted in the North Atlantic since the Middle Ages, and is now considered to be among the most endangered of the large whale species.

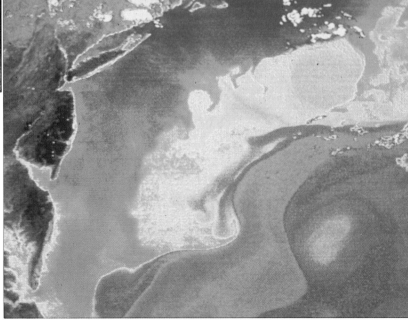

Captured at the point when it turns toward the open Atlantic and flows past Chesapeake Bay, New York, and Cape Cod, the Gulf Stream appears as a pink band (left) in this false-colour satellite image. The colours represent the surface temperature of the water. Farther offshore, the current's flow becomes unstable, and meanders or eddies, known as Gulf Stream rings, break off from its margins. In the photograph, one ring appears north of the Gulf Stream, and another lies to the south of it.

These rings continue to circulate for up to two years to the north and south of the main flow. The northern rings follow a clockwise motion, and the southern ones an anticlockwise motion. As it moves east, the Gulf Stream becomes part of the North Atlantic Current which warms the coasts of north-western Europe. Although the Gulf Stream itself breaks up off the Grand Banks of Newfoundland, its influence helps to moderate the climate of both northern and western Europe.

Mediterranean

The Mediterranean is one of the world's busiest seas. Over 70 per cent of the world's tourists are drawn by its sandy beaches, historical sites, food and wine, and the warm, dry climate. It is also a major shipping route, particularly for oil from the Middle East.

The current population of the countries around the Mediterranean coast numbers some 360 million, of which 37 per cent (133 million people) live on the coast. This population is expected to reach 520-570 million by the year 2025. The greatest increases will occur along the coasts of Algeria, Morocco, Turkey and Egypt. Urban populations in coastal areas will expand by up to 80 per cent. Even today, facilities which are adequate for a year-round population of hundreds are inadequate for seasonal populations of many thousands.

Fishing and mariculture

The fisheries of the Mediterranean are relatively poor and overexploited. The annual yield of less than 2 million tonnes can meet only half of the region's demand. However, mariculture has great potential for further development, and up to 10,000 square kilometres (3,860 square miles) of coastal lagoons provide potential for further production. The most important mariculture species is the Mediterranean mussel (*Mytilus galloprovincialis*), of which the prin-

cipal producer is Italy. Other important species include mullets (*Mugilidae*), the gilthead sea bream (*Sparus aurata*), and the sea bass (*Dicentrarchus labrax*). Fish are raised in enclosed lagoons, using techniques which date back to the Roman empire. Mariculture specialists are also experimenting with the possibility of raising sea bream (*Pagellus centrodontus*) using cages suspended from anchored vessels.

At least 80 per cent of the half billion tonnes of sewage entering the Mediterranean is untreated. Beaches showing visible signs of pollution and water covered in sludgy algal blooms are beginning to drive away tourists. Public health is also threatened by an increase in the number of microorganisms, which spread hepatitis, cholera, dysentery and enteritis.

Under the auspices of the United Nations Environment Programme (UNEP), the Mediterranean Action Plan was formulated in the 1970s by 17 coastal countries as a strategy to improve the Mediterranean environment. In spite of underfunding, the plan has had some success in areas such as sewage treatment and pollution monitoring. The first three protocols of the Barcelona Convention are designed to deal with pollution. These concern dumping from ships and aircraft, pollution from land-based sources, and cooperation in the event of pollution incidents.

France and Spain – Around 600 dead or dying dolphins (Stenella coeruleoalba) *were washed up in autumn 1990. The deaths were caused by a virus similar to that which hit North Sea seals in 1988, and which has not yet spread beyond the north-western waters of the Mediterranean. Lack of food and the effects of pollution may have reduced the ability of the dolphins to fight off the virus. Lesions found on many of the dead animals were possibly caused by toxic agents.*

Camargue, France – *This wetland area provides an important resting and feeding area for migratory waterfowl and is a key breeding area for some species. The Camargue is a vast delta, formed at the mouth of the Rhône, where the river divides into two arms. This Biosphere Reserve provides a breeding ground for 15-20,000 greater flamingos (Phoenicopterus ruber) which derive their pink colour from the shrimp they feed upon. More than 300 species of migratory birds visit the Camargue each year.*

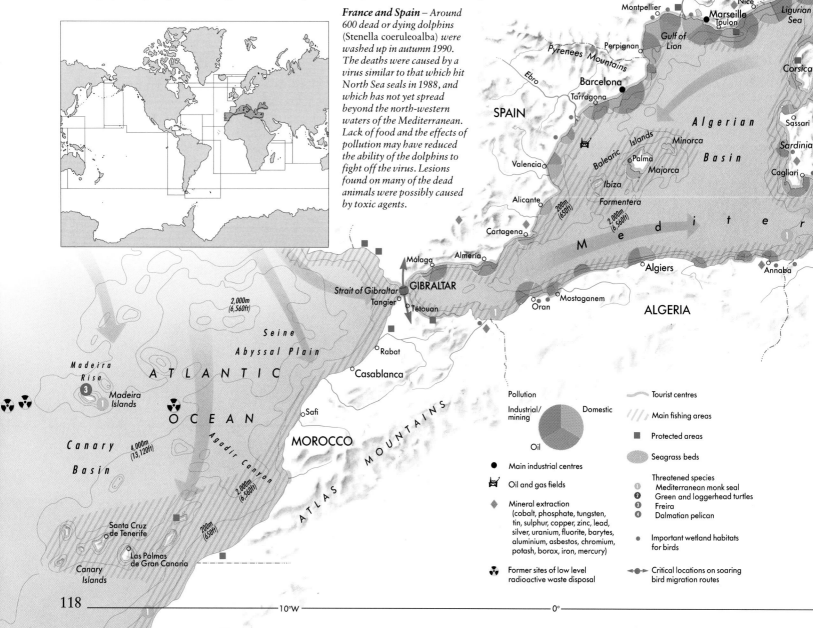

Pollution

Industrial/mining — Domestic

Oil

● Main industrial centres

⚒ Oil and gas fields

◆ Mineral extraction (cobalt, phosphate, tungsten, tin, sulphur, copper, zinc, lead, silver, uranium, fluorite, barytes, aluminium, asbestos, chromium, potash, borax, iron, mercury)

☢ Former sites of low level radioactive waste disposal

⌇ Tourist centres

/// Main fishing areas

■ Protected areas

Seagrass beds

Threatened species
1 Mediterranean monk seal
2 Green and loggerhead turtles
3 Freira
4 Dalmatian pelican

● Important wetland habitats for birds

Critical locations on soaring bird migration routes

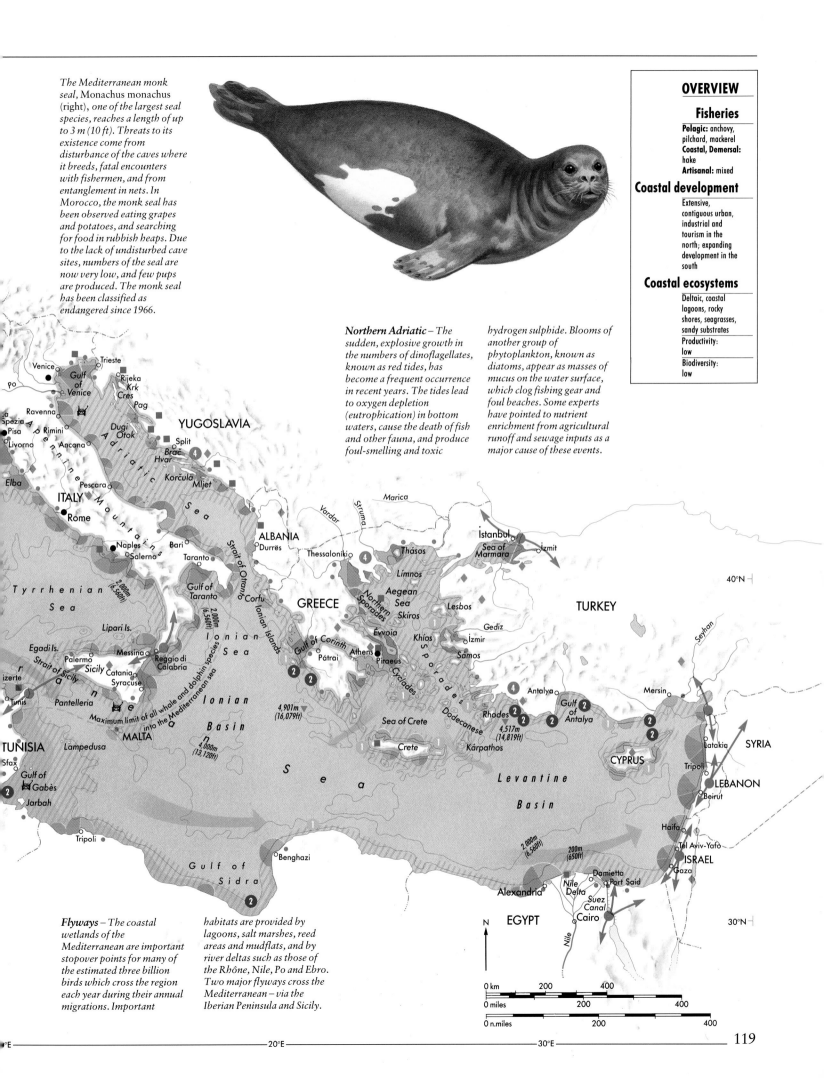

The Mediterranean monk seal, Monachus monachus (right), one of the largest seal species, reaches a length of up to 3 m (10 ft). Threats to its existence come from disturbance of the caves where it breeds, fatal encounters with fishermen, and from entanglement in nets. In Morocco, the monk seal has been observed eating grapes and potatoes, and searching for food in rubbish heaps. Due to the lack of undisturbed cave sites, numbers of the seal are now very low, and few pups are produced. The monk seal has been classified as endangered since 1966.

Northern Adriatic – The sudden, explosive growth in the numbers of dinoflagellates, known as red tides, has become a frequent occurrence in recent years. The tides lead to oxygen depletion (eutrophication) in bottom waters, cause the death of fish and other fauna, and produce foul-smelling and toxic hydrogen sulphide. Blooms of another group of phytoplankton, known as diatoms, appear as masses of mucus on the water surface, which clog fishing gear and foul beaches. Some experts have pointed to nutrient enrichment from agricultural runoff and sewage inputs as a major cause of these events.

Flyways – The coastal wetlands of the Mediterranean are important stopover points for many of the estimated three billion birds which cross the region each year during their annual migrations. Important habitats are provided by lagoons, salt marshes, reed areas and mudflats, and by river deltas such as those of the Rhône, Nile, Po and Ebro. Two major flyways cross the Mediterranean – via the Iberian Peninsula and Sicily.

119

Exploiting the Mediterranean

The increasing population density around the Mediterranean is paralleled by increasing demands and stresses on the natural environment. Coastal development, intensive tourism and land reclamation for agriculture place pressures on key wildlife habitats such as turtle nesting beaches and wetlands. Local and regional problems created by pollution arising from domestic and industrial effluent, oil transportation and refineries, and agricultural runoff, are beginning to have an impact on wildlife as well as on human populations and fisheries. Waterborne diseases and substandard beaches are beginning to deter tourists, who are essential to the economic well-being of many Mediterranean countries.

A number of endangered species are found in the Mediterranean. The Mediterranean monk seal (*Monachus monachus*) now numbers only a few hundred individuals. They are scattered from Cap Blanc on the west coast of Africa to the Greek islands. Other threatened marine mammals found in the warm Mediterranean waters include the fin whale (*Balaenoptera physalus*), the harbour porpoise (*Phocoena phocoena*) and dolphins. Green and loggerhead turtles nest along the shores of the eastern and southern Mediterranean (see pages 118-119). The disturbances caused by economic development and tourist activity are making peaceful nesting sites scarcer.

Domestic and industrial pollution

The Mediterranean is an almost entirely enclosed sea, with complete water turnover through the Strait of Gibraltar taking up to 150 years. Because this "residence time" is so long, the Mediterranean is particularly vulnerable to pollution. Few of the 56 coastal cities with populations over 100,000 have adequate sewage treatment facilities – 80 per cent of sewage released into the Mediterranean is untreated, which leads to organic and bacterial pollution.

Coastal industries release industrial effluent which creates extensive pollution at sites such as Portman

Mediterranean tourism (right) is heavily concentrated on the coastal areas. A total of 100 million visitors per year spend 1,400 million guest-nights in the region. Seasonal pressures on water supplies and waste disposal facilities are considerable and space is becoming limited. France, Italy and Spain are the most popular holiday destinations, but tourism is a growing industry in east Mediterranean countries and in North Africa. Tourism provides an incentive to protect the environment, both natural and historical, since the industry is dependent on visitors continuing to be attracted to the region.

Tuna (right) are an important food species in the Mediterranean. Many are caught by teams of fishermen who drive the fish into shallow channels with nets at the bottom. As the nets are raised, individual fishermen jump into the water and haul the massive fish out.

Sea grass beds (above) are being degraded and destroyed by pollution and mechanical disturbance. The sea grasses trap and stabilize sediment, providing a habitat for rich detritivore and herbivore food chains. Posidonia oceania *is the most extensive of the Mediterranean sea grasses, but* Zostera marina *is also important.* Halophila stipulacea, *which is now found around the coasts of the eastern Mediterranean, colonised from the Indian Ocean via the Suez Canal.*

Bay in southern Spain. The wastes dumped here by a single mining company account for over 90 per cent of Spain's toxic waste. Inland industries are also major sources of pollutants which are carried to the sea by rivers. As well as causing environmental degradation, pollutants have a direct impact on wildlife. The fin whale is threatened by heavy metals which are present in its favourite food, krill. In this case, the metals are from industrial wastes dumped off Corsica. Greenpeace has recently found high levels of PCBs in dolphins which had died of a viral disease.

At nearly 2 million tonnes per annum the existing Mediterranean fishery is far in excess of the estimated sustainable yield of 1.09-1.41 million tonnes. Many local fisheries are declining as a consequence of indiscriminate trawl fishing. The effects of pollution have almost certainly contributed to the reduction in yields and quality of fish. Many fishermen blame the monk seal for stealing fish from nets and consequently kill seals they encounter.

MARINE ARCHAEOLOGY

The Greek, Phoenician, Roman, Etruscan, Byzantine and Islamic civilizations have all left the remains of their activities on the Mediterranean coastline. Trade in goods and people has crisscrossed the waters of the Mediterranean for centuries. A wreck dating from the 14th century BC was recently excavated off Ulu Burun, on the Turkish coast. Its rich collection of artifacts, including many copper ingots, revealed information on trade patterns throughout the Mediterranean region. As well as being of great historical value, such sites can be used to obtain data on past sea levels and resource utilization. Archaeological diving in the Mediterranean started in 1960. Wrecks are now detected with the use of sonar and deep-sea excavation is carried out with the aid of unmanned submersibles.

How the Mediterranean Works

The Mediterranean is an almost completely enclosed sea covering an area of 2.54 million square kilometres (0.98 million square miles), and with a mean depth of 1.5 kilometres (0.93 miles). It is linked to the Atlantic through the Strait of Gibraltar, to the Black Sea by the Dardanelles, and to the Red Sea by the Suez Canal which was opened in 1869. Water entering the Mediterranean remains there for 150 years or more before being flushed out.

Atlantic water, which enters the Mediterranean through the Strait of Gibraltar, has a greater volume than the outflow of more saline, cooler Mediterranean water. This deep-water current was, according to legend, harnessed by the Phoenicians who lowered the sails of their ships several fathoms into the sea in order to enter the Atlantic against surface currents. Today, this strong underwater current is used by submarines, which can turn their engines off to pass silently through the Strait.

The impact of the warm Mediterranean climate leads to a transformation, over decades, of the Atlantic water which enters the basin. The most marked change is in salinity, which increases eastwards to as high as 39.5 parts per thousand. In summer, the warming of surface waters leads to a marked temperature change (thermocline) at 20-40 metres (66-131 feet) which separates warm, high-salinity water from cooler, less saline water. Warm, dry winds lead to evaporation and to the concentration of waters above the thermocline. Dry winds are also a feature of the winter climate and have the effect of removing both heat and moisture from the surface waters. These sink into the waters below as a consequence of their increased density. Three winter water masses are formed which flow westwards to the Gibraltar Strait or form the dense bottom water of the eastern basin.

The study of Mediterranean hydrography is now aided by satellite imagery which reveals local and regional circulation features such as upwelling, eddies, thermal fronts, and plankton productivity. Conventional plankton studies have revealed that zooplankton species characteristic of the Aegean are spreading into the Black Sea communities. This is caused by the damming of rivers which feed freshwater to the Black Sea and the consequent increased influx of Aegean water. Mediterranean plankton communities have themselves been altered by the entry of Red Sea species through the Suez Canal.

The impact of the "greenhouse effect"

The potential impacts of climate change on the Mediterranean were discussed by the United Nations Environment Programme at a major conference in Split, Yugoslavia, in 1988. A change in climate would change the circulation patterns of the sea, while sea level rise would have major impacts on low-lying coasts and delta areas. The Po Delta is an area where coastlines have been in retreat for decades owing to land subsidence – a consequence of clay compaction and groundwater extraction. The nearby city of Venice could be further threatened by an increase in the mean high tide level.

The Mediterranean (below) is composed of a series of basins which are separated from the Atlantic by a sill at the Strait of Gibraltar. The warm, dry Mediterranean climate means that the amount of water lost through evaporation exceeds the amount entering the sea from precipitation and runoff.

Water flows in from the Atlantic through the Strait of Gibraltar to compensate for this loss. This results in an increase in salinity from west to east. The Black Sea has a low level of salinity owing to high river influxes – especially from the Danube. The Black Sea's deep, dense waters are

renewed slowly, and become anoxic. Hydrogen sulphide reacts with minerals to form black metal oxides which have given the sea its name. Fallout radionuclides released after the accident at Chernobyl in April 1986 have been used as tracers to examine Black Sea circulation.

High tide (right) in Venice floods St Mark's Square. The acqua alta *is caused by the piling up of the waters of the Adriatic at its enclosed northern end by the south-easterly scirocco wind. The historic city is also threatened by subsidence due to compacting of the sand and mud underlying the city. Groundwater extraction has added to the problem. A small rise in sea level would threaten Venice even further.*

28°C 24°C 20°C 16°C 12°C 8°C 4°C 0°C

A false-colour satellite image (above) of the Mediterranean shows the distribution of phytoplankton in the surface waters. Red indicates dense areas, whereas parts of the sea with less phytoplankton show up as blue. Parts of the Atlantic (top left) and the Black Sea (top right) contain higher densities of plankton than the Mediterranean. Within the Mediterranean itself, phytoplankton density tends to be higher in areas where nutrients are available for algal growth. Red areas along the Adriatic coast reflect sewage inputs and agricultural runoff, which increase nutrient availability. Recent algal blooms in the Adriatic have been blamed on phosphorous loading, and result in anoxia, benthos death, and hydrogen sulphide production. The construction of the Aswan High Dam between 1960-70 reduced the volume of nutrients being fed into the Mediterranean by the river Nile. This led to the collapse of the sardine fishery in delta areas.

Wider Caribbean

The Wider Caribbean region occupies the southwestern margin of the North Atlantic Ocean. It includes both tropical and subtropical waters, with Cape Hatteras as the northern limit of tropical fauna. The eastern boundary of the Caribbean is defined by the Bahamas and the Greater and Lesser Antilles. The Gulf of Mexico is a single basin separated by the Straits of Florida and Cuba. The region is linked by the warm Guiana Current which sweeps northwards from Recife, joins the North Equatorial Current, then flows between the southern Caribbean islands and into the Gulf of Mexico, where loop currents form. It eventually joins the Gulf Stream off the Florida coast.

Primary productivity is greatest in coastal waters near coral reefs, sea grass beds and mangroves. These areas provide habitats and rich feeding grounds for fish. About 14 per cent of the world's coral reefs are found in the region. Fringing and patch reefs are the most common around islands, on the side facing the prevailing wind. Of note is the long barrier reef system off Belize, which from end to end measures about 220 kilometres (140 miles).

Closely associated with coral reefs are the highly productive sea grass beds. The sea grass colonizes bottom sediments produced by the erosion of the reef and they trap abrasive sediments which could otherwise damage corals. Sea grasses such as *Thalassia* provide grazing for sea turtles, manatees, fish and invertebrates.

Coastal mangroves fulfil a similar role to sea grass beds. Mangroves trap sediments and export nutrients, and in this way support a grazing food chain and provide nursery grounds for fish and shellfish. The high flow rates of the Amazon curbs sediment deposition which limits mangrove development.

Human impacts

Coastal lagoons are an important mainland feature in the Wider Caribbean region. Common to the many islands are salinas, or shallow tidal ponds. Both systems protect reefs, since they trap sediments, serve as nursery areas for fish, and provide wetland habitats for birds. Local people use these areas to produce salt. However, the lagoons are increasingly targeted for such developments as marinas, or ponds for aquaculture and mariculture. Coastal lagoons and salinas were probably important feeding grounds for the Caribbean monk seal (*Monachus tropicalis*). The animal is now believed to be extinct, as a result of over-exploitation during the 19th century, and through disturbance of its habitat in more recent times. The threatened Amazonian manatee (*Trichechus inunguis*), which is exploited for its meat, is now limited to the lower reaches of the Amazon River as far north as Cabo Norte. The numbers of the West Indian or Caribbean manatee (*Trichechus manatus*) are also severely depressed.

Industrial development in the region as a whole is quite limited, but localized pollution problems exist around coastal cities. Contamination by metals and organic chemicals is likely to worsen as industrial development continues. On many islands, the discharge of untreated sewage endangers public health and fouls the region's valuable beaches. Runoff from inland areas contains pesticides and fertilizers which are heavily applied to bananas, tobacco and sugar cane. Alkaline effluent produced by the sugar industry encourage the growth of algae, which uses up dissolved oxygen in coastal waters, and exacerbates the depletion of oxygen already caused by nutrient inputs from sewage and fertilizers.

Belize – the barrier reef is one of the most important of the country's assets. Second in length only to Australia's Great Barrier Reef, the reef supports valuable but declining conch and spiny lobster fisheries, and now attracts increasing numbers of foreign tourists. To resolve legal, administrative and use conflicts, management of the reef is now a priority for Belize's fisheries department and some local non-government organizations.

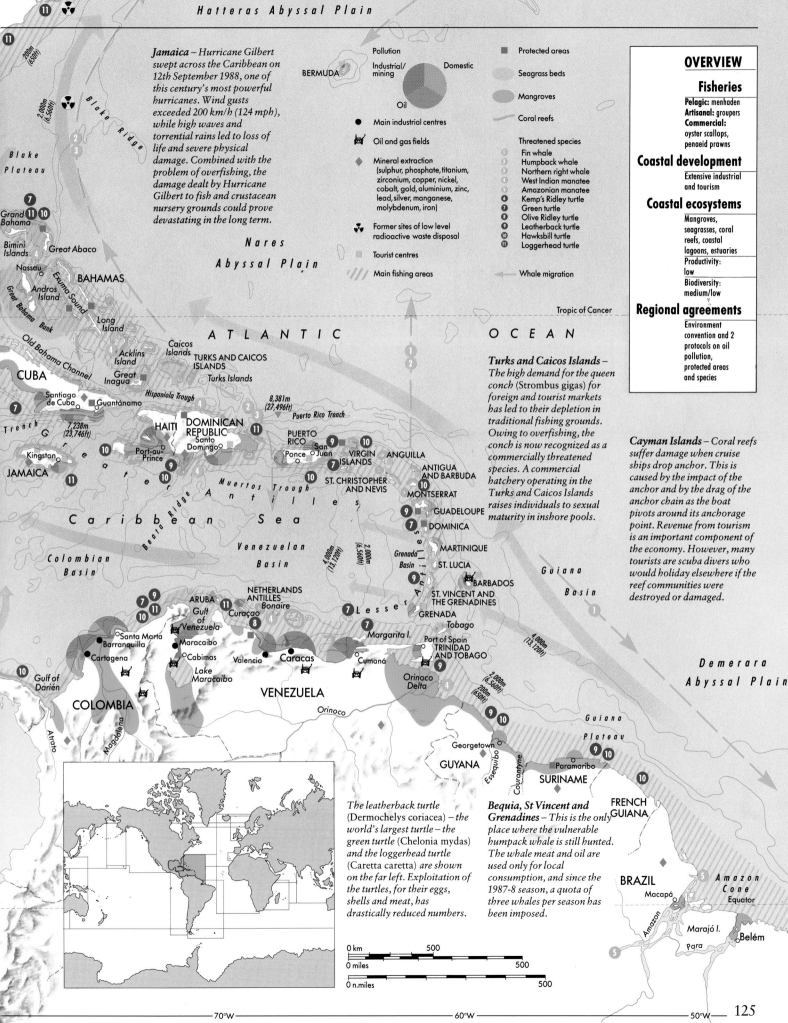

Cape Hatteras

Hatteras Abyssal Plain

Jamaica – Hurricane Gilbert swept across the Caribbean on 12th September 1988, one of this century's most powerful hurricanes. Wind gusts exceeded 200 km/h (124 mph), while high waves and torrential rains led to loss of life and severe physical damage. Combined with the problem of overfishing, the damage dealt by Hurricane Gilbert to fish and crustacean nursery grounds could prove devastating in the long term.

BERMUDA

Pollution
Industrial/mining
Domestic
Oil

■ Protected areas
Seagrass beds
Mangroves
Coral reefs

● Main industrial centres
Oil and gas fields
Mineral extraction (sulphur, phosphate, titanium, zirconium, copper, nickel, cobalt, gold, aluminium, zinc, lead, silver, manganese, molybdenum, iron)
Former sites of low level radioactive waste disposal
Tourist centres
Main fishing areas

Threatened species
① Fin whale
② Humpback whale
③ Northern right whale
④ West Indian manatee
⑤ Amazonian manatee
⑥ Kemp's Ridley turtle
⑦ Green turtle
⑧ Olive Ridley turtle
⑨ Leatherback turtle
⑩ Hawksbill turtle
⑪ Loggerhead turtle

→ Whale migration

Nares Abyssal Plain

OVERVIEW

Fisheries

Pelagic: menhaden
Artisanal: groupers
Commercial: oyster scallops, penaeid prawns

Coastal development
Extensive industrial and tourism

Coastal ecosystems
Mangroves, seagrasses, coral reefs, coastal lagoons, estuaries
Productivity: low
Biodiversity: medium/low

Regional agreements
Environment convention and 2 protocols on oil pollution, protected areas and species

200m (650ft)
2,000m (6,560ft)

Blake Ridge
Blake Plateau

Grand Bahama
Bimini Islands
Great Abaco
Nassau
BAHAMAS
Andros Island
Exuma Sound
Long Island
Great Bahama Bank
Old Bahama Channel
CUBA
Acklins Island
Great Inagua
Caicos Islands
TURKS AND CAICOS ISLANDS
Turks Islands

A T L A N T I C   O C E A N

Tropic of Cancer

Turks and Caicos Islands – The high demand for the queen conch (Strombus gigas) for foreign and tourist markets has led to their depletion in traditional fishing grounds. Owing to overfishing, the conch is now recognized as a commercially threatened species. A commercial hatchery operating in the Turks and Caicos Islands raises individuals to sexual maturity in inshore pools.

Cayman Islands – Coral reefs suffer damage when cruise ships drop anchor. This is caused by the impact of the anchor and by the drag of the anchor chain as the boat pivots around its anchorage point. Revenue from tourism is an important component of the economy. However, many tourists are scuba divers who would holiday elsewhere if the reef communities were destroyed or damaged.

Santiago de Cuba
Guantánamo
7,238m (23,746ft)
Kingston
JAMAICA
Port-au-Prince
HAITI
DOMINICAN REPUBLIC
Santo Domingo
Hispaniola Trough
8,381m (27,496ft)
Puerto Rico Trench
PUERTO RICO
Ponce
San Juan
VIRGIN ISLANDS
ANGUILLA
ANTIGUA AND BARBUDA
ST. CHRISTOPHER AND NEVIS
MONTSERRAT
GUADELOUPE
DOMINICA
MARTINIQUE
ST. LUCIA
BARBADOS
ST. VINCENT AND THE GRENADINES
GRENADA
Tobago

C a r i b b e a n   S e a
Beata Ridge
Muertos Trough
Venezuelan Basin
Colombian Basin
4,000m (13,120ft)
2,000m (6,560ft)
Grenada Basin
G r e a t e r   A n t i l l e s
L e s s e r   A n t i l l e s

Guiana Basin

Demerara Abyssal Plain

ARUBA
NETHERLANDS ANTILLES
Bonaire
Gulf of Venezuela
Curaçao
Margarita I.
Port of Spain
TRINIDAD AND TOBAGO
Santa Marta
Barranquilla
Cartagena
Maracaibo
Cabimas
Lake Maracaibo
Valencia
Caracas
Cumaná
Orinoco Delta
Gulf of Darién
COLOMBIA
VENEZUELA
Orinoco
Atrato
Magdalena
4,000m (13,120ft)
2,000m (6,560ft)
200m (650ft)

Guiana Plateau

Georgetown
GUYANA
Essequibo
Courantyne
Paramaribo
SURINAME
FRENCH GUIANA

The leatherback turtle (Dermochelys coriacea) – the world's largest turtle – the green turtle (Chelonia mydas) and the loggerhead turtle (Caretta caretta) are shown on the far left. Exploitation of the turtles, for their eggs, shells and meat, has drastically reduced numbers.

Bequia, St Vincent and Grenadines – This is the only place where the vulnerable humpack whale is still hunted. The whale meat and oil are used only for local consumption, and since the 1987-8 season, a quota of three whales per season has been imposed.

BRAZIL
Macapá
Amazon Cone
Equator
Amazon
Marajó I.
Pará
Belém

0 km   500
0 miles   500
0 n.miles   500

70°W   60°W   50°W

125

Pollution and Problems

Economic development in the Wider Caribbean is uneven, ranging from the wealthy United States through the rapidly developing economies of Mexico, Colombia and Venezuela, to the extreme poverty of Haiti. Fishing is an important activity for many communities, but owing to rapid population growth and development, local fisheries face problems of excessive demand and pollution of the coastal environment.

Small-scale inshore fisheries are diverse and productive, but in many areas the use of outboard motors and nylon or plastic nets has led to over-exploitation of some marine resources. Although dynamite fishing and the use of poisons have been widely prohibited, other fishing methods can severely damage the coastal environment, especially coral reefs. Industrial fisheries which operate from the mainland and larger islands have wiped out some artisanal fisheries through the efficiency of trawling and purse seining operations. The fisheries with the highest yields are those of the demersal grouper (*Epinephalus*) and the Gulf menhaden (*Brevoortia patronus*). In terms of yield, the most important shellfish are the American cupped oyster (*Crassostrea virginica*) and the calico scallop (*Argopecten gibbus*). In some areas, there is potential for expansion of the fishery, in particular for pelagic species such as tuna and flying fish. Current levels of exploitation of two species of spiny lobster – *Panulirus guttatus* and *Panulirus argus* – and the queen conch (*Strombus gigas*) are so high that these animals are considered to be commercially threatened.

The impact of development

The Wider Caribbean region attracts around 100 million tourists each year, mainly from the United States, of whom 3 million arrive on cruise ships. Because of the abundance of sun, clear waters, white sandy beaches and lush vegetation, most visitors remain unaware of the region's social and economic problems. These include overpopulation, inadequate public health, widespread unemployment, unequal trade balances and chronic debt. In addition, the region is plagued by natural disasters such as earthquakes, volcanic eruptions and typhoons. In September 1988 Hurricane Gilbert cut a wide swathe of devastation across much of the Caribbean, and destroyed more than 100,000 homes in Jamaica.

Tourist revenue plays a vital part in the economies of many Caribbean states. In the Cayman Islands, tourist income accounts for 70 per cent of the gross national product. The tourist industry depends on the maintenance of a pristine environment, but the provision of facilities for tourists creates problems. Reefs are damaged when boats run aground or anchor on them, and when visitors trample them and break pieces off. Reef communities have been damaged by spearfishing and by collections for the curio trade. The growth of cities and the construction of airports, ports and marinas encroaches on fragile coastal mangroves and wetlands. Even small-scale developments, such as jetties for local fisheries, have an impact on reefs since they alter water circulation patterns. However, by far the greatest problem comes from the mining of beach and coral sands. These are extracted for use in the production of lime, in construction and road building and as landfill. Sea grass beds and corals suffer most as a result of this mining, since the removal of sand changes water circulation patterns and makes beaches vulnerable to erosion. Mining increases the amount of material suspended in the water, and thereby affects photosynthesis.

Flare stacks burn off surplus gas at an oil production complex (right) *off Ciudad del Carmen in the southern Gulf of Mexico. Since the late 1930s, the Gulf has become an important centre for the extraction of oil and natural gas, as well as the production of petrochemicals. The development of oil resources has led to increasing levels of contamination in the Gulf, particularly along beaches and in mangroves and coastal lagoons. Important oil and gas fields lie off the coast of Louisiana and the Mexican states of Veracruz and Campeche. Other major oil producers in the Wider Caribbean region include Venezuela and the island state of Trinidad and Tobago.*

Tourism is a major industry for many states in the Wider Caribbean region, creating jobs and providing vital foreign exchange. The construction of recreational facilities, like this marina (below) *in the Bahamas, poses a grave threat to coastal environments. Coral reefs suffer damage from increased traffic, while mangroves are removed to make way for port facilities. Dredging beach sands for use in construction degrades sea grass beds, and by increasing the amount of material suspended in the water, harms coral reefs.*

Mexican fishermen land their catch at a harbour near Progreso on the Yucatan Peninsula (above). The Campeche Bank, which lies offshore, is one of the richest fishing grounds in the Wider Caribbean region. The wide continental shelf round much of the Gulf of Mexico supports extensive fisheries.

A fisherman (right) on Jamaica's southern coast holds up a crevalle jack (Caranx hippos). Although nutrient levels in much of the Wider Caribbean are relatively low, coastal waters are highly productive. Most fisheries are small, and artisanal fishing is extremely important for coastal communities. However, population growth in the region means that demand for fish and marine products now threatens to exceed available stocks of some species.

Gulf of Mexico

The Gulf of Mexico forms the north-eastern component of the Wider Caribbean. Surrounded by the Yucatan Peninsula, the island of Cuba and the coast of Florida, the Gulf contains rich marine habitats and major petroleum reserves. The continental shelf is wide, and the Campeche Bank off the Yucatan Peninsula provides a rich fishing ground, particularly for penaeid prawns.

The northern shoreline of the Gulf of Mexico consists mostly of sedimentary material derived from the Mississippi Basin. Over the last 7,000 years, the coastal plain has increased in width by as much as 150 kilometres (93 miles), the result of shifts and expansion in the Mississippi's delta. During the 19th century, engineers attempted to control the rate of flow of the river, in order to prevent new shifts in its course. The rate of flow has increased as the Mississippi's course has become streamlined. The river formerly deposited its huge load of sediment mainly in the delta region. However, sediments and nutrients carried from inland are now washed far out into the Gulf. In recent years, this has led to coastal erosion and the loss of wetland areas.

The western and southern coasts of the Gulf of Mexico are characterized by large lagoons separated from the sea by barrier beaches. The salinity of these areas varies with tidal action, evaporation, freshwater input from rain and runoff from the land. The lagoons are an important habitat for numerous animals, including crocodiles and manatees, as well as for birds such as flamingos, ibises and pelicans. The endangered Kemp's Ridley turtle (*Lepidochelys kempii*) nests only on the barrier beach of Rancho Nuevo, on the west coast of the Gulf.

The Gulf coast of the United States is densely populated and heavily industrialized. In Mexico, the expansion of tourism and the exploitation of the country's petroleum resources have been economically important. Pollution problems affect coastal waters and estuaries around busy industrial and shipping centres such as Houston and New Orleans. The depletion of oxygen in bottom waters, or eutrophication, is a growing problem. Sea grass beds are found along much of the coast. They are particularly susceptible to the effects of thermal pollution, such as that caused by power plants. Such discharges alter water temperature and encourage algal growth. In the northern Gulf, dredging spoil and chemical wastes are dumped. Wastes from the petrochemical industry are known to be toxic to marine fauna. One major dump site is located on the edge of the "fertile fisheries crescent", which lies off the Mississippi, Louisiana and Texas coasts.

Oil pollution

An important pollution problem in the Gulf arises from the oil industry. Oil reserves in the Gulf are estimated to total over five billion tonnes. Conditions are generally considered to be favourable for exploitation. The coastal areas off Louisiana and the Mexican states of Veracruz and Campeche are the centres of Gulf oil production. Shipping accidents and well blowouts have given the pollution problems a high profile. Steady losses of oil during normal operations are perhaps more serious, and are exacerbated by natural seeps, discharges from refineries and losses during transportation. Oil residues decompose very slowly in coastal lagoons, sandy beaches and mangroves, which shed their leaves on exposure to oil. Many animals, including turtles, have been shown to take in oil during feeding.

Rancho Nuevo – The endangered Kemp's Ridley turtle (Lepidochelys kempii) nests only at a few sites on a 20-km (12-mile) stretch of barrier beach. Up to 2,000 clutches of eggs are removed each year to hatcheries in Mexico and the United States. The principal threat to the population is shrimp trawls. A longer-term problem may be the presence of toxic tar balls, which some turtles eat.

Gulf of Campeche – The Ixtoc I oil well blowout in 1980 spilled some 475,000 tonnes of oil into the Gulf of Mexico, a greater volume than from any previous spill. Because of the extremely high pressure of the oil, two relief wells had to be drilled before the well could be capped. An estimated area of 15,000 sq km (5,790 sq miles) was contaminated, threatening marine life.

Cape Hatteras
Pamlico Sound
Onslow Bay
Wilmington
Cape Fear
Long Bay
Pee Dee
Santee
Savannah
Altamaha
Charleston
Savannah
Sea Islands
200m (650ft)

Major oil and gas production

⛏ high production

⛏ low production

🚢 Tanker terminals

〰️ High-risk offshore pollution areas

🛢 Petroleum refineries

OIL Petrochemical plants

/// Main fishing areas

■ Protected areas

░ Seagrass beds

〜 Coral reefs

0 km 100 200 300
0 miles 100 200 300
0 n.miles 100 200 300

N

Blake Plateau

ATLANTIC

OCEAN

STATES
🛢 OIL
Mobile
Biloxi
OIL Pensacola
Panama City
Chandeleur Islands
Mississippi Delta
Apalachicola
Cape San Blas
Apalachee Bay
Suwannee
Waccassa Bay
Jacksonville
Saint Johns
Cape Canaveral
OIL Tampa
St. Petersburg
Tampa Bay
Lake Okeechobee
200m (650ft)
2,000m (6,560ft)
Charlotte Harbor
West Palm Beach
Fort Lauderdale
Ten Thousand Islands
The Everglades
Miami
Cape Sable
Florida Bay
Key Largo
Florida Keys
Straits of Florida
200m (650ft)

Cay Sal Bank

200m (650ft)

The gentle Caribbean manatee, or Trichechus manatus (above left), is an aquatic mammal which inhabits shallow coastal waters, or lagoons, swamps and rivers. Together with the dugong, the manatee belongs to the order or group of animals known as Sirenia. This name comes from belief once held by sailors that the animals were sirens or mermaids. The manatee feeds on aquatic plants. Along the west coast of Florida, the animal faces threats to its survival from the development of marinas and housing around coastal lagoons or estuaries. Many animals are injured by propellers.

Mexico

Yucatan – Tourism in Mexico and most Central American countries has been concentrated on the Pacific coast, but in recent years efforts have been made to develop the northern Yucatan Peninsula as a tourist destination. Tourist visits pose problems for the nearby Rio Largartos wildlife reserve, the only regular breeding site of the Yucatan population of the greater flamingo.

Nicholas Channel
Archipiélago de Sabana
Havana
200m (650ft)
Ensenada de la Broa
Cienfuegos
Gulf of Guanahacabibes
Gulf of Batabanó
Bay of Pigs
CUBA
2,000m (6,560ft)
200m (650ft)
Canal de los Indios
Archipiélago de los Canarreos
Isle of Youth
Gulf of Ana Maria
Jardines de la Reina
2,000m (6,560ft)
Yucatan Channel

Cozumel I.

Ascensión Bay

C a r i b b e a n   S e a

Y u c a t a n
B a s i n

CAYMAN ISLANDS
Cayman Brac
Grand Cayman
Little Cayman
7,238m (23,746ft)
6,000m (19,680ft)
Cayman Trench
6,000m (19,680ft)
2,000m (6,560ft)
200m (650ft)

Banco Chinchorro

4,000m (13,120ft)

4,000m (13,120ft)

2,000m (6,560ft)

BELIZE
Chetumal Bay
Belize City
Turneffe Islands

85°W   80°W

129

South-West Atlantic

The South-West portion of the Atlantic Ocean extends from 9° to 52°S, and spans tropical to temperate waters. Along the coast of South America, the Brazil Current flows southward from around 10°S. At the mouth of the Río de la Plata it converges with the north flowing Falkland Current and turns eastward as the Southern Tropical Gyre.

The Río de la Plata forms an important boundary between warm temperate and cold temperate regions. Productivity is greater in the south, especially in the cool temperate area south of the Río de la Plata. Tropical marine animals of the north include corals and sea turtles, while the south is home to various species of seals and penguins.

The largest area of coral reefs lies between Recife and Maceió, on Brazil's north-eastern tip. The Abrolhos Islands boast a unique development of the mushroom-shaped *chapieroes* (*Mussismilia braziliensis*), each of which stands some 2-3 metres (6-10 feet) high. Reef fauna includes loggerhead, green and leatherback turtles and 16 species of sponges. The rare queen conch (*Strombus gigas*) lives in stony areas between the reefs.

Coastal habitats

Mangroves, lagoons and estuaries in the north of the region provide nurseries for fish and shellfish, and support local artisanal fisheries. While production in the south is higher, the fauna is less diverse. Salt marshes and large algal beds are common.

Magellan's penguin (*Sphensiscus magellanicus*) breeds south of latitude 41°S. The southern sea lion (*Otaria byronia*, formerly *flavescens*) breeds as far north as Recife dos Torres. Because they sometimes steal fish from nets, they are killed by fishermen. In Uruguay, controlled exploitation of the sea lion yields meat and leather. The southern fur seal (*Arctocephalus australis*) is found on the Falkland Islands, and on the mainland from Recife dos Torres southward. A major breeding colony is based on Isla de Lobos, in the La Plata estuary. Commercial sealing began in Uruguay as early as 1515, and the government still organizes an annual hunt. Although the seal's numbers are low, stocks are now stable.

Fisheries

On Brazil's north-east coast, fishermen use traps to capture fish in lagoons, where they are then cultivated. In the Mandau and Manguaba lagoons near Maceió, a "bush park" (*caicera*) system is used. Fishermen lay branches in selected areas of the lagoon, which then attract fish through the enhanced growth of algae in the feeding grounds.

Coastal fish benefit from the large quantities of plankton which are created by the mangrove system. Since the late 1960s, exploitation of the Atlantic seabob in coastal waters has grown in importance. However, this fishery depends on the use of powerful boats equipped with otter trawl nets, and is of little value to local artisanal fishermen.

Commercial species include the Patagonian hake (*Merluccius hubbsi*), the Argentine anchovy (*Engrualis anchoita*), the common squid (*Loligo*) and the shortfin squid (*Illex argentinus*). In the warmer northern waters, crustaceans such as penaeid shrimps and molluscs such as the white seabob are more important. At present, there is little danger of overfishing, as fleets take only the older classes of species. But careful management is vital in order to avoid depletion of species such as the shortfin squid, whose annual recruitment varies from year to year.

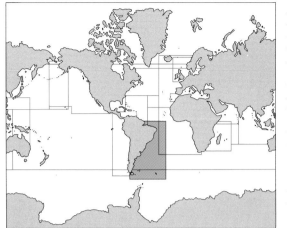

Banados del Este Biosphere Reserve, Uruguay – *This low-lying reserve in Uruguay supports a diverse indigenous flora and fauna. But it is threatened by changes in land use, in particular the change from grazing to rice culture, and by tourism. The fauna are threatened by hunting, although trade in the vulnerable La Plata otter (*Lutra longicaudis*) has been reduced. The value of the fur is sufficient for hunters to dedicate weeks to obtaining a single skin .*

Magellan's penguin
Spheniscus magellanicus *(above, centre) is one of the most northerly of the penguins, ranging as far as southern Brazil. It nests in burrows dug several metres into turf banks – a strikingly different habit to that of the chinstrap penguin* Pygoscelis antarctica *(above left) which builds a simple scoop nest, or the king penguin* Aptenodytes patagonica *(above, right) which incubates a single egg on its feet.*

Patagonia – *The kelp beds of the Patagonian Shelf and Tierra del Fuego, along with those of southern Chile, constitute one of the largest seaweed ecosystems of the world. The dominant alga is the giant* Macrocystis *which is closely related to the forest kelps of California. The kelps are a valuable habitat and feeding ground for numerous species including Magellan's penguin (*Spheniscus magellanicus*) which feeds on cuttlefish.*

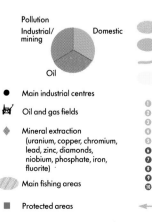

Pollution
Industrial/mining — Domestic
Oil

- ● Main industrial centres
- 🗡 Oil and gas fields
- ◆ Mineral extraction (uranium, copper, chromium, lead, zinc, diamonds, niobium, phosphate, iron, fluorite)
- ▨ Main fishing areas
- ■ Protected areas

- Seaweed beds
- Mangroves
- Coral reefs
- Saltmarsh areas

Threatened species
- ① Southern right whale
- ② Fin whale
- ③ Humpback whale
- ④ Amazonian manatee
- ⑤ La Plata otter
- ⑥ Green turtle
- ⑦ Olive Ridley turtle
- ⑧ Leatherback turtle
- ⑨ Hawksbill turtle
- ⑩ Loggerhead turtle

← Whale migration

ARGENTINA
Bahía Blanca
Colorado
Negro
San Matía Gulf
Chubut
Golfo Nuevo
Chico
San Jorge Gulf
Comodoro Rivadavia
Chico
Patagonia
Bahía Grande
Río Gallegos
200m (650ft)
Strait of Magellan
CHILE
Tierra del Fuego
Staten Island
70°W
Cape Horn
Falkla

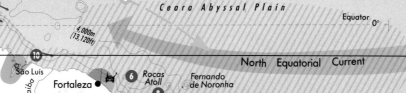

Ceara Abyssal Plain

Equator 0°

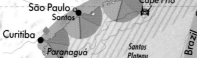

Mouths of the Amazon

4,000m (13,120ft)

North Equatorial Current

Belém

São Luís

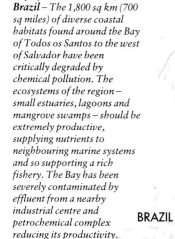

Bay of Todos os Santos, Brazil – The 1,800 sq km (700 sq miles) of diverse coastal habitats found around the Bay of Todos os Santos to the west of Salvador have been critically degraded by chemical pollution. The ecosystems of the region – small estuaries, lagoons and mangrove swamps – should be extremely productive, supplying nutrients to neighbouring marine systems and so supporting a rich fishery. The Bay has been severely contaminated by effluent from a nearby industrial centre and petrochemical complex reducing its productivity.

Parnaíba

Fortaleza

Rocas Atoll

Fernando de Noronha

South Equatorial Current

10°S

Cape São Roque

Natal

João Pessoa

Recife

Maceió

São Francisco

Aracaju

Salvador

BRAZIL

Abrolhos Bank

B r a z i l

Vitória

Trindade Spur

Trindade I.

Martin Vaz Is.

20°S

Campos

B a s i n

Rio de Janeiro

Tropic of Capricorn

São Paulo

Santos

Cape Frio

Brazil Current

Curitiba

Paranaguá Bay

Santos Plateau

Santa Catarina I.

Pôrto Alegre

Paraná

Uruguay

Patos Lagoon

Pelotas

Rio Grande Plateau

30°S

4,000m (13,120ft)

Mirim Lake

URUGUAY

Mangueira Lake

S O U T H

Buenos Aires

Montevideo

La Plata

Río de la Plata

A T L A N T I C

Mar del Plata

4,000m (13,120ft)

O C E A N

Bahía Blanca

2,000m (6,560ft)

200m (650ft)

Shelf

South Atlantic Current

40°S

A r g e n t i n e

B a s i n

Valdes Peninsula – Surveys of known individual animals, which are recognized by white growths on the skin, indicate that around 1,200 of the estimated 1,500 surviving southern right whales may overwinter off the Valdes Peninsula in Argentina. The right whales are known for their antics, including leaping out of the water and raising their flukes. The bays behind the peninsula are where the whales mate, calve and raise their young – the birth of about 100 calves each year has produced an encouraging annual growth in the Atlantic population, which was decimated by hunters between 1775 and 1939. Two bays off the Peninsula are protected but further habitat protection may be necessary in the future. The proposed development of oil and gas fields or a tidal barrage could adversely affect the calving bays.

A r g e n t i n e

A b y s s a l

6,000m (19,680ft)

6,245m (20,488ft)

P l a i n

G e o r g i a

50°S

B a s i n

Maurice Ewing Bank

F a l k l a n d

FALKLAND ISLANDS

P l a t e a u

North Scotia Ridge

West Wind Drift

SOUTH GEORGIA

W e s t   S c o t i a

2,000m (6,560ft)

Burdwood Bank

B a s i n

4,000m (13,120ft)

60°W   50°W   40°W   30°W

0 km   600
0 miles   200   400   600
0 n.miles   200   400   600

N

OVERVIEW

Fisheries

Pelagic: squid, anchovy;
Demersal: hake, whiting;
Coastal artisanal: mixed

Coastal development

Several large urban and industrial centres

Coastal ecosystems

Deltas, coastal lagoons, soft bottom habitats, sandy and rocky coasts

Productivity: medium

Biodiversity: low

Regional agreements

None

Problems and Pollution

Many species found in the South-West Atlantic are harvested for food, pelts or other by-products. Exploitation of some species, like the sea lion and the southern fur seal, is controlled, but others face depletion or even extinction. Increasing industrialization, population growth and the development of tourism all cause severe environmental problems, which inevitably affect the fauna of the region.

Hunting threatens the La Plata otter (*Lutra platensis*), which is found in rivers, lakes and deltas in Brazil, Argentina and Uruguay. Although protected by law in all the countries in which it occurs, the otter is still hunted for its valuable fur. The destruction of its habitat, and the decline in fish numbers due to pollution, also affect otter populations.

The South-West Atlantic is important to a number of the threatened southern populations of whales. These include the southern right whale (*Eubalaena australis*), as well as the fin whale (*Balaenoptera physalus*), blue whale (*Balaenoptera musculus*) and humpback whale (*Megaptera novaeangliae*), which migrate through the region.

Industrial impacts

Although the economy of Argentina has traditionally been based on agriculture, large-scale industrialization began in the early 20th century. However, the legacy of this economic development has been severe coastal pollution, particularly around urban centres where the treatment of sewage and industrial wastes is inadequate.

Industrial development in Brazil and Uruguay began later than in Argentina. Nevertheless, pollution is already a problem for these countries. Brazil's explosive urbanization, which has averaged 65 per cent per decade since the 1960s, has been accompanied by massive industrial expansion. As a consequence of this rapid growth, lagoons, estuaries and coastal waters have all been fouled by untreated sewage and industrial wastes. Coastal wetlands have been destroyed to make way for both industrial and leisure developments. The tourist industry has promoted the development of marinas, beach housing, and the sale of plots of reclaimed land to speculators.

These pressures on coastal lands also have social implications, since they threaten not only marine resources but also traditional life styles. When land is designated for other uses, communities such as the *Caicaras* of Brazil – whose way of life depends on the sea – are evicted from coastal areas.

The estuary of Santos, in the Brazilian state of São Paulo, has suffered severe damage. There is a vast input of nitric acid and ammonia from fertilizer processing plants. The high level of pollution from chemical factories around Santos has given the area the name of the "Valley of Death". Fish and crabs caught and sold locally may be severely contaminated by heavy metals. Mangroves have been destroyed, while sewage from domestic and industrial sources spills into the estuary at the rate of 90 cubic metres (118 cubic yards) per second.

Inland activities also threaten the coastal environment. In Brazil, deforestation increases the sediment load carried by rivers, which in turn poses a threat to coastal habitats. Sport fishing, spear-fishing, coastal development and tourism cause further problems. However, the damming of rivers to develop hydroelectric power actually has the opposite effect, since it reduces sediment input to estuaries and may alter tidal patterns. Economic losses could follow, as fisheries suffer through the loss of breeding grounds.

The industrial centre of Santos (below), in Brazil, lies on an estuary contaminated with acids, ammonia, heavy metals and sewage.

The South American sea lion, or southern sea lion (Otaria byronia) (far right), lives on both the east and west coasts of South America. About 230,000 breed on the mainland, and another 30,000 on the Falkland Islands in the South Atlantic Ocean. Overall, their numbers are thought to be declining in some parts of their range and stable in others. The sea lion is hunted for its valuable fur, as well as being persecuted by fishermen who blame it for stealing fish from their nets. They feed mostly on fish, cephalopods and crustaceans.

Fishermen land a massive catch of tarpon (Tarpon atlanticus) (right) off the coast of Brazil. These large, powerful fish are a valuable food source in the tropical and subtropical waters off South America and West Africa, where they tend to swim in large shoals. The juvenile tarpons spend much of their early life in the shallow, calm waters of mangroves or lagoons. As they mature, they migrate towards the open ocean, where they increase in size, sometimes reaching lengths of more than 2 m (6.6 ft).

West African Seas

The West African region stretches over 9,000 kilometres (5,600 miles) from 21°N to 34°S. The climate varies from humid, tropical around the Equator to arid in the north and south. Coastal features are diverse, ranging from drowned river valleys to sand dunes, lagoons, mudflats and – in the far south – algal beds. The width of the continental shelf varies from 70 kilometres (45 miles) in the Gulf of Guinea to only four kilometres (2.5 miles) off Angola.

Flora and fauna

Dolphin and porpoise species are present as well as the West African manatee (*Trichechus senegalensis*), found in rivers, estuaries and coastal regions from Senegal to Angola. The manatee lives in shallow, swampy areas, where it feeds on submerged vegetation. Despite local protection, it is threatened by hunting and incidental trapping in shark nets.

Coastal areas and lagoons are important wildlife habitats and are visited seasonally by millions of migratory birds such as the black-tailed godwit (*Limosa limosa*), dunlin (*Calidris alpina*), spoonbill (*Platalea leucordia*) and roseate tern (*Sterna dougallii*). Beaches provide nesting for the green and olive Ridley turtles (*Chelonia mydas* and *Lepidochelys olivacea*), and for three other turtle species.

Mauritania marks the northern limit of the African mangrove (*Avicennia africana*) and the southern limit of cord grass (*Spartina maritima*). Over 25,000 square kilometres (9,650 square miles) of mangroves, containing six different species, extend around the West African coast to Angola.

The rich fisheries result from high primary productivity based on upwellings of cold, nutrient-rich waters. There are two permanent areas of upwelling off Senegal and Zaire, driven by the Canary and Benguela Currents. Each July and August, a seasonal, wind-driven upwelling occurs between the Ivory Coast and Ghana. Another area of high productivity surrounds the outflow of the massive Congo-Zaire River drainage system.

The most important fishes are the sardine (*Sardinops ocellata*), which dominates the Benguela Current region, the pilchard (*Sardina pilchardus*) in the north, the Spanish sardine (*Sardinella aurita*) and the horse mackerel (*Tracharus* sp.) found throughout the region. Hake (*Merluccius* spp.) is the most important demersal fish. Lobsters are fished in the north and south of the region, deep-water shrimp are trawled off Senegal and Angola, and prawns in the Gulf of Guinea. Intertidal molluscs are harvested off Senegal, Sierra Leone and Nigeria.

Living marine resources are central to the economies of countries such as Mauritania, where fisheries provide 66 per cent of the national revenue. Seafood represents a significant source of protein: in Ghana, consumption of fish exceeds that of meat. A wide range of inshore and lagoon species is exploited using small boats, push nets and hand-held trawls, as well as a range of fixed gear from wicker cages to stake net barriers. Overfishing is a growing problem.

Pressures on the region

The environmental problems of the region include rapid population expansion, oil pollution, coastal erosion, discharge of raw sewage, and release of pesticides and fertilizers. A new problem is the export of toxic wastes to the region by more developed countries. The dumping of hazardous industrial and municipal wastes is likely to have serious consequences for terrestrial and the marine environments.

Cape Verde Islands – There is no coral reef development, but coral is found around the archipelagoes of the Gulf of Guinea and the Cape Verde Islands, and on parts of the mainland. About 18 species of coral are present: of these, five are the same as, or closely related to, Caribbean species, while nine are endemic.

Guinea Bissau – The Bijagós archipelago is an area of immense biological diversity and productivity. It supports numerous wildlife species, including regionally important populations of turtles and a wide variety of birds, and is one of the few places where the hippopotamus (Hippopotamus amphibius) ventures into the sea. Licensed foreign vessels exploit the fisheries, but do little for the local economy since profits are exported. A coastal Biosphere Reserve to encompass much of the archipelago is currently under development to ensure that the region is administered in a way that minimizes conflicts and promotes sustainable development.

Oranjemund diamond deposits – Some of the finest diamonds in the world are found on the marine terraces off the south-west coast of Africa. The diamonds were carried to the coast in the alluvial sediments of ancient rivers and became concentrated in coastal gravels by wave action. Gem quality diamonds are now obtained from raised beaches as well as from placers below the tideline.

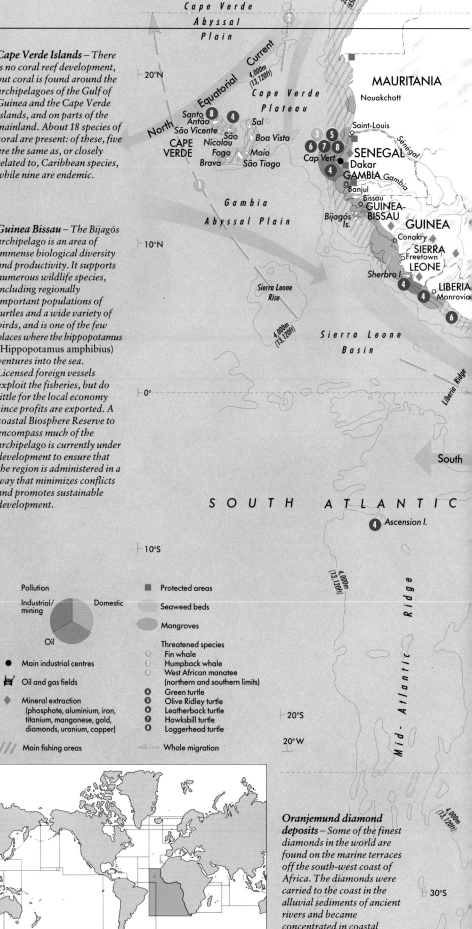

Pollution

Industrial/mining — Domestic

Oil

● Main industrial centres

⚓ Oil and gas fields

◆ Mineral extraction (phosphate, aluminium, iron, titanium, manganese, gold, diamonds, uranium, copper)

/// Main fishing areas

■ Protected areas

Seaweed beds

Mangroves

Threatened species
1 Fin whale
2 Humpback whale
3 West African manatee (northern and southern limits)
4 Green turtle
5 Olive Ridley turtle
6 Leatherback turtle
7 Hawksbill turtle
8 Loggerhead turtle

← Whale migration

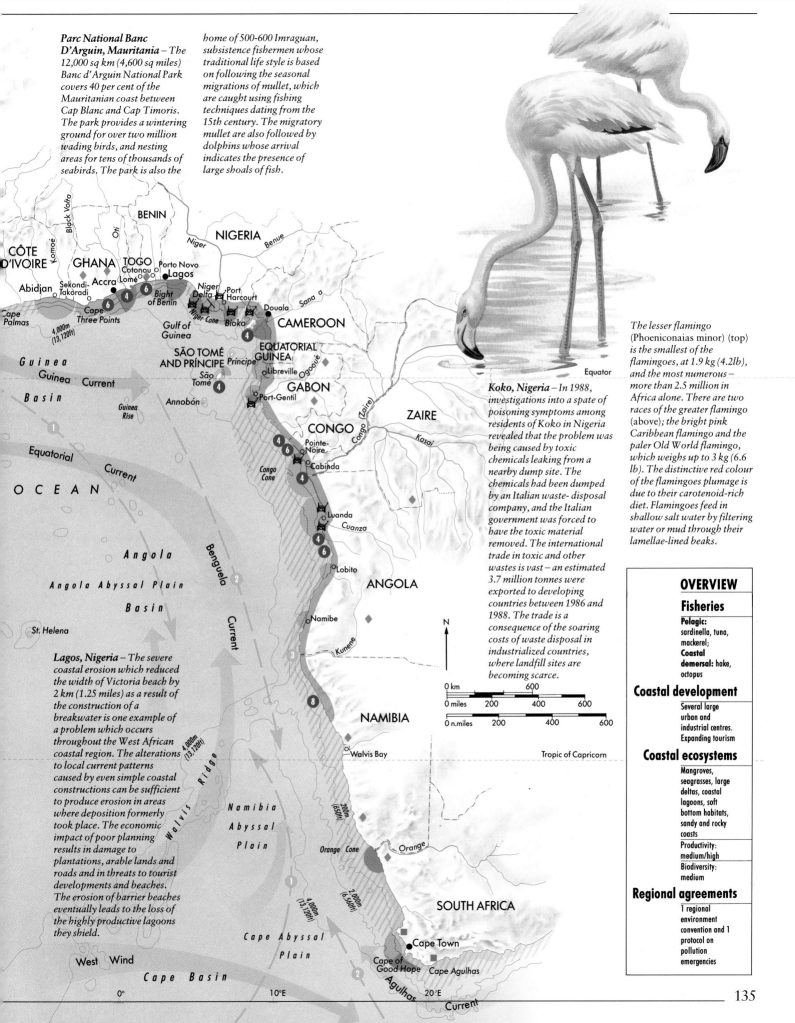

Parc National Banc D'Arguin, Mauritania – The 12,000 sq km (4,600 sq miles) Banc d'Arguin National Park covers 40 per cent of the Mauritanian coast between Cap Blanc and Cap Timoris. The park provides a wintering ground for over two million wading birds, and nesting areas for tens of thousands of seabirds. The park is also the home of 500-600 Imraguan, subsistence fishermen whose traditional life style is based on following the seasonal migrations of mullet, which are caught using fishing techniques dating from the 15th century. The migratory mullet are also followed by dolphins whose arrival indicates the presence of large shoals of fish.

Lagos, Nigeria – The severe coastal erosion which reduced the width of Victoria beach by 2 km (1.25 miles) as a result of the construction of a breakwater is one example of a problem which occurs throughout the West African coastal region. The alterations to local current patterns caused by even simple coastal constructions can be sufficient to produce erosion in areas where deposition formerly took place. The economic impact of poor planning results in damage to plantations, arable lands and roads and in threats to tourist developments and beaches. The erosion of barrier beaches eventually leads to the loss of the highly productive lagoons they shield.

Koko, Nigeria – In 1988, investigations into a spate of poisoning symptoms among residents of Koko in Nigeria revealed that the problem was being caused by toxic chemicals leaking from a nearby dump site. The chemicals had been dumped by an Italian waste-disposal company, and the Italian government was forced to have the toxic material removed. The international trade in toxic and other wastes is vast – an estimated 3.7 million tonnes were exported to developing countries between 1986 and 1988. The trade is a consequence of the soaring costs of waste disposal in industrialized countries, where landfill sites are becoming scarce.

The lesser flamingo (Phoeniconaias minor) (top) is the smallest of the flamingoes, at 1.9 kg (4.2lb), and the most numerous – more than 2.5 million in Africa alone. There are two races of the greater flamingo (above); the bright pink Caribbean flamingo and the paler Old World flamingo, which weighs up to 3 kg (6.6 lb). The distinctive red colour of the flamingoes plumage is due to their carotenoid-rich diet. Flamingoes feed in shallow salt water by filtering water or mud through their lamellae-lined beaks.

OVERVIEW

Fisheries

Pelagic: sardinella, tuna, mackerel; **Coastal demersal:** hake, octopus

Coastal development

Several large urban and industrial centres. Expanding tourism

Coastal ecosystems

Mangroves, seagrasses, large deltas, coastal lagoons, soft bottom habitats, sandy and rocky coasts
Productivity: medium/high
Biodiversity: medium

Regional agreements

1 regional environment convention and 1 protocol on pollution emergencies

Human Pressures

Today, only one tenth of the West African population lives near the coast. This proportion is expected to grow as coastal capital cities expand rapidly. As well as being densely populated, coastal cities are important industrial and transportation centres. Lagos, for example, is the location of over 85 per cent of Nigeria's industry, and houses eight million people.

Few of the coastal cities have adequate drainage and sewage treatment facilities, and consequently sewage pollution of coastal waters and lagoons has become a severe problem, degrading the environment and threatening public health and fisheries. Organic and nutrient enrichment cause deoxygenation of waters, both directly and through the promotion and subsequent decay of algal blooms. Diseases can be spread to humans through direct contact with water and seafood, particularly oysters, contaminated with faecal waste. Waterborne diseases such as hepatitis, cholera, typhoid and dysentery are all endemic to the West African coastal region.

Oil exploitation

There are significant oil reserves in the Gulf of Guinea, and oil is important to the economies of several surrounding countries, in particular Nigeria, Gabon, Cameroon, Congo, Zaire and Angola. Petroleum products account for more than 90 per cent of Nigeria's exports, making its economy very sensitive to fluctuations in the world market. High hydrocarbon concentrations in inshore waters and lagoons, and tar balls on beaches, are a consequence not only of oil exploitation in the Gulf, but also of pollution by tanker traffic and untreated refinery and engineering effluent.

There has been a rapid growth in the number of visitors to parts of the region. Around 85,000 tourists visit The Gambia each year. However, beach pollution by sewage and oil threatens the future of the tourist industry, and the loss of actual and potential incomes could be substantial.

Coastal erosion is an area requiring priority action in this region. Erosion is aggravated by lagoon channel alterations, seashore construction, and by the construction of dams which reduce sediment inputs from rivers. Coastal erosion is posing serious problems in Ivory Coast, Nigeria, Benin, The Gambia, Liberia, Sierra Leone and Togo.

Coastal mangroves have been cleared to make way for other land uses. In Benin, mangrove systems have been almost entirely destroyed by the construction of evaporation ponds for salt extraction from sea water. In Senegal, The Gambia and Sierra Leone, acid sulphate conditions developed in mangrove soils after they were cleared and drained for rice cultivation. In Senegal, the loss of mangroves was associated with declines in shrimp and other seafood, and with the occurrence of diseases such as typhoid and schistosomiasis, previously absent from the area.

Lagos, the capital of Nigeria (main picture), *is typical of many large coastal cities in developing countries. Nearly 70 per cent of the world's cities with more than 2.5 million inhabitants are located in coastal, delta and estuarine areas. Their rate of growth is seriously affecting the state of marine and coastal environments.*

Beach seining (inset) *is often used to catch fish in areas where sandy or soft bottoms allow the net to be drawn on-shore without tangling or tearing on rocks. Populations in coastal areas depend on open access to living marine resources for their survival. As populations grow in coastal areas so does the pressure on living resources.*

Western Indian Ocean

The Indian Ocean is the third largest of the world's oceans. Under the influence of the monsoon winds, its currents change direction twice each year. The climate systems are also dominated by the monsoon winds, which carry a low or a high moisture content, depending on whether they arise in the eastern and southern section of the Indian Ocean or the Arabian Peninsula.

The East African coastline runs diagonally from the north-east tip of Somalia through Kenya, Tanzania, Mozambique and South Africa. The continental shelf is almost non-existent in this area, so the inshore waters are heavily influenced by the deep water of the northern Indian Ocean. From Mogadishu to southern Mozambique the shelf extends further from shore. Common features of this coast include fringing coral and patch reefs, sea grass beds and tidal estuaries which support mangrove stands.

Rivers such as the Limpopo and the Zambezi carry sediments from inland areas, which suppress coral growth around the river mouths. These provide natural channels through the offshore reefs into inlets and bays, where ports such as Mombasa and Dar es Salaam have been developed.

Reef and mangrove systems

The coral reef system of East Africa forms an intermediate stage between the varied and extensive systems of the Pacific and the more limited and less diverse systems of the Wider Caribbean. Dominant genera include *Porites, Acropora, Goniastrea, Favia, Pocillopora, Stylophora, Millepora* and *Platygyra.* Mangroves are also not as widespread or as diverse in comparison to the Pacific and Caribbean. The largest stands of mangrove consist of around 460 sq km (180 sq miles) near Lamu in northern Kenya and around 700 sq km (270 sq miles) in the central delta area of Mozambique. However, these are small in comparison with other mangrove areas of the Indian Ocean region, such as the Indus Delta or the Sundarbans region on the Bay of Bengal. The coral reef and mangrove systems support a variety of crabs, molluscs, sea birds, dugongs, sea turtles and many species of fishes.

Fisheries

With the exception of a few urban centres which grew up around ports, the coast of East Africa is not densely populated. Small villages dot the coastline, and the local populations depend on the resources of the reef system and local coastal waters for much of their food. Fishermen use lines from small dugout boats, propelled either by oars or by lateen sails. Some larger sailing vessels, which are closely related to the Arab dhow, ply offshore waters where groupers, marlin, sailfish, sharks and tuna are caught. In the inshore area, the catch is mainly reef fish, such as parrotfish, snappers and wrasses, caught in nets or in traps positioned along the shoreline. Shrimp and prawns are caught in estuaries.

In some areas, like the coastal strip around Mombasa, Kenya the rapid development of tourism has put pressure on the sustainable use of the reef system. Demand from tourists has risen for seafood, shells and coral fragments. As local supplies become depleted, the pressure on the reef system extends farther from the resorts. Lobsters served to tourists in Kenya are caught in southern Somalia, while shells gathered along the north coast of Tanzania supply Kenya's tourist trade and shell and coral brokers who sell to overseas markets.

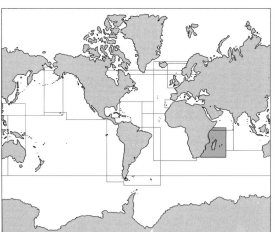

Reef destruction – In a number of locations dynamite is used to stun reef fishes which are collected when they float to the surface. In some areas large craters caused by the blasts are common. In one case the fringing reef was so badly damaged that an island inside the reef was washed away. The lack of fishing nets and line, coupled with readily available dynamite and increased demand for seafood, promotes this practice.

The coelacanth (Latimeria chalumnae) (below) belongs to a remarkable group of fishes, the crossopterians, from which the land vertebrates evolved. They had long been known as fossils and scientists believed them extinct until one was accidentally caught in a trawl net off southern Africa in 1938. Sionce then many other specimens have been caught in the Indian Ocean.

Curio collecting – Many tourist beaches and adjacent reefs have been denuded of their shells and small coral heads. Thus collecting is no longer possible for many tourists, so they resort to buying from hawkers or souvenir shops. Many dealers are former fisherman who are trying to enhance their livelihood by giving up fishing for the village market in favour of catering to the lucrative tourist trade. Thus tourists are degrading the very environment they come to see.

Indian Ocean whale sanctuary – This sanctuary was created in 1979 following an outline proposed to the International Whaling Commission (IWC) by the Republic of Seychelles. The sanctuary covers most of the Indian Ocean, a region in which nearly all the species of baleen whales and 33 species of toothed cetaceans breed. Among the smaller toothed whales are the bottlenose dolphin (Tursiops truncatus), and the Indo-Pacific humpbacked dolphin (Sousa chinensis). Baleen whales include Bryde's whale and the humpback whale. Blue whales have been sighted in the Gulf of Aden and sperm whales have been sighted off Oman.

TANZANIA

10°S

MALAWI

Zambezi

20°S

Beira

Sofala Bay

Save

Bazaruto I.

Limpopo

Tropic of Capricorn

Ponta da Barra

5
7

Maputo

SWAZILAND

Mozambique Current

SOUTH AFRICA

7

LESOTHO

5

30°S
Durban

30°E

Argulhas Ridge

0°

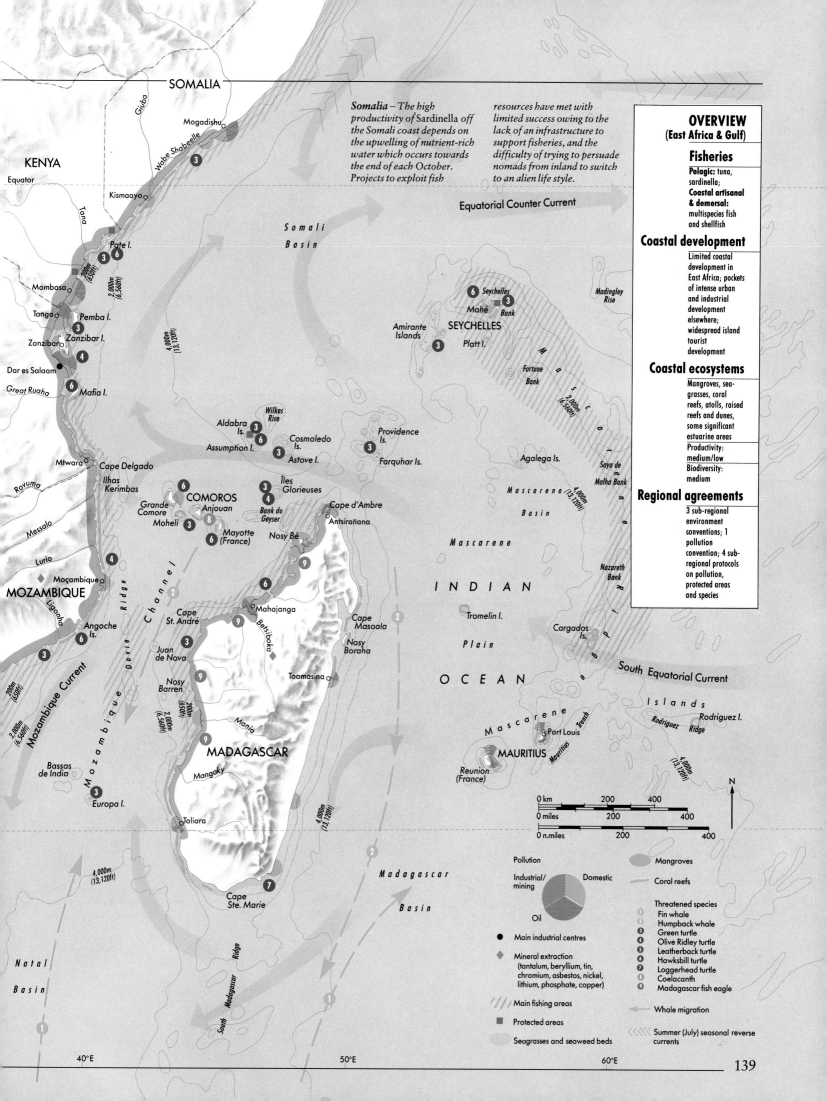

SOMALIA

KENYA

Equator

Giuba

Mogadishu

Wobe Shabeelle

③

Kismaayo

Tana

Pate I.

③ ⑥

200m
(650ft)

2,000m
(6,560ft)

Mombasa

Tanga

Pemba I.

③

Zanzibar

Zanzibar I.

④

Dar es Salaam •

⑥ Mafia I.

Great Ruaha

Mtwara

Cape Delgado

Ilhas
Kerimbas

Rovuma

Messalo

COMOROS

⑥

Grande
Comore

⑧

Anjouan

Moheli

③

⑥ Mayotte
(France)

Lurio

④

Moçambique

MOZAMBIQUE

Ligonha

⑥ Angoche
Is.

③

200m
(650ft)

2,000m
(6,560ft)

Bassas
de India

③

Europa I.

4,000m
(13,120ft)

Natal

Basin

Somalia – *The high
productivity of Sardinella off
the Somali coast depends on
the upwelling of nutrient-rich
water which occurs towards
the end of each October.
Projects to exploit fish*

*resources have met with
limited success owing to the
lack of an infrastructure to
support fisheries, and the
difficulty of trying to persuade
nomads from inland to switch
to an alien life style.*

Equatorial Counter Current

Somali

Basin

4,000m
(13,120ft)

Wilkes
Rise

Aldabra
Is.

③

⑥

Assumption I.

Cosmoledo
Is.

③

Astove I.

Îles
Glorieuses

③

④

Bank du
Geyser

Cape d'Ambre

Antsirañana

Nosy Bé

⑨

Mahajanga

Cape
St. André

⑨

Betsiboka

Juan
de Nova

③

Nosy
Barren

⑨

Mania

⑨

MADAGASCAR

Mangoky

4,000m
(13,120ft)

Toliara

Madagascar

Basin

Cape
Ste. Marie

⑦

South Madagascar Ridge

⑥ Seychelles

Mahé
Bank

③

Amirante
Islands

③

SEYCHELLES

Platt I.

Providence
Is.

③

Farquhar Is.

Fortune
Bank

Madingley
Rise

Agalega Is.

Saya de
Malha Bank

Mascarene

Basin

Mascarene

I N D I A N

Plain

O C E A N

Tromelin I.

Nazareth
Bank

Cargados
Is.

South Equatorial Current

Islands

Rodriguez I.

Rodriguez
Ridge

Port Louis

MAURITIUS

Reunion
(France)

4,000m
(13,120ft)

Cape
Masoala

Nosy
Boraha

Toamasina

②

②

②

②

①

①

Mascarene Ridge

Mauritius Trench

Mozambique Channel

Davie Ridge

Mozambique Current

OVERVIEW
(East Africa & Gulf)

Fisheries

Pelagic: tuna,
sardinella;
**Coastal artisanal
& demersal:**
multispecies fish
and shellfish

Coastal development

Limited coastal
development in
East Africa; pockets
of intense urban
and industrial
development
elsewhere;
widespread island
tourist
development

Coastal ecosystems

Mangroves, sea-
grasses, coral
reefs, atolls, raised
reefs and dunes,
some significant
estuarine areas

Productivity:
medium/low
Biodiversity:
medium

Regional agreements

3 sub-regional
environment
conventions; 1
pollution
convention; 4 sub-
regional protocols
on pollution,
protected areas
and species

---

0 km   200   400

0 miles   200   400

0 n.miles   200   400

N

Pollution

Industrial/
mining   Domestic

Oil

● Main industrial centres

◆ Mineral extraction
(tantalum, beryllium, tin,
chromium, asbestos, nickel,
lithium, phosphate, copper)

/// Main fishing areas

■ Protected areas

Seagrasses and seaweed beds

Mangroves

Coral reefs

Threatened species
① Fin whale
② Humpback whale
③ Green turtle
④ Olive Ridley turtle
⑤ Leatherback turtle
⑥ Hawksbill turtle
⑦ Loggerhead turtle
⑧ Coelacanth
⑨ Madagascar fish eagle

← Whale migration

<<< Summer (July) seasonal reverse
currents

40°E   50°E   60°E   **139**

Arabian Seas

The waters of the Arabian Peninsula and neighbouring countries form a distinctive subregion of the Indian Ocean. This area includes the Red Sea and Gulf of Aden, the Arabian Sea, and the Persian Gulf. The shores of this region have attracted human activity for thousands of years. The prosperous trading civilization of Dilmun flourished some 4,000-5,000 years ago, and encompassed what is now Bahrain and eastern Saudi Arabia. Before the 10th century AD, Arab mariners had established a trade network which extended from the Persian Gulf as far east as China. Long voyages were made possible by the Arabs' sophisticated knowledge of astronomy and navigation. The trade in textiles, frankincense and pepper led to contacts between distant cultures and the exchange of scientific knowledge and religious ideas.

The marine environment

The Red Sea, together with its associated arm, the Gulf of Aqaba, is very deep, reaching more than 2,000 metres (6,560 feet) in some places. However, the Gulf of Suez is quite shallow. The clear waters of the Red Sea have favoured the development of an extensive coral reef system along both its western and eastern seaboard. The reefs run for a distance of nearly 2,000 kilometres (1,240 miles). Some 220 species of coral have been recorded. The variety of species of marine organisms is invariably greater in the Red Sea than in either the Arabian Sea or the Persian Gulf. Along the intertidal zone, mangrove vegetation is important, particularly in the south. Elsewhere in the region, mangroves are less extensive, with the exception of parts of Iran.

The Arabian Sea is much deeper than the Red Sea, and reaches a maximum depth of more than 4,000 metres (13,000 feet). The major influence on the climate of this region is the monsoon system. From November to April, the North East Monsoon prevails, but from April to October the system reverses and the South West Monsoon predominates. The latter results in water movements that create cold water upwelling, a process that is responsible for the remarkably high productivity associated with the region. Studies carried out on rocky shores in Oman during the 1980s revealed a unique biological community, dominated by two species of macroalgae, *Sargassopsis zanardinii* and *Ecklonia radiata*. These algal communities sustain important local abalone and crustacean fisheries.

In contrast to the Arabian Sea, the Persian Gulf has an average depth of only 35 metres (115 feet). Because of its shallowness, the Gulf also experiences higher levels of salinity (40-70 parts per thousand) and wider seasonal changes in sea temperature (15-38°C) than the Red Sea and most parts of the Arabian Sea. The number of marine species found only in the Gulf is high, and reaches 12 per cent for species groups such as echinoderms, which include starfish, sea urchins and sea cucumbers.

While coastal use in much of the Red Sea and Arabian Sea has so far been limited, development pressures have been substantial along much of the Gulf's shoreline. The construction of ports and other facilities for the oil industry has exacerbated the problems created by infilling and dredging. The extraction and transport of oil results in a constant input of oil into the waters of the Gulf. In 1991, the outbreak of war in the region led to the discharge of millions of gallons of oil into the Gulf, which posed a potentially devastating threat to an already stressed marine environment.

The dugong (Dugong dugon) (above) *belongs to one of the world's few remaining species of sirenian. These are the only marine mammals which are entirely vegetarian (feeding on sea grasses), and may live for up to 70 years. The dugong is especially vulnerable to extinction owing to its low reproductive rate and late sexual maturity.*

Bahrain – Historical references to the pearl oysters found off the shores of Bahrain date back over 2,000 years. The pearls were known to the Assyrians, and it was the desire for the pearls which spurred the Portuguese invasion of the region in 1522. Pearl collecting continued into the 1930s, using methods little changed from those first described two thousand years before. The divers collected baskets of oysters, as well as leather bottles of freshwater from underwater springs.

Bahrain and Qatar – During the early 1980s, the Gulf was believed to contain only about 50 dugongs. However, the sighting of a herd of 674 dugongs between Bahrain and Qatar during the aerial surveys of 1985 and 1986 resulted in a total reassessment of their numbers. There are believed to be around 7,000 dugongs living in the Persian Gulf and over 4,000 in the Red Sea, making this the most important region for dugongs outside Australia.

Persian Gulf – Following hostilities during the 1991 Gulf war, around 5 million barrels of oil were released into the sea. Coastal infrastructures and resources at particular risk included desalination plants and the fisheries, the latter a multi-million dollar industry and of much social importance. Also at risk were birds and other wildlife including turtles, dugongs and many other species. Smoke and atmospheric pollutants, together with unburnt oil, have also reached the marine environment.

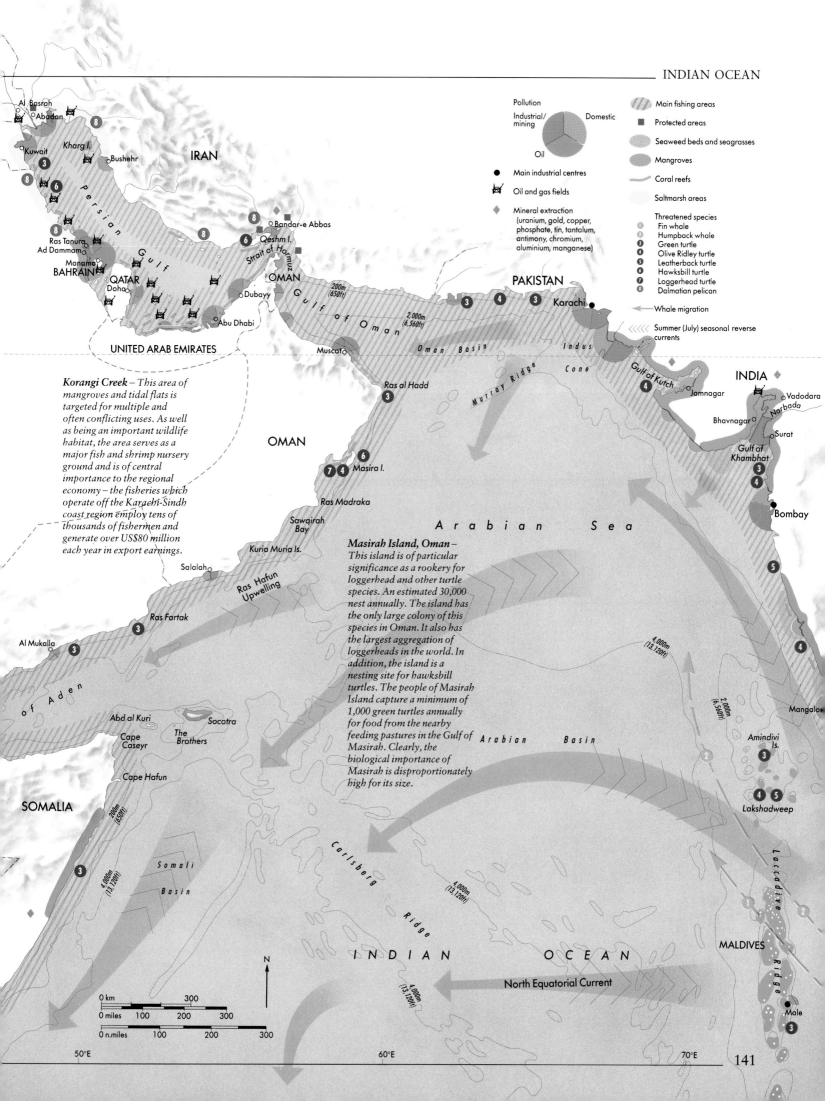

Al Basrah
Abadan
Kuwait
Kharg I.
Bushehr
IRAN
Ras Tanura
Ad Dammam
Manama
BAHRAIN
QATAR
Doha
Dubayy
Abu Dhabi
UNITED ARAB EMIRATES

Persian Gulf

Bandar-e Abbas
Qeshm I.
Strait of Hormuz
OMAN
Gulf of Oman
200m (650ft)
2,000m (6,560ft)
Oman Basin
PAKISTAN
Karachi
Indus
Gulf of Kutch
Jamnagar
INDIA
Vadodara
Narbada
Bhavnagar
Surat
Gulf of Khambhat
Bombay

Muscat
Ras al Hadd
OMAN
Masira I.
Ras Madraka
Sawqirah Bay
Kuria Muria Is.
Salalah
Ras Hafun Upwelling
Ras Fartak
Al Mukalla
of Aden
Abd al Kuri
Socotra
Cape Caseyr
The Brothers
Cape Hafun
SOMALIA

Murray Ridge
Cone

Arabian   Sea

Arabian   Basin

Mangalor
Amindivi Is.
Lakshadweep

Korangi Creek – *This area of mangroves and tidal flats is targeted for multiple and often conflicting uses. As well as being an important wildlife habitat, the area serves as a major fish and shrimp nursery ground and is of central importance to the regional economy – the fisheries which operate off the Karachi-Sindh coast region employ tens of thousands of fishermen and generate over US$80 million each year in export earnings.*

Masirah Island, Oman – *This island is of particular significance as a rookery for loggerhead and other turtle species. An estimated 30,000 nest annually. The island has the only large colony of this species in Oman. It also has the largest aggregation of loggerheads in the world. In addition, the island is a nesting site for hawksbill turtles. The people of Masirah Island capture a minimum of 1,000 green turtles annually for food from the nearby feeding pastures in the Gulf of Masirah. Clearly, the biological importance of Masirah is disproportionately high for its size.*

Somali Basin
4,000m (13,120ft)
4,000m (13,120ft)
Carlsberg Ridge
4,000m (13,120ft)
4,000m (13,120ft)
2,000m (6,560ft)
Laccadive Ridge

INDIAN   OCEAN
North Equatorial Current
MALDIVES
Male

N

0 km		300
0 miles	100	200	300
0 n.miles	100	200	300

Pollution
Industrial/ mining
Domestic
Oil

● Main industrial centres
Oil and gas fields
◆ Mineral extraction (uranium, gold, copper, phosphate, tin, tantalum, antimony, chromium, aluminium, manganese)

Main fishing areas
Protected areas
Seaweed beds and seagrasses
Mangroves
Coral reefs
Saltmarsh areas

Threatened species
1 Fin whale
2 Humpback whale
3 Green turtle
4 Olive Ridley turtle
5 Leatherback turtle
6 Hawksbill turtle
7 Loggerhead turtle
8 Dalmatian pelican

← Whale migration
Summer (July) seasonal reverse currents

50°E   60°E   70°E

141

Island Life

The Indian Ocean contains a number of unique island environments which differ in their physical characteristics. They range from the large atoll systems of the Maldives, where tiny islands perch precariously on coral reefs, to the granite and coral islands in the Seychelles group and Madagascar which is the world's fourth largest island. The ancient geological history of Madagascar contrasts with the recent volcanic origin of the Comoros, Mauritius and Rodrigues islands, as well as the island of Reunion.

Like the islands, the peoples of the region trace their origins back to a number of sources. The languages of Madagascar show links with those of South-East Asia and New Guinea. Many of the other island peoples show evidence of an African heritage. In contrast, the linguistic and cultural ties of the inhabitants of the Maldives and the Laccadive Islands lie with Sri Lanka, South and North India and the Arabian Peninsula.

Despite these differences, islands share many of the same environmental problems. As a result of population growth on very small land areas, problems such as solid waste disposal, and the contamination of bathing beaches through the discharge of untreated sewage are widespread. On islands with mountainous or highland areas, such as Madagascar and Mauritius, the clearance of inland forest leads to soil erosion. Rivers transport eroded sediments to coastal areas, which then smother reefs and fill harbours. In the early 1980s, annual soil losses through erosion on Madagascar reached between 25 and 250 metric tonnes per hectare. Most island societies depend heavily on fishing and the harvesting of marine resources which provide food for local communities and export products. In terms of exports, tuna is the region's most important fish resource.

Threatened reefs

The marine fauna of the Indian Ocean is not as diverse as South-East Asia and the Western Pacific. However, the central part of the Indian Ocean is home to some 1,000 species of fish, 140 species of coral, 63 species of marine benthic algae and between 11 and 14 species of nesting seabirds. This diversity lessens to the west and north. The Indian Ocean's profusion of marine life, together with coral reefs, deserted islands and white sand beaches under a tropical sun form the major reasons for the increasing popularity of these islands as tourist destinations for winter-weary Europeans. The tiny Republic of the Maldives welcomes some 158,000 tourist arrivals every year, a figure which nearly equals the indigenous population of 214,000. In Seychelles, revenue from tourism in 1988 amounted to about 50 per cent of gross domestic product.

Few tourists realize the extent of environmental problems in small islands. Ironically, tourists themselves contribute to the degradation of the very reefs they come to see, when divers break off living corals or when anchor chains scar the reef surface and break down the coral colonies. The populations of reef fish decrease through spear-fishing and the collection of shells and bleached coral as souvenirs.

Construction also poses a threat to small atoll islands since the only sources of building material are the reef itself and coral sands from the lagoon. Demand for building materials increases with population growth, the expansion of tourism and economic development. In order to supply Male, the capital of the Maldives, around 2,000 cubic metres (70,600 cubic feet) of living coral is harvested annually. Esti-

mates indicate that by the year 2014 no suitable coral supplies will be found in North Male Atoll. Without a healthy reef, tourism will die and the country will no longer be able to sustain its present rate of economic development.

Male is a a mere 1,700 metres (5,580 feet) in length and 700 metres (2,300 feet) in width. This has been extended by pumping sand from the lagoon onto the reef flat, which now covers the entire reef area almost to its edge. Over 56,000 people live on the island and the population has doubled in just 13 years. Land is scarce and the government plans to develop a nearby island as a "suburb". In response to such threats to their coral reefs, the governments of many of the island nations of the Indian Ocean have passed laws and regulations to control, or even ban, such practices as the harvesting of corals, spear-fishing and the sale of corals. Some authorities have tried to provide alternative sources of income for the islanders. One interesting development with important implications for the future was the 1979 decision to turn the Indian Ocean into an ocean whale sanctuary. This move reflected the growing concern among governments in the region with the conservation of the marine environment and its resources.

An ambitious hotel development covers a small island (left) in Mauritius, and reflects the increasing importance of tourism for the economies of the island nations of the Indian Ocean. Tourism now furnishes a significant portion of the national income of the Maldives and Seychelles. However, the growth of the tourist industry threatens to destroy the spectacular marine environment that now attracts so many visitors. The destruction of coral reefs to provide construction materials has had a great impact in the Comoros, Maldives, Mauritius and Seychelles. Removal of coral reefs leaves beaches and coasts vulnerable to the action of the sea. Coral reefs also suffer damage from increased tourist traffic, spear-fishing and the collection of souvenirs. However, many remote islands in Seychelles, such as the island of Aldabra, still remain free from such negative impacts.

The variety of marine curios for sale to tourists at this stall (far left, top) in Seychelles includes sea turtles and objects carved from their shell, as well as coco de mer. Together with the collection and sale of coral and shells, the trade in such curios poses a threat to the coastal environment of the Indian Ocean's islands.

A group of islanders recover a piece of drifting timber (far left, bottom) from the shallow waters of a lagoon in the Maldive Islands. Traditional fishing boats or dhonis in the Maldives ae usually constructed from coconut since timber is in short supply on small atoll islands. Floating timbers such as this one represent a valuable windfall.

The coco de mer (Lodoicea maldivica), or double coconut (left), weighs up to 22 kg (48lbs). The species is native to the Seychelles, but the palm is now found only on Praslin Island, on the tiny Curieuse Island, and is under cultivation in a few sites and botanical gardens. It is now protected in its most well-known locality, the Vallée de Mai, which became a World Heritage site in 1983. The collection of the coco de mer is specifically controlled by law, and the government maintains a monopoly on its exploitation.

Indian Ocean Basin

The Indian Ocean lies across the Equator, extending from the Tropic of Cancer in the north to the Tropic of Capricorn in the south. Its western boundary is the African coast at around 45°E, while the Malay Peninsula and the Indonesian Archipelago at approximately 100°E define its eastern boundary. The semi-enclosed Persian Gulf and Red Sea are extensions of the Indian Ocean in the north, and together with the Arabian Sea, the Gulf of Aden and the Gulf of Oman, they define the boundaries of the Arabian Peninsula.

There are two surface current systems that dominate the Indian Ocean, one in the north, the other in the south. In the south, a large anticyclonic gyre predominates, which results in a westward-flowing equatorial current in lower latitudes and an eastward-flowing current in higher latitudes. A component of the South Equatorial Current, the Mozambique Current, flows southward between Madagascar and the East African coast. Another component, the Agulhas Current, flows south of Madagascar, along the south African coast. In the north, the surface currents undergo a seasonal reversal under the influence of the monsoon system. During the North-East Monsoon (November to April), the North Equatorial Current flows west and produces the Somali Current which moves from the Horn of Africa to southern Tanzania. In the South-West Monsoon (May to October) the surface current direction is reversed and flows eastward and splits to form clockwise currents in the Arabian Sea and the Bay of Bengal. During this season, the monsoon winds generate upwellings of deep, nutrient-rich water off the coasts of Somalia and Oman.

Over most of its surface, temperatures vary between 25° and 30°C (77° and 86°F), but because of the direction of circulation, the temperatures tend to be higher in the west than in the east. The annual variation in surface temperature is only 2-3°C (3.6-5.4°F) near South-East Asia, and 4-6°C (7.2-10.8°F) near the East African Coast. The most dramatic changes occur during the Somali and Omani upwelling periods when the colder, deep water flowing to the surface is sometimes 18°C (32°F) lower than that at the surface.

The climate and the monsoon system

The climate of the region varies both seasonally and according to location, but like the current systems is generally dominated by the monsoon cycle. This results in a dry season during the first quarter of the year, then gradually develops more frequent rain systems, particularly in the Bay of Bengal, in the second quarter. During the third quarter, when the South-West Monsoon predominates, wind speeds and rainfall reach their maximum. The monsoon gradually shifts back to its north-easterly origins during the fourth quarter, but heavy rainfall still prevails in some parts of the region during this time.

The climatic and oceanographic conditions, including the seasonal upwellings they bring about, coupled with wide variation in the terrestrial conditions prevailing in the region, are responsible for the highly significant regional differences in the levels of nutrients in the surface waters.

Beyond the highly productive continental margins and the Somali upwelling, the primary productivity of the Indian Ocean is extremely low. But the diversity of the marine fauna is high – over 4,000 pelagic fish species alone have been recorded. The Indian Ocean is a key area for marine mammals – almost all of the baleen whales breed here and 33 species of the toothed cetaceans live here. The ocean is crossed by other large migratory species, including marine turtles and a number of the commercially important tuna species, which are exploited by longline fleets. The ocean currents of the regions play an important part in the homogeneity of the flora and fauna across the region. These are dispersed at different stages in their life cycles throughout the Indian Ocean and in some cases the western Pacific.

Concern for the state of the marine environment is generally high in this region. Several action plans and regional conventions have been developed by the countries surrounding the Indian Ocean, including those of East Africa, the Red Sea and Gulf of Aden, the Persian Gulf and South Asian Seas regions. Recent initiatives involve discussions on broader, collaborative efforts to address the marine environmental problems of the entire Indian Ocean Basin.

This south Indian fish market (right) is typical of many found around the Indian Ocean Basin. Tuna, shrimp, barracuda and sea bream are commonly caught along most coastal areas of Africa, Arabia and south Asia.

The shipment of mangrove poles (below) from Lamu Island and the Rufigi Delta basin northwards to the Arabian Peninsula is a leftover of the ancient trade practices developed by some of the region's earliest civilisations. They also carry charcoal and spices north, and Persian carpets south.

Coral reefs (far right) border the barren desert shores of the Red Sea. Some 350 species of coral occur in the Red Sea. This diversity is greater than in the Caribbean and among the highest for coral reefs in the Indian Ocean. An estimated 6 per cent of coral species are endemic to the Red Sea. In some groups of reef fish, endemism may even reach 90 per cent. Human pressures on Red Sea coral reefs are still generally low and the majority remain relatively pristine. However, increased coastal development, oil and mineral exploration, have begun to exert some adverse efforts.

TRADING ROUTES

The Indian Ocean has long served as an important trade route both internally between India, Africa and Arabia and externally with trade and sailing routes passing by the southern tip of India to the rich spice islands of the East Indies. Arab dhows have been a feature of the Indian Ocean for over 4,000 years, and even the most recent designs resemble the wooden ships of the 17th century. These teak sailing boats were suitable for lengthy voyages or simple ferrying purposes. Their cargoes included among other things: Chinese pottery, dates, grains, spices, ointments, cowries shells and slaves. Arab traders would carry cowries from the Maldives to northern India, Arabia and south to Africa, and such shells have even been found in European prehistoric burial sites. Rice from India was traded for dried fish and shells from the Maldives. Arab traders also ventured into South-East Asia as far as the island of New Guinea. They established trading bases, empires and sultanates and spread the influence of Islam, long before European sailors reached the area. Cultural linkages between East Africa and Arabia are maintained even today. Along the African coast such traders still carry mangrove poles and charcoal to the Arabian peninsula where wood is in short supply.

East Asian Seas

The seas of East Asia support a wide variety of animals and plants. Although the primary productivity of the region is generally low, coral reefs, mangroves and sea grass beds provide rich habitats. Coral reef development is most extensive around the Philippines and Indonesia, which together have over 20,000 islands. In the western portion, the main reef systems surround the Andaman, Nicobar and Chagos Islands.

Important species

Mangroves and mud flat areas are important feeding grounds for some of the 155 species of seabirds which live in the region. Seven genera of sea grasses occur, which provide grazing areas for sea turtles and the dugong (*Dugong dugon*), as well as serving important ecological and physical functions because of their high productivity, structure and habitat.

Some reef species, including sea hares and sea fans, are an important source of antibiotic and anticoagulant drugs. Unfortunately, the predatory crown-of-thorns starfish (*Acanthaster planci*) has caused damage to reefs in some areas, especially where the corals have been rendered vulnerable because of other sources of environmental stress. Six species of sea turtle nest in the East Asian Seas region: the flatback (*Chelonia depress*), the green (*Chelonia mydas*), hawksbill (*Eretmochelys imbricata*), leatherback (*Dermochelys coriacea*), olive Ridley (*Lepidochelys olivacea*) and the loggerhead (*Caretta caretta*). The last five are classed as vulnerable or endangered.

Marine resources

The communities of organisms which depend on the reefs offer a rich harvest. Fish taken from reef communities within 15 kilometres (9 miles) of the shore contribute up to 60 per cent of local protein intake, and in the Philippines over 50 species of algae from the reef flat are exploited for protein, vitamins, agar and carrageenin. Inshore fisheries focus on small fish such as mackerel, scad and sardine; demersal fish such as snapper, croaker and bream; and also shrimp and cephalopods. King mackerel and tuna are fished further offshore, and sea cucumbers are prized for their high export values.

A variety of fishing methods are used to exploit the many different species of the region. In the mangrove areas, these range from lines of up to 400 metres (440 yards), armed with hundreds of hooks, to barrier nets strung across tidally drained creeks. The fish are sometimes intoxicated using derris root (*Derris elliptica*). Jellyfish are also collected, using a rake, net or hands. Prawns are caught using a method known as *merigis*: a nypa leaf stalk, with a curtain of midribs attached, is dragged across the water surface, causing the prawns to leap out of the water and into the boat.

Human influences

The coastal populations of all the East Asian Seas countries are high – more than 180 million people live on the 13,677 islands of the Indonesian archipelago alone. There is an ever-increasing demand for land in coastal zones. Since 1905, more than 2.5 million people have moved or been moved under transmigration programmes from the densely-populated and environmentally degraded islands of Java, Bali, Madura and Lombok to other Indonesian islands.

Brunei, Indonesia, Malaysia, the Philippines, Singapore and Thailand have coordinated efforts in developing a regional action plan and in 1990 all six countries signed the Baguio Declaration on Managing Coastal Resources for Sustainable Development.

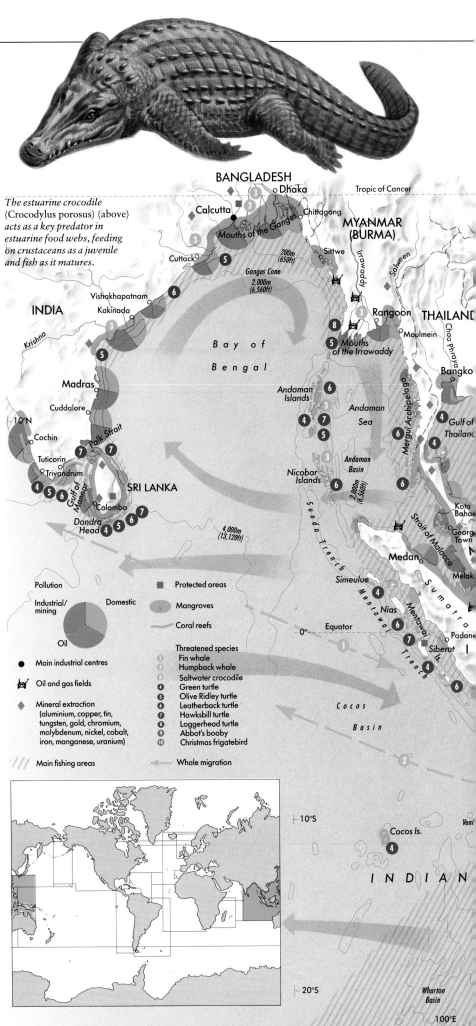

The estuarine crocodile (Crocodylus porosus) (above) acts as a key predator in estuarine food webs, feeding on crustaceans as a juvenile and fish as it matures.

Pollution

Industrial/mining — Domestic

Oil

- ● Main industrial centres
- Oil and gas fields
- ◆ Mineral extraction (aluminium, copper, tin, tungsten, gold, chromium, molybdenum, nickel, cobalt, iron, manganese, uranium)
- /// Main fishing areas

- ■ Protected areas
- Mangroves
- Coral reefs

Threatened species
- ① Fin whale
- ② Humpback whale
- ③ Saltwater crocodile
- ④ Green turtle
- ⑤ Olive Ridley turtle
- ⑥ Leatherback turtle
- ⑦ Hawksbill turtle
- ⑧ Loggerhead turtle
- ⑨ Abbot's booby
- ⑩ Christmas frigatebird

Whale migration

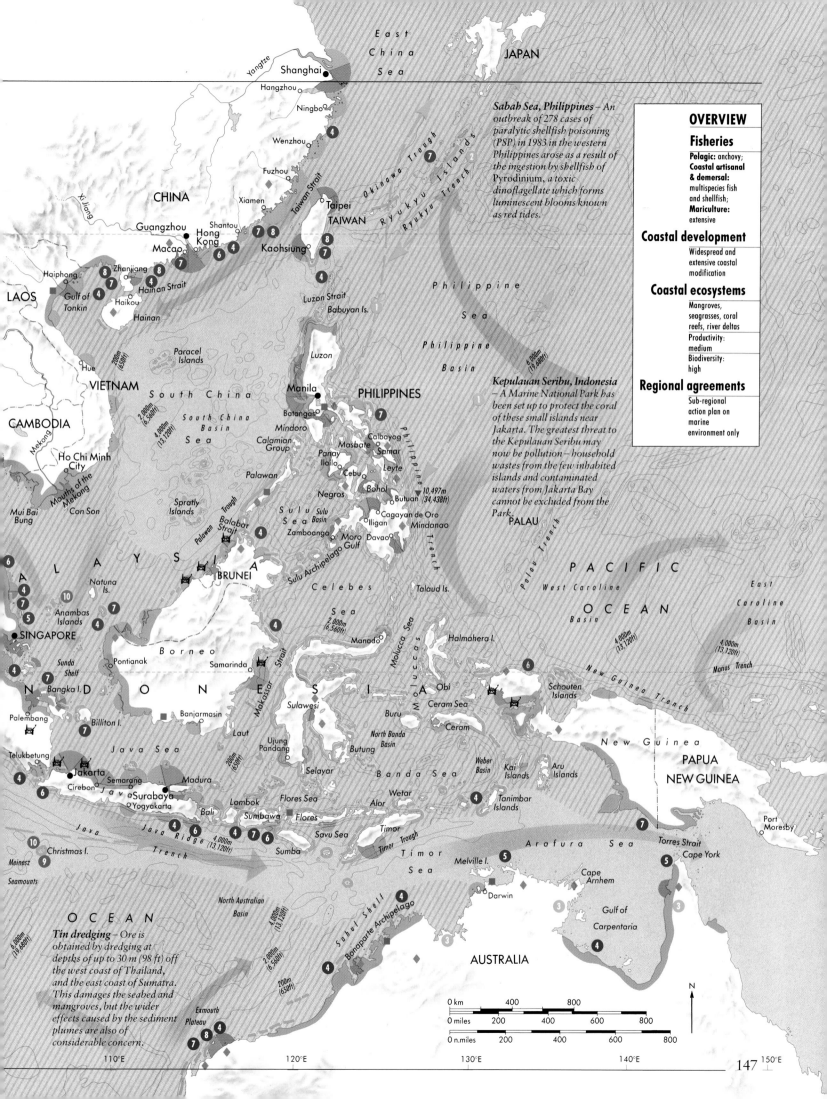

East China Sea

JAPAN

Shanghai
Yangtze
Hangzhou
Ningbo
Wenzhou
Fuzhou
CHINA
Xiamen
Taipei
TAIWAN
Guangzhou
Shantou
Hong Kong
Macao
Kaohsiung
Zhanjiang
Haiphong
Hainan Strait
Gulf of Tonkin
Haikou
Hainan
Luzon Strait
Babuyan Is.

LAOS

Okinawa Trough
Ryukyu Islands
Ryukyu Trench

Philippine Sea

Philippine Basin

6,000m (19,680ft)

VIETNAM
Xi Jiang
Hue
Paracel Islands
700m (650ft)
Luzon

South China Sea
2,000m (6,560ft)
South China Basin
4,000m (13,120ft)

Manila
PHILIPPINES
Batangas
Mindoro
Calamian Group
Masbate
Panay
Iloilo
Cebu
Calbayog
Samar
Leyte
Bohol
10,497m (34,438ft)
Butuan

CAMBODIA
Mekong
Ho Chi Minh City
Mouths of the Mekong
Mui Bai Bung
Con Son
Palawan
Negros
Cagayan de Oro
Iligan
Mindanao
Zamboanga
Moro Gulf
Davao

Spratly Islands
Palawan Trough
Balabar Strait

PALAU

Philippine Trench

MALAYSIA
Natuna Is.
BRUNEI
Sulu Sea
Sulu Basin
Sulu Archipelago
Talaud Is.

PACIFIC OCEAN

West Caroline Basin
East Caroline Basin

Anambas Islands
SINGAPORE
Sunda Shelf
Pontianak
Borneo
Samarinda
Makassar Strait
Celebes Sea
2,000m (6,560ft)
Manado
Halmahera I.
Molucca Sea
4,000m (13,120ft)
4,000m (13,120ft)
Manus Trench
New Guinea Trench

INDONESIA
Bangka I.
Palembang
Billiton I.
Banjarmasin
Sulawesi
Buru
Obi
Ceram Sea
Ceram
Schouten Islands

Telukbetung
Java Sea
200m (650ft)
Ujung Pandang
Butung
North Banda Basin

New Guinea

Jakarta
Semarang
Cirebon
Surabaya
Yogyakarta
Bali
Madura
Lombok
Sumbawa
Flores Sea
Selayar
Banda Sea
Weber Basin
Kai Islands
Aru Islands

PAPUA NEW GUINEA

Java Ridge
4,000m (13,120ft)
Java Trench
Sumba
Flores
Savu Sea
Timor
Wetar
Alor
Tanimbar Islands
Timor Trough
Port Moresby

Christmas I.
Meinesz
Seamounts
6,000m (19,680ft)

Timor Sea
Arafura Sea
Torres Strait
Cape York

OCEAN

North Australian Basin
4,000m (13,120ft)
2,000m (6,560ft)
200m (650ft)
Sahul Shelf
Bonaparte Archipelago
Melville I.
Darwin
Cape Arnhem
Gulf of Carpentaria

AUSTRALIA

Exmouth Plateau

Sabah Sea, Philippines – An outbreak of 278 cases of paralytic shellfish poisoning (PSP) in 1983 in the western Philippines arose as a result of the ingestion by shellfish of Pyrodinium, a toxic dinoflagellate which forms luminescent blooms known as red tides.

Kepulauan Seribu, Indonesia – A Marine National Park has been set up to protect the coral of these small islands near Jakarta. The greatest threat to the Kepulauan Seribu may now be pollution – household wastes from the few inhabited islands and contaminated waters from Jakarta Bay cannot be excluded from the Park.

Tin dredging – Ore is obtained by dredging at depths of up to 30 m (98 ft) off the west coast of Thailand, and the east coast of Sumatra. This damages the seabed and mangroves, but the wider effects caused by the sediment plumes are also of considerable concern.

OVERVIEW

Fisheries

Pelagic: anchovy;
Coastal artisanal & demersal: multispecies fish and shellfish;
Mariculture: extensive

Coastal development

Widespread and extensive coastal modification

Coastal ecosystems

Mangroves, seagrasses, coral reefs, river deltas
Productivity: medium
Biodiversity: high

Regional agreements

Sub-regional action plan on marine environment only

---

0 km 400 800
0 miles 200 400 600 800
0 n.miles 200 400 600 800

N

110°E   120°E   130°E   140°E   150°E

Exploiting Marine Resources

East Asian coastal areas have suffered severe environmental stress as a result of population growth and economic development. This has led to the destruction and degradation of major coastal and marine habitats, the loss of fisheries, and toxic algal blooms in the waters of Malaysia, the Philippines and Brunei.

The mangroves which were once a major feature of the coasts of the East Asian Seas region have been exploited directly for timber, firewood, charcoal, poles, bark (for tannin) and woodchips (for rayon). Other plants in the mangrove system, such as the nypa palm (*Nypa fruticans*) are also valuable. The fronds are used for roof thatching, matting and the manufacture of cigarette papers, while the flowering stems are tapped for nypa sugar, which is used in Sarawak for the commercial production of alcohol. Mangrove areas are converted to agricultural land; reclaimed for industrial, urban and aquacultural development; or clear felled, often illegally.

Mineral exploitation

Tin and other mineral deposits are exploited by dredging, especially off the west coast of Thailand. There are considerable offshore gas and oil reserves in the region, and petroleum and related products are important exports from Malaysia, Indonesia and Brunei. Placer mining in mangrove areas causes complete destruction, and destroys the chemical balance of the substrate. Mangroves and sea grasses also suffer as a result of oil spills, because they trap oil, which kills invertebrate animals and damages seedlings.

Offshore tin mining poses a major threat to corals, through siltation, while mine tailings from inland mines are dumped into rivers, passing downstream to the coast where they smother corals or retard their growth by increasing the turbidity of the water. This prevents photosynthesis by the zooxanthellae, and results in coral bleaching. The turbidity of water entering the sea from rivers has also been increased because of poor land-use practice. and forest clearance inland.

Damage caused by fishing

In some regions, corals have been severely damaged by destructive fishing methods, both artisanal and commercial. Despite being banned in 1972, blast fishing – using ammonium nitrate or dynamite to stun or kill fish – remains widespread in the Philippines. The explosion kills fish of all sizes indiscriminately, and shatters corals. The Danajan Bank reef in the Philippines has been blast-fished since the 1950s, leading to its destruction and the loss of a valued fishery resource. Physical damage to reefs is also caused by trawling, purse seining and *Muro-ami:* a traditional fishing method whereby up to 200 swimmers drag weighted lines across the reef surface. The collection of aquarium specimens can also kill corals and fish, as the process involves aiming sodium cyanide at coral heads to disable small fish such as the polkadot grouper (*Cromileptes altivelis*) and the giant labrid (*Cheilinus undulatus*), as they swim out.

The destruction of habitats by industrial, agricultural and maricultural pollution and overfishing has degraded the fishery resource. East Asian trawlers are small and fish mainly in inshore waters, usually making round trips in just one day and exploiting the valuable shrimp resources and demersal fish to a depth of up to 50 metres (164 feet). Where trawling bans have been imposed, stocks have been able to recover, and projects are currently under way to reconstruct habitats by building artificial reefs.

A typical fish market in Maricet, South Thailand (top). The Gulf of Thailand provides important spawning grounds for many of the region's commercial fish species, shrimp and cephalopods, and is a valued inshore fishery which provides an annual yield of more than 1,000 kg/sq km (5,700 lb/sq mile).

This stilt village, Kampung Kinabalu in Borneo (above), is set on the fringe of the largest expanse of mangrove forests in the world – the Sunda Shelf, a region encompassed by Vietnam, Kampuchea, Thailand, Malaysia, Sumatra, Java and Borneo. Mangroves form important nursery areas for fish and crustaceans such as penaeid shrimps.

Jakarta (right), the capital city of Indonesia, has a population of around 7.5 million people which is rapidly expanding. Fish are the major source of dietary protein, and this fishing village is part of the vast sprawling city which now covers over 650 sq km (250 sq miles) along 32 km (20 miles) of coast, and over 300 islands in Jakarta Bay. The sanitation facilities of the city are minimal and untreated sewage runs into the Bay via the city's canals and rivers. Pathogens found in the filter-feeding clams Anadara and oysters Saccostrea make these unfit for human consumption.

Mariculture

The East Asian Seas region has a long tradition of mariculture, utilizing a wide range of fish, crustaceans, molluscs and plants. Traditional maricultural and aquacultural techniques provide cheap protein and employment to rural people, and for these reasons are regarded as a valuable component of development schemes. However, intensive production for commercial gain of species with a high market value can be environmentally damaging. It also offers little to local people and may be socially disruptive as it causes the marginalization of small-scale, artisanal fisheries.

Traditional culture methods, such as the *tambak* system of Indonesia, are extensive. The density of the stock is kept relatively low and artificial foods are not used. Tidal flushing of the ponds provides a natural turnover of the water. In these systems, polyculture (farming a variety of species) is common because mixed stocks of young fish and shrimps are collected from the wild together.

In contrast, intensive commercial production makes use of artificial food and depends on pumps to provide adequate water turnover. Stock densities may be ten times higher than in extensive systems. The waste products from intensively stocked ponds create local pollution problems, and may damage offshore fisheries.

Mariculture species

The giant tiger prawn (*Penaeus monodon*), which weighs up to 500 grams (1.1 pounds), is typical of the species cultured in the intensive system. Freshwater is used for salinity regulation, at the expense of domestic and agricultural supplies. Saltwater is beginning to intrude into the groundwater system in many areas, as a result of overextraction of ground water. In Taiwan the government has banned new prawn farms following severe land subsidence. Prawn culture in Asia currently accounts for three-quarters of world production, but producers may be hard hit in the future as the world market is becoming saturated.

In the Philippines, the extent of mangrove coverage has declined from over 400,00 hectares in the 1920s to only 140,000 hectares today. At least 60 per cent of this loss is due to conversion to milkfish farms. A vicious cycle operates where mangrove areas are cut down to make room for fish farms, consequently removing their ability to function as nursery grounds for young fish and other species, and as a source of nutrients. Floating net cages can be used for fish culture in mangrove waterways and estuaries, to avoid these destructive effects. This system was introduced to Malaysia in 1973, and cultured species include the grouper (*Epinephelus tauvina*) and the seabass (*Lates calcifer*), which tolerate crowding of 300-500 fish per cage. The brown mussel (*Mytilus viridis*) is cultured on ropes strung between rafts, and yields up to 30 kilograms (66 pounds) per rope over six to seven months. Around peninsular Malaysia, the culture of cockles (*Anadara granosa*), using larvae collected from the wild, is an important activity among the Chinese fishing community.

Seven giant clams, belonging to the genera *Tridacna* and *Hippopus*, have their centre of distribution in the Indo-West Pacific. The giant clam (*Tridacna gigas*) has a shell up to one metre (three feet) in length. Apart from the poisonous kidney, all of the flesh is edible, and the adductor muscle is prized in China as an aphrodisiac. Unfortunately, collection of the colourful shells of smaller species has led to a serious reduction in numbers, and several species are now considered vulnerable. Recent research into the culture of giant clams has proved promising.

The estuarine crocodile (*Crocodylus porosus*) is an endangered species which appears in the IUCN Red List. Numbers have fallen because of habitat destruction, hunting and egg collection, and breeding programmes have been set up in several countries for both commercial and conservation purposes. The Food and Agricultural Organization of the United Nations (FAO) has set up a project in Irian Jaya, Indonesia, to rear the estuarine crocodile and the freshwater crocodile (*Crocodylus novaeguineae*) for their skins and flesh, which have a high commercial value.

Red algae of the genus *Eucheuma* are farmed in the Philippines to produce carrageenin, a cell wall component used as a thickening agent in foods. Production in 1987 amounted to 222,549 tonnes. Many small-scale farms are run by artisanal fishermen to supplement their incomes. The algae is grown from cuttings attached to nylon ropes forming a grid across the sea bed or reef flat. Farms can be destroyed by starfish, sea urchins, sea cucumbers, puffer fish and rabbit fish. Seaweed farming is threatening Tubbataha Reef, the largest coral atoll of the Philippines, in spite of its protected status as a national marine park.

Prawn farming (left) *has traditionally provided a valuable sideline to fish culture. Prawns are often farmed in* tambaks. *The banana prawn* (Penaeus merguiensis) *is farmed in Indonesia, Malaysia, Thailand and the Philippines, which have a combined annual production of over 25,000 tonnes. Intensive systems are environmentally damaging, and clearance of the mangrove system for pond development is affecting offshore fisheries, since many offshore species spawn in mangroves.*

Farming of fin fish (above) *in small pens has a number of advantages over the use of ponds on cleared land. They make use of existing water bodies, are fairly inexpensive to construct, and require comparatively low levels of maintenance. A floating "collar" of buoyant material, usually bamboo or plastic, holds up a nylon or polythene net. Pens are usually anchored in shallow water with ropes or poles fixed to the bottom.*

South Pacific

The Pacific islands (Melanesia, Micronesia and Polynesia) are home to just over five million people. Their combined land area is no greater than 500,000 square kilometres (193,000 square miles), and the Pacific Basin contains some of the world's smallest states. About 85 per cent of the land and 66 per cent of the population lie within the boundaries of Papua New Guinea. For most Pacific countries, land forms only a tiny part (as little as 0.001 per cent) of the total area under their jurisdiction. Therefore, they depend upon marine resources both for subsistence and commercial use.

Pacific islands range from low-lying atolls, up to four metres (13 feet) above sea level, to high volcanic islands with steep profiles. Atolls are living coral reefs growing on submerged volcanic cones; the atoll islands, or *motu*, are formed of piles of sand derived from weathered coral skeletons and other reef organisms such as the alga *Halimeda*. These islands are formed in long, narrow strips, either entirely enclosing a central lagoon or forming a series of small islets around the edges of it. They are unstable, susceptible to destruction by hurricanes, and have only a limited underground supply of freshwater.

Raised coral islands are composed of reef limestone. They tend to have poor soils and little or 'no surface freshwater, in contrast to volcanic islands which are densely vegetated and have rich soils. Island relief affects rainfall and runoff patterns, which in turn affect the distribution of coastal habitats such as mangroves and coral reefs. Volcanic islands are among the highest in the Pacific and generally have a steep off-shore gradient, dropping rapidly to the ocean depths. Within the tropics and subtropics, these islands are usually surrounded by highly-productive fringing or barrier reefs.

Pacific peoples

The island states of the Pacific are remarkable for their cultural and linguistic diversity. Over a third of the world's languages are spoken in just four Melanesian countries – Papua New Guinea, the Solomons, Vanuatu and New Caledonia – and each Pacific island group is home to distinctive human cultures, with their own social and cultural mores, dance, dress, traditional knowledge and technologies.

Human population densities are generally high in the South Pacific, with up to 386 people per square kilometre (1,000 per square mile). Population growth rates also tend to be high; but several countries, including Pitcairn and Tonga, have negative growth rates because of emigration. As a result of such emigration, the largest Polynesian city in the world is Auckland, New Zealand, and more Tokelauans now live in New Zealand than live in Tokelau. Nevertheless, emigration is an important source of revenue through remittances. Many insular communities depend upon the export of labour to maintain their standard of living.

Internal migration is also high, and populations tend to gather round centres of services, such as Majuro in the Marshall Islands, which now has a population density of 2,188 per square kilometre (5,666 per square mile). This leads in many cases to over-exploitation of living resources, and environmental degradation. High density aggregations of people on small islands leads to sewage pollution of enclosed lagoons and coastal waters; habitat clearance for construction, both residential and tourist; inappropriate coastal developments and problems of solid waste disposal.

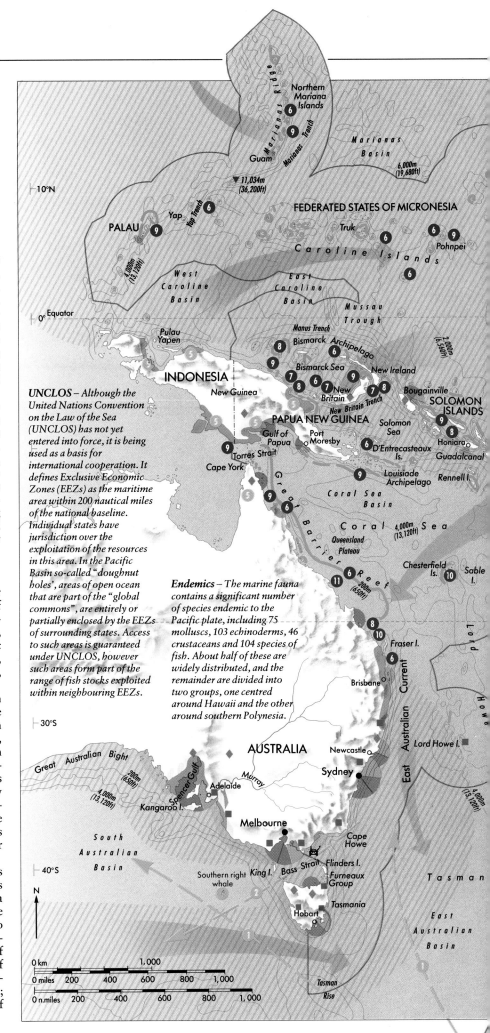

UNCLOS – Although the United Nations Convention on the Law of the Sea (UNCLOS) has not yet entered into force, it is being used as a basis for international cooperation. It defines Exclusive Economic Zones (EEZs) as the maritime area within 200 nautical miles of the national baseline. Individual states have jurisdiction over the exploitation of the resources in this area. In the Pacific Basin so-called "doughnut holes', areas of open ocean that are part of the "global commons", are entirely or partially enclosed by the EEZs of surrounding states. Access to such areas is guaranteed under UNCLOS, however such areas form part of the range of fish stocks exploited within neighbouring EEZs.

Endemics – The marine fauna contains a significant number of species endemic to the Pacific plate, including 75 molluscs, 103 echinoderms, 46 crustaceans and 104 species of fish. About half of these are widely distributed, and the remainder are divided into two groups, one centred around Hawaii and the other around southern Polynesia.

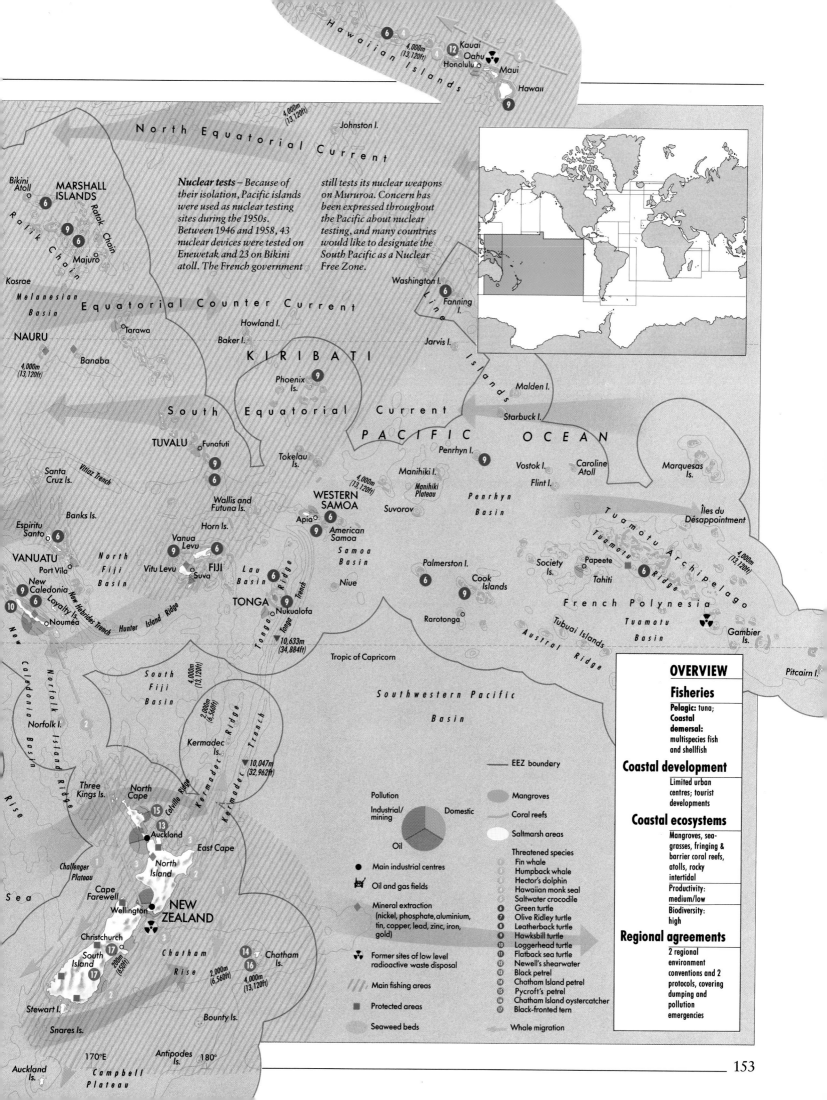

Nuclear tests – Because of their isolation, Pacific islands were used as nuclear testing sites during the 1950s. Between 1946 and 1958, 43 nuclear devices were tested on Enewetak and 23 on Bikini atoll. The French government still tests its nuclear weapons on Mururoa. Concern has been expressed throughout the Pacific about nuclear testing, and many countries would like to designate the South Pacific as a Nuclear Free Zone.

OVERVIEW

Fisheries

Pelagic: tuna; **Coastal demersal:** multispecies fish and shellfish

Coastal development

Limited urban centres; tourist developments

Coastal ecosystems

Mangroves, seagrasses, fringing & barrier coral reefs, atolls, rocky intertidal

Productivity: medium/low

Biodiversity: high

Regional agreements

2 regional environment conventions and 2 protocols, covering dumping and pollution emergencies

---

EEZ boundary

Pollution
Industrial/mining
Domestic
Oil

Mangroves
Coral reefs
Saltmarsh areas

Threatened species
1 Fin whale
2 Humpback whale
3 Hector's dolphin
4 Hawaiian monk seal
5 Saltwater crocodile
6 Green turtle
7 Olive Ridley turtle
8 Leatherback turtle
9 Hawksbill turtle
10 Loggerhead turtle
11 Flatback sea turtle
12 Newell's shearwater
13 Black petrel
14 Chatham Island petrel
15 Pycroft's petrel
16 Chatham Island oystercatcher
17 Black-fronted tern

● Main industrial centres
Oil and gas fields
◆ Mineral extraction (nickel, phosphate, aluminium, tin, copper, lead, zinc, iron, gold)
Former sites of low level radioactive waste disposal
Main fishing areas
■ Protected areas
Seaweed beds
Whale migration

153

Marine Resources

Most Pacific societies have one important feature in common; their dependence upon marine resources for survival. Without the diversity of marine organisms and the knowledge of how to catch and utilize such resources, many of the smaller islands of Micronesia would have been uninhabitable. For many modern Pacific island societies tuna forms an important economic resource, which is often exploited under license by the fishing fleets of major powers such as Japan and the United States.

Historically, traditional societies guarded their resources jealously. On the island of Ponam in the Manus Province of Papua New Guinea, ownership of different fishing grounds, fish species and fishing techniques was formally divided between different clans. A fisherman catching a species belonging to another clan, even in his own fishing grounds, was obliged to make a gift of the catch to the owner clan on his return. Such complex patterns of exploitation reduced the pressure on individual resources and ensured distribution of each catch throughout the society concerned.

The concepts of communal ownership, "limited entry" and "closed seasons" for particular fisheries were once widespread throughout Pacific cultures. They depended upon a detailed knowledge of the biology and ecology of individual species, and an individual's knowledge of where, when and how to fish often determined his status in traditional society. For example, in the Lau islands of Fiji the head or *dau-goli* of the fishing clan was in charge of communal fish drives and turtle fishing, and had the power to declare restrictions on times and areas of fishing. To achieve the status of master fisherman a long apprenticeship had to be served; many skills and techniques had to be mastered if the full range of available species was to be effectively exploited. In the South Pacific, some techniques were localized, such as harpooning dugong in Papua New Guinea and the noosing of mangrove lobsters in Fiji, while others were more widespread including the use of lures for catching pelagic tuna, large wooden hooks for the deep-water oil fish (*Ruvettus*) and nooses for catching sharks.

Traditional societies exploited a wide variety of marine species. The Motu people of southern Papua New Guinea were known to eat more than 90 different species of mollusc. Archaeologists digging near Port Moresby have discovered the remains of sea urchins, crabs, dugong, fin-fish and whale. The longest continuous record of marine resource use in the world is at New Ireland, Papua New Guinea, where at one site a community exploited local fish and shellfish resources for more than 20,000 years.

Past extinctions and modern pressures

Interestingly, the belief that exploitation by traditional societies preserved resources is not true. In Fiji, the horseshoe clam (*Hippopus hippopus*) has been extinct throughout living memory, though archaeologists have unearthed its shells in middens dating back 2,000 years. With population growth, technological innovation and contact with European cultures, species such as dugong, turtles and some types of fish, have been over exploited and local populations are now extinct. One valuable but threatened resource is the giant clam; the danger is now receding due to the development of successful clam mariculture. As resources are now sold for money, instead of being exchanged in a traditional small-scale barter system, there is an incentive to over-harvest for profit.

Resources such as mangrove crabs, lobsters and barramundi, are now purchased from local fishermen for export.

Drift-net fishing is not a new concept, yet recent technological developments are causing concern among environmentalists and pelagic fisheries managers. Living resources face severe damage because some Asian countries are now using drift nets several kilometres long to harvest tuna in the Pacific Basin. These nets also catch many non-commercial species, including smaller marine mammals and turtles. Lost sections of net may continue to "ghost fish" for years, as they are made of artificial fibres which do not degrade. South Pacific countries are calling for a convention banning drift-net fishing in the South Pacific.

Changes in land use are also affecting coastal environments, with nickel mining in New Caledonia and copper and gold mining in Papua New Guinea resulting in increased sediment flow in sensisitive coral reef areas. Aggregations of people in coastal cities and around centres of services result in sewage pollution of coastal waters and concentrates harvesting of resources into the immediate neighbourhood.

The island of Nauru (above) covers only 20 sq km (8 sq miles) and most of this raised limestone island is covered by rich deposits of phosphate. This view shows loading of a large vessel, with small traditionally designed outrigger canoes in the foreground. Although the income from the phosphate extraction provides Nauruans with a high per capita income, destruction of the island's environment deprives the islanders of a sustainable way of life.

Freshly caught tuna and a dolphin fish are landed on the quay at Bora Bora (below) in French Polynesia. Pelagic fish were important items in the traditional catch of artisanal fishermen and now form a vital source of export income for the economies of small island states. Fears have been expressed that large-scale drift-net fishing by fleets from Asia may adversely affect the stocks on which these islands depend. Drift-nets tens of kilometres in length result in the deaths of turtles, marine mammals, and non-commercial fish species, and threaten the very tuna stocks which form the basis of the fishery.

FARMING GIANT CLAMS

Despite its reputation for trapping unwary divers, the giant clam *Tridacna gigas* is incapable of completely closing the two halves of its shell. But its reputation has not protected it against fishermen collecting its adductor muscle, which is considered a delicacy and fetches around US$150 a kilogram (2.2 pounds) in the markets of Singapore. Illegal harvesting of giant clams (family Tridacnidae) on isolated islands and reefs throughout the Pacific has severely depleted stocks of the larger species. To combat this, the farming of these great bivalves has been under development in a number of South Pacific countries including Micronesia, the Solomons, Papua New Guinea and Australia. Recent successful attempts mean that restocking of depleted reefs and supplying international demand are now possible in the near future, especially since giant clams grow fast and the adductor muscle can be harvested within four years.

Mangroves and Sea Grasses

Mangroves and sea grass beds display their greatest variety of species in the Indo-West Pacific region. The farther an area is from this region, the lower the species diversity. In New Guinea, mangrove communities are composed of 37 different species in 13 genera, whereas in the Caribbean such communities contain only seven species in four genera. At the most northerly and southerly limits of their distribution mangroves often contain a single species. Sea grasses are more widely distributed, with some species forming important habitats in the temperate and Mediterranean regions.

Mangroves

Within the Pacific Basin, the diversity of mangrove species declines to the north and south of the Equator, and from west to east across the Pacific. It was once thought that the distribution of mangroves could be explained fully by the effects of distance and island areas, with larger islands closer to the centre of diversity in the Indo-West Pacific having more mangroves than smaller islands farther away. A closer examination of the data suggests that other factors may also be important. In the Federated States of Micronesia, of those islands that cover more than 20 square kilometres (eight square miles) only two out of the 28 atoll islands and one of the 14 raised limestone islands have mangroves. In contrast, mangroves are found on five out of six volcanic islands of similar size. This suggests that higher rainfall on volcanic islands, leading to higher runoff and increased amounts of sediment entering coastal environments, may determine the successful establishment and maintenance of mangrove communities.

Extensive mangroves grow on prograding shorelines in Melanesia, and display a characteristic

The estuarine crocodile (Crocodylus porosus) (below) is the largest of the living crocodiles, which as its name suggests occurs in saline coastal areas. Inhabiting mangroves swamps in Melanesia, northern Australia and Indonesia, this species is now farmed for its skin. Young males migrate along the coasts in search of suitable areas in which to establish their territories, and a single individual is known to have reached Fiji probably from the Solomon Island. Females lay eggs in a nest built above the high-tide level which they guard against intruders.

pattern of zonation. The distribution of mangrove tree species reflects differences in their tolerance to salinity and the tidal regime on different parts of the shore. The mangrove fauna also shows similar zonation: penaeid prawns are characteristic of the more saline reaches of mangroves, while *Macrobrachium* shrimps complete the whole of their life cycle in freshwater areas. The fish fauna shows similar differences, with a large number of mud-feeding species and few herbivores or plankton feeders, reflecting the availability of food resources within the habitat. Mangroves also provide an important habitat for other animals. In southern New Guinea and northern Australia, pig-nosed turtles (*Carettochelys insculpta*) feed on mangrove seedlings and lay their eggs in sand banks that have mangroves nearby. Both the freshwater crocodile and the endangered saltwater species (*Crocodylus porosus*) live in mangroves

which, like sea grass beds, act as nurseries for a variety of fish and crustanceans.

Sea grass beds

Throughout the South Pacific, sea grasses are important in stabilizing sands in intertidal zones, often in lagoons and other sheltered areas associated with reef systems and on the seaward side of mangroves. The underground stems and low growth forms of many sea grasses create a dense surface cover in which small animals can hide from predators. Sea grasses also grow rapidly and their leaves are colonized by many different epiphytic plants and animals, which are in turn grazed by small fish such as rabbitfishes (Siganidae). In addition to providing feeding grounds for various marine turtles and the dugong (*Dugong dugon*), they are grazed by the sea urchin *Tripneustes gratilla* which is harvested by local people for food.

Mangroves of the genus Rhizophora (below) are characteristic of the seaward fringes of mangrove swamps, where their extensive prop root systems help support the trees in soft, muddy substrates. Breathing cells on prop roots and specially modified breathing roots, the pneumatophores, aid oxygen uptake in the sulphurous soils characteristic of such swamps.

This photograph of Rhizophora from Fiji (left) shows the enlarged propagules which aid mangrove dispersal. The seed of the mangrove actually germinates while still attached to the parent plant, a condition known as vivipary. When mature, the propagule drops into the mud or water below the parent and is moved by water currents to other areas. As it develops further, small roots emerge from the tip, assisting it in anchoring once it has been deposited in the intertidal. The high salt and sulphide concentrations, acidity and lack of oxygen, make mangrove soils a hostile environment for seedlings, and vivipary may be one way of overcoming the problems of growth during the early stage of development.

Coral Reefs in the South Pacific

The Pacific Ocean is renowned for its coral reefs and small islands with coconut palms and white coral sand beaches. Indeed, some of the most diverse and dramatic reef structures in the world are found in the South Pacific. Reefs are of three basic types: fringing reefs, which grow directly adjacent to island and continental land masses, and are the most widespread; extended barrier reefs, such as the Great Barrier Reef, which occur some distance offshore and are separated from the mainland by a deep-water channel; and atolls, ring-like reefs characteristic of Micronesia and Polynesia which are found in the open ocean.

Charles Darwin was one of the first to propose the theory of atoll formation in which he suggested that the upward growth of the corals kept pace with the slowly sinking land beneath. Nearly one hundred years later evidence to support this theory came when in 1952 two deep drill holes were bored on Enewetak, and about 1,300 metres (4,300 feet) of carbonate limestone was found to overlay the summit of an ancient volcanic cone, which was itself 5,000 metres (16,400 feet) above the ocean floor. Atolls are therefore the remains of volcanic islands which have gradually sunk below the sea surface. Elsewhere in the region active' uplift has stranded reef systems above the present sea level in a series of terraces, perhaps the most spectacular of which are on the Huon Peninsular in northern New Guinea.

The reef itself represents a remarkably complex habitat of high species diversity, which owes its existence to the symbiotic relationship between the tiny coral animals or polyps and dinoflagellates that inhabit their tissues (see pp. 68-69). Coral colonies are composed of numerous individuals, which feed on plankton, grow and reproduce to form a complex skeleton. Coral skeletons take many forms from the fine, delicate branches of *Stylophora* and *Acropora* which grow in sheltered waters, to the massive, boulder-like structures of *Porites* in the warmer lagoon areas. Various hemispherical brain corals are characteristic of areas exposed to wave action and broad, flattened plate-like forms of *Acropora* are found in deeper water on the reef face where there is less light.

The complex three-dimensional structure of a coral reef provides a multiplicity of micro-habitats occupied by small crabs, shrimps, starfishes, brittle stars, molluscs and a host of fishes. Primary producers include a number of different kinds of algae: filamentous green algae which provide food for small herbivorous fishes. Forms such as *Halimeda* provide much of the sand that fills the lagoons, and multicoloured encrusting forms cement together the sand and skeletal fragments of the reef flat. The complex web of life on coral reefs is typified by the multitude of symbiotic, commensal and parasitic relationships found there. These range from small crabs which remain in *Acropora* branches until the coral grows around them to the long, thin, colourless fish which live inside the mantle cavity of bivalve molluscs or the anal chambers of sea cucumbers.

In the Pacific, coral reefs diversity declines as one moves away from the equator, and from west to east across the Pacific. It has long been recognized that the western Pacific is an area of high species diversity

A small Acropora *head (above right) serves as a refuge for a school of small angel fish. When a large predatory fish approaches or a shadow passes overhead, the fish dart* in among the protective branches of the coral. Such schools are often associated with individual corals, moving away only short distances to feed.

A large elkhorn coral (below) provides shelter for a variety of fish and a Diadema *sea urchin. Growing in deeper water, the elkhorn's branches are broad and flattened to provide a large surface area to the light which filters down. Small colonies of the massive coral* Porites *are also shown in the foreground, while pink and red encrusting algae can be seen on the surface of the dead coral. These algae are important in cementing loose coral fragments together, and providing a solid surface for recolonization by reef-building corals.*

among various marine groups, partly as a consequence of the area accumulating species that have differentiated in either the Indian Ocean or the eastern Pacific. During the Eocene and Miocene times, a single fauna extended virtually around the world, such that cones, cowries, *Nautilus*, giant clams and reef-building corals were found from the Mediterranean through the Indian Ocean to the Pacific and Caribbean. The Pacific-Caribbean connection was lost in the late Eocene, while the Mediterranean-Indian connection closed during the Miocene. Tectonic events in the Indo-Malayan region effectively severed the Indian-Pacific connection, and species evolved separately in the two oceans, with an overlap in the western Pacific. As a result of this, on average 28 per cent of the species of gastropods, crustaceans, fishes and echinoderms are restricted to the western Pacific, 37 per cent are widespread over the entire Indo-West Pacific, 18 per cent are found in both the Indian Ocean and the western Pacific, and 16 per cent in both the Pacific plate area and the western Pacific.

CORALS FOR JEWELLERY

Despite their name, black corals are only distantly related to the reef-building corals. They grow in deep water in the form of branched tree-like colonies and are harvested by divers. These slow growing, colonial animals produce a skeleton of horny material which when polished is used for jewellery, key rings, and decorative items sold largely through the tourist trade. Only the main stems and branches provide large enough pieces for working, and most of the finer branches are discarded. Unfortunately due to their slow growth rate colonies large enough to produce materials for jewellery may be many tens and often hundreds of years old. The rate of harvest exceeds natural replacement rates and results in depletion and loss of these resources in many islands throughout the Pacific.

This male sea snake (Laticauda colubrina) (above) is resting on a shore in Fiji. Sea snakes are venomous and males of this species are predators of small moray eels on reefs, while the larger females prey on conger eels in deeper waters. L. colubrina comes inshore to digest its food and lay eggs in moist areas of decaying vegetation.

North-East Pacific

The North-East Pacific coast extends from Alaska through the densely populated state of California to the tropical waters off southern Mexico. Major urban-industrial centres include Vancouver, Seattle, San Francisco, Los Angeles and San Diego.

The fisheries of the North-East Pacific are not nearly as productive as those of the west. In terms of quantity, the Alaska pollock is the most important single species. However, the catch is only about 20 per cent of that in the North-West Pacific. Other commercially important species include the various Pacific salmon (*Oncorhynchus* spp.), the yellowfin sole (*Limanda aspera*) and the Pacific cod (*Gadus macrocephalus*). As in the North-West Pacific, bivalves dominate shellfish catches. Several foreign fishing fleets operate in the North-East Pacific, including those of China, Japan, the Soviet Union and North and South Korea. However, in numbers the US fishing fleet is by far the largest.

The rich kelp forests along the California coast support a varied fauna, which includes such commercially exploited species as abalone, spiny lobster, sea bass and red urchin. The giant kelp (*Macrocystis pyrifera*) itself yields algin, a gelatinous substance used as a thickening agent in the food industry. There is potential for the development of kelp harvesting further north, but this could be destructive to salmon habitats in that area.

Although construction associated with development has destroyed some coastal vegetation, the North-East Pacific coast has retained significant areas of salt marsh. However, habitat loss is a threat to species such as the burrowing starlet sea anemone (*Nematostella vectensis*). Found in salt marshes along the coast of California, the species is of scientific interest chiefly for its unusual distribution.

Endangered species

The islands of the North-East Pacific support a number of endangered and vulnerable populations of marine birds and mammals. The only known breeding colonies of the Guadalupe fur seal (*Arctocephalus townsendii*) lie on Mexico's Guadalupe Island, 256 km (159 miles) west of Baja California. Commercial sealing almost reduced the seal to extinction, but its numbers are believed to be on the increase. However, fishing boats, cruise ships and the island's wild goats disturb its breeding grounds.

There has been a steady reduction of the California sea otter population, initially through fur trapping and subsequently through loss of habitat and food, particularly abalone, which is now heavily exploited in most areas. Attempts are now being made to reintroduce the species.

Townsend's shearwater (*Puffinus auricularis*) breeds only on the Revillagigedos Islands, south of Baja California, where it suffers as a result of nest destruction by pigs and predation by cats, and on the Hawaiian Islands where the introduced mongoose is the principal threat.

The region's coastal waters have become polluted, especially around major cities such as Los Angeles and San Francisco, leading to problems of contaminated seafood. However, oil pollution is not generally a major problem in the North-East Pacific. The greatest threat comes from shipping accidents. In March 1989, the tanker *Exxon Valdez* spilled crude oil into the waters of Alaska's Prince William Sound. The logging industries of British Columbia pollute the waters with wood debris and floating logs which can cause considerable damage to small boats.

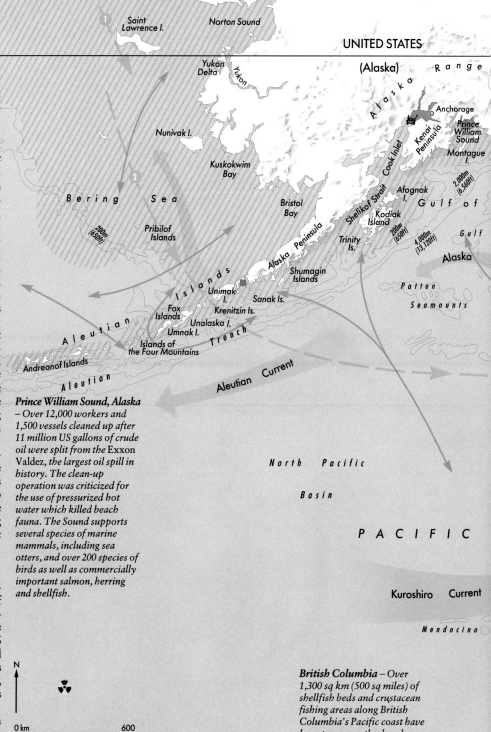

Prince William Sound, Alaska
– Over 12,000 workers and 1,500 vessels cleaned up after 11 million US gallons of crude oil were split from the Exxon Valdez, *the largest oil spill in history. The clean-up operation was criticized for the use of pressurized hot water which killed beach fauna. The Sound supports several species of marine mammals, including sea otters, and over 200 species of birds as well as commercially important salmon, herring and shellfish.*

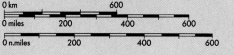

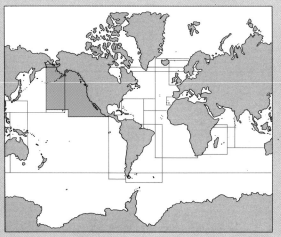

British Columbia *– Over 1,300 sq km (500 sq miles) of shellfish beds and crustacean fishing areas along British Columbia's Pacific coast have been permanently closed owing to contamination by bacteria and toxins, leading to losses in potential income worth millions of dollars each year. The most widespread problem is posed by the discharge of untreated sewage, which contains high numbers of bacteria and viruses – a health hazard to consumers of raw or partially cooked shellfish. The sedentary bivalves pump hundreds of litres of water through their gills each day as they filter feed and water contaminants become concentrated in their tissues. The shellfish themselves are unaffected by sewage microorganisms but consumers may be exposed to numerous diseases.*

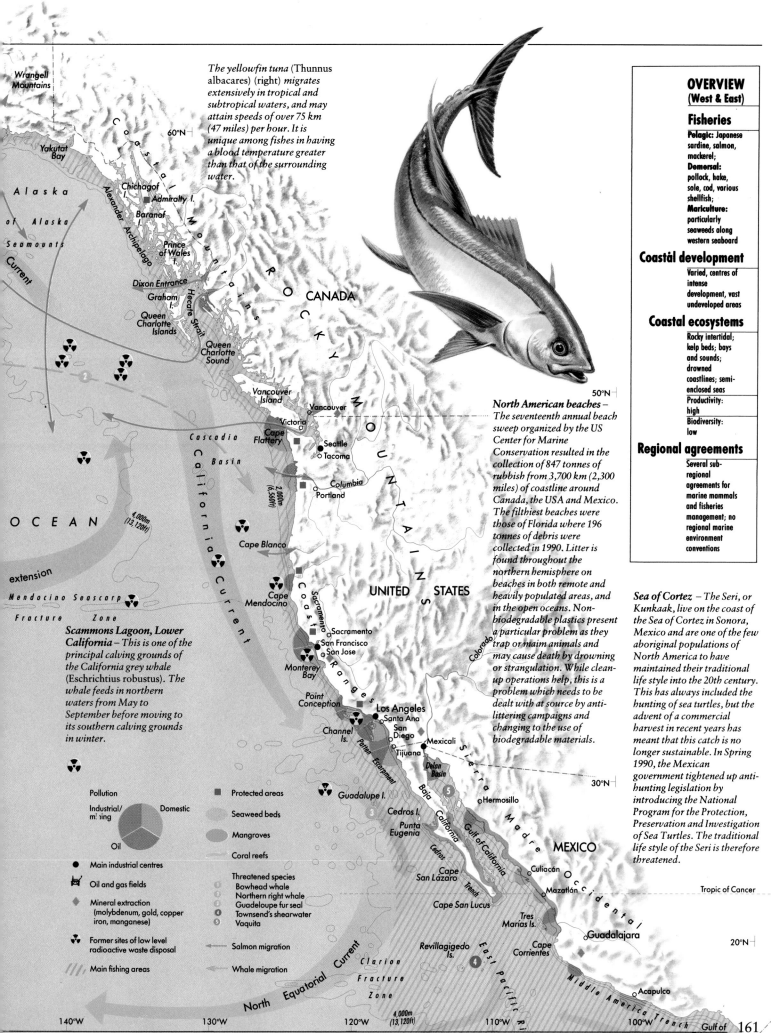

The yellowfin tuna (Thunnus albacares) (right) migrates extensively in tropical and subtropical waters, and may attain speeds of over 75 km (47 miles) per hour. It is unique among fishes in having a blood temperature greater than that of the surrounding water.

OVERVIEW (West & East)

Fisheries

Pelagic: Japanese sardine, salmon, mackerel; **Demersal:** pollock, hake, sole, cod, various shellfish; **Mariculture:** particularly seaweeds along western seaboard

Coastal development

Varied, centres of intense development, vast undeveloped areas

Coastal ecosystems

Rocky intertidal; kelp beds; bays and sounds; drowned coastlines; semi-enclosed seas
Productivity: high
Biodiversity: low

Regional agreements

Several sub-regional agreements for marine mammals and fisheries management; no regional marine environment conventions

North American beaches – The seventeenth annual beach sweep organized by the US Center for Marine Conservation resulted in the collection of 847 tonnes of rubbish from 3,700 km (2,300 miles) of coastline around Canada, the USA and Mexico. The filthiest beaches were those of Florida where 196 tonnes of debris were collected in 1990. Litter is found throughout the northern hemisphere on beaches in both remote and heavily populated areas, and in the open oceans. Non-biodegradable plastics present a particular problem as they trap or maim animals and may cause death by drowning or strangulation. While clean-up operations help, this is a problem which needs to be dealt with at source by anti-littering campaigns and changing to the use of biodegradable materials.

Sea of Cortez – The Seri, or Kunkaak, live on the coast of the Sea of Cortez in Sonora, Mexico and are one of the few aboriginal populations of North America to have maintained their traditional life style into the 20th century. This has always included the hunting of sea turtles, but the advent of a commercial harvest in recent years has meant that this catch is no longer sustainable. In Spring 1990, the Mexican government tightened up anti-hunting legislation by introducing the National Program for the Protection, Preservation and Investigation of Sea Turtles. The traditional life style of the Seri is therefore threatened.

Scammons Lagoon, Lower California – This is one of the principal calving grounds of the California grey whale (Eschrichtius robustus). The whale feeds in northern waters from May to September before moving to its southern calving grounds in winter.

Pollution
Industrial/mining
Domestic
Oil

- Main industrial centres
- Oil and gas fields
- Mineral extraction (molybdenum, gold, copper iron, manganese)
- Former sites of low level radioactive waste disposal
- Main fishing areas

- Protected areas
- Seaweed beds
- Mangroves
- Coral reefs

Threatened species
1 Bowhead whale
2 Northern right whale
3 Guadeloupe fur seal
4 Townsend's shearwater
5 Vaquita

→ Salmon migration
← Whale migration

North-West Pacific

The North Pacific Ocean extends from the Equator to the Bering Strait, the narrow passage which links it to the Arctic Ocean. On its western edge lie the heavily populated countries of China, Korea and the island groups of the Philippines and Japan. In the northwest lies the Kamchatka Peninsula.

As a result of climate conditions and ocean currents, the fisheries of the North-West Pacific are among the world's most productive. The confluence of the warm, north-flowing Kuroshio Current and the south-flowing Oyashio Current contributes to an enormous profusion of fish species. Commercial fishermen in the North-West Pacific region harvest up to 1,000 demersal, or bottom-dwelling, species. Although the bulk of the catch consists of less than 50 species, local fish markets offer a massive range of seafood. The most important species is the widely distributed Alaska pollock (*Theragra chalcogramma*), with a catch that exceeded five million tonnes in 1988. North-West Pacific fisheries operate on the region's extensive continental shelves, as well as over seamounts in the central Pacific.

Two species dominate the pelagic, or open ocean, fishery – the Japanese sardine (*Sardinops melanostictus*) and the chub mackerel (*Scomber japonicus*). The Japanese sardine fishery underwent explosive growth during the 1970s, and catches exceeded even those of the Alaska pollock. The sardine is fished in the warm waters of the Kuroshio Current and Tsumima Warm Current region. The last boom period for the sardine fishery occurred in the 1930s. The reason for its fluctuation is uncertain, but may be linked with fluctuations in other stocks, including the mackerel. Among shellfish, bivalves produce the highest yields.

Mariculture

The countries of the North-West Pacific are centres of mariculture. Important species include the Japanese amberjack (*Seriola quinqueradiata*) and the Pacific cupped oyster (*Crassostrea gigas*). A number of oyster species are cultured for pearls.

The cultivation of algae is important in the region. Species include the red and green lavers, and the *wakame*. The kelp *Laminaria japonica* was introduced by accident to China in 1927, and that country has since become the largest producer. The annual kelp harvest has grown to more than one and a half million tonnes. As well as being a valuable food product and a source of raw materials for industry, kelp is prized for its curative effect on swollen thyroid glands.

Pollution

Industrial pollution, domestic sewage and agricultural runoff affect mariculture and inshore fisheries. As a result of nutrient inputs from fertilizers and sewage, which encourage the growth of algae, Japan's Seto Naikai (Inland Sea) suffers from oxygen depletion. Red tides, which are sudden increases in the density of single-celled algae (phytoplankton), are now an annual occurrence in the Inland Sea.

Coastal waters are polluted by a wide range of contaminants, ranging from chemicals such as PCBs and DDT, to tar balls and heavy metals. Such contaminants degrade very slowly and may enter the human food chain through seafood. During the 1950s, consumption of seafood contaminated by methyl mercury led to "Minamata disease", named after Minamata Bay in Japan. It causes impaired vision, speech and hearing, trembling, and in some cases, hallucinations. More than 900 cases were reported between 1953 and 1975, and around 100 people died.

The killer whale (Orcinus orca) (below) feeds opportunistically on almost all marine organisms including other cetaceans, turtles and fish. Perceived conflicts with fisheries have led to ill-informed campaigns to control its numbers.

Bohai Bay – The discovery of necklaces dating back more than 20,000 years on the shores of Bohai Bay has provided evidence of China's ancient coastal settlement. The extensive use of the coastal zone for food collecting and fishing in the New Stone Age, some 5,000 years ago, is evident in mounds of shells, arrow heads and fishing spears. Coastal management also has ancient roots in China – the first recorded fish protection edict, which prevented fishing during the spawning season, was issued 4,000 years ago when trade in marine products began.

Jinzhou Bay, China – The semi-enclosed Jinzhou Bay has been described as the most polluted in China, a problem reflected in the poor health of the region's inhabitants and in damage to fisheries, salt pan areas and tourist spots. Action is now under way to ameliorate the problem by pre-treatment of wastes and by removal of the most contaminated sediments. Such actions are expected to increase in the near future.

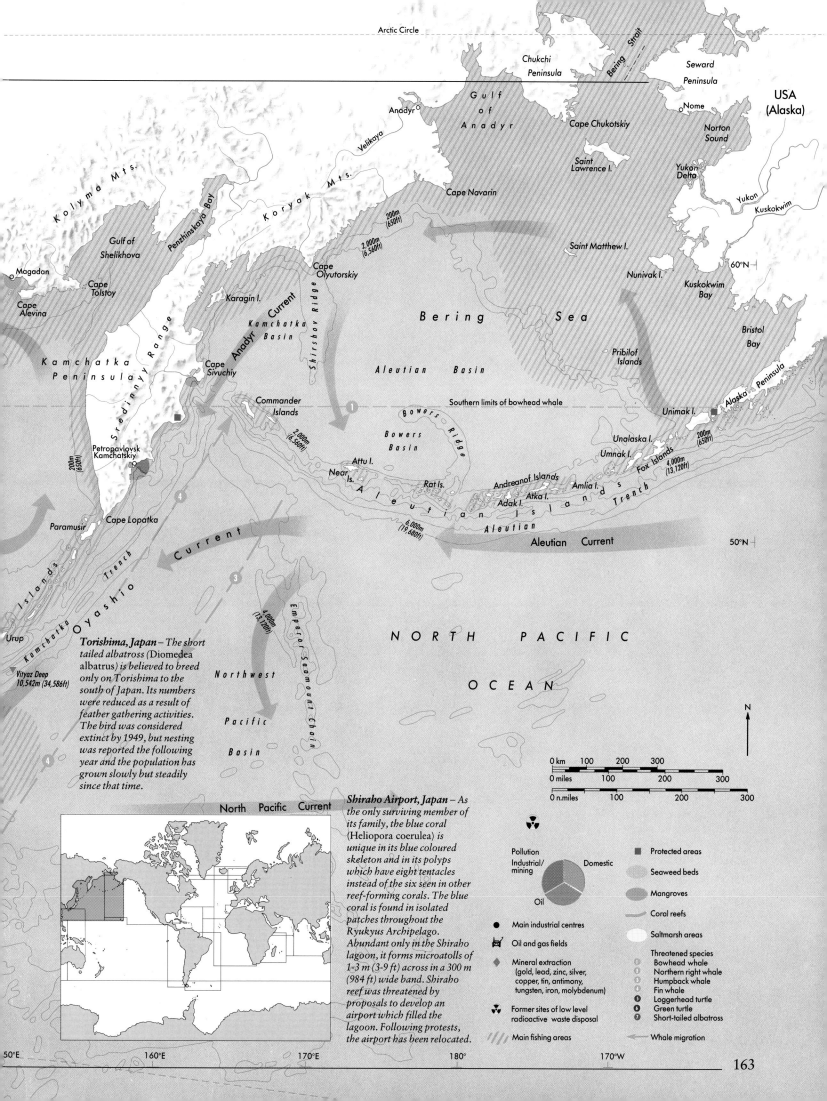

Arctic Circle

Chukchi Peninsula

Bering Strait

Seward Peninsula

USA (Alaska)

Gulf of Anadyr

Anadyr

Cape Chukotskiy

Nome

Norton Sound

Kolyma Mts.

Velikaya

Koryak Mts.

Cape Navarin

Saint Lawrence I.

Yukon Delta

Yukon

Kuskokwim

Gulf of Shelikhova

Penzhinskaya Bay

200m (650ft)

2,000m (6,560ft)

Saint Matthew I.

60°N

Magadan

Cape Tolstoy

Cape Olyutorskiy

Kamchatka Basin

Karagin I.

Kuskokwim Bay

Nunivak I.

Cape Alevina

Sredinny Range

Anadyr Current

Shirshov Ridge

Bering Sea

Bristol Bay

Kamchatka Peninsula

Cape Sivuchiy

Aleutian Basin

Pribilof Islands

Commander Islands

①

Southern limits of bowhead whale

Unimak I.

Alaska Peninsula

2,000m (6,560ft)

Bowers Ridge

Bowers Basin

Unalaska I.

200m (650ft)

200m (650ft)

Petropavlovsk Kamchatskiy

Attu I.

Near Is.

Rat Is.

Andreanof Islands

Amlia I.

Umnak I.

Fox Islands

4,000m (13,120ft)

④

Adak I. Atka I.

Aleutian Islands Trench

Cape Lopatka

Kamchatka Trench

Oyashio

Current

6,000m (19,680ft)

Aleutian Current

Aleutian Current

50°N

Paramusir

③

Urup

④

Emperor Seamount Chain

NORTH PACIFIC

Vityaz Deep 10,542m (34,586ft)

Northwest

Torishima, Japan – The short tailed albatross (Diomedea albatrus) is believed to breed only on Torishima to the south of Japan. Its numbers were reduced as a result of feather gathering activities. The bird was considered extinct by 1949, but nesting was reported the following year and the population has grown slowly but steadily since that time.

4,000m (13,120ft)

OCEAN

Pacific

Basin

North Pacific Current

Shiraho Airport, Japan – As the only surviving member of its family, the blue coral (Heliopora coerulea) is unique in its blue coloured skeleton and in its polyps which have eight tentacles instead of the six seen in other reef-forming corals. The blue coral is found in isolated patches throughout the Ryukyus Archipelago. Abundant only in the Shiraho lagoon, it forms microatolls of 1-3 m (3-9 ft) across in a 300 m (984 ft) wide band. Shiraho reef was threatened by proposals to develop an airport which filled the lagoon. Following protests, the airport has been relocated.

N

0 km 100 200 300
0 miles 100 200 300
0 n.miles 100 200 300

☢

Pollution
Industrial/ mining — Domestic
Oil

● Main industrial centres

⚒ Oil and gas fields

◆ Mineral extraction (gold, lead, zinc, silver, copper, tin, antimony, tungsten, iron, molybdenum)

☢ Former sites of low level radioactive waste disposal

⫽⫽ Main fishing areas

■ Protected areas

Seaweed beds

Mangroves

Coral reefs

Saltmarsh areas

Threatened species
① Bowhead whale
② Northern right whale
③ Humpback whale
④ Fin whale
⑤ Loggerhead turtle
⑥ Green turtle
⑦ Short-tailed albatross

→ Whale migration

50°E 160°E 170°E 180° 170°W

North Pacific Basin

A massive clockwise circulation drives the waters of the North Pacific, and carries warm southern waters northward along the coast of mainland Asia. In the east, cooled water flows southward along the west coast of the United States and Mexico. The range of temperature is much more marked on the western coasts and seasonal fish migrations are characteristic of stocks in this region. Extensive migrations of salmon (*Oncorhynchus* spp.), billfish (*Istiophoridae* spp.) and tuna (*Thunnus* spp.) take place across the North Pacific. Over 50 species of marine mammals are found in the North Pacific, including the polar bear (*Ursus maritimus*), fur seals, the walrus, dolphins and the sea otter. Threatened whales include the bowhead whale (*Balaena mysticetus*) and the northern right whale (*Eubalaena glacialis*), believed to be near extinction in the North-East Pacific.

The North Pacific albacore tuna (*Thunnus alalunga*) undergoes one of the longest migrations. In less than a year, it travels the 8,500 kilometres (5,300 miles) from California to Japan. The United States and Japan operate the two largest tuna fisheries, and harvest the albacore at both ends of its range. Although the mass of tuna harvested is relatively low, the high price fetched by tuna flesh makes the value of the fishery disproportionately greater than that of other fisheries. Most tuna meat is canned, but the raw flesh of old, fat tuna is particularly prized and fetches exceptionally high prices.

Human influences

In addition to pollution from coastal activities, the North Pacific has suffered damage from the deliberate dumping of a range of wastes, including dredging spoil, domestic and industrial residues, and other materials. Sea dumping presents a cheap alternative to land disposal, and the ocean is regarded as having a vast capacity to assimilate and dilute wastes. The currents of the Pacific do disperse wastes, but they also spread debris such as plastics and tar balls far from their original source. National legislation and the London Convention on Ocean Dumping help regulate these activities. A moratorium now limits the dumping of nuclear waste.

Plastics create a particularly difficult problem. Fishing operations are hampered by floating plastic litter or discarded fishing nets. Since they are not biodegradable, plastics remain a long-term problem. Discarded plastics entangle seabirds, mammals and fish, and cause death by strangulation, drowning or infected wounds.

In addition to target species such as albacore tuna, the drift nets used in North Pacific fishing operations kill or maim many non-target species. In international waters, Japanese, Korean and Taiwanese fleets use these in the seasonal squid fishery. Further south, Japanese, Taiwanese and United States vessels operate a "large mesh" fishery for billfish and albacore tuna. However, these fisheries also trap dolphins, porpoises, whales, seals, seabirds and turtles. Vessels operating in the north may illegally take migrating salmon, which are then processed by distant canning factories.

Steller's sea cow (*Hydrodamalis gigas*) was named after the shipwrecked doctor who first described it. The animal was hunted to extinction by the beginning of the 18th century, owing to its lack of fear of man. Once an inhabitant of the waters around Bering and Cooper Islands, the sea cow was the only known sirenian (aquatic placental mammal) to live outside tropical waters.

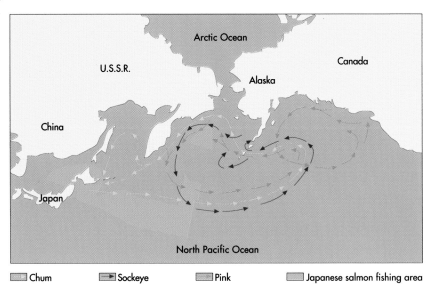

Chum   Sockeye   Pink   Japanese salmon fishing area

The six species of Pacific salmon migrate (left) from their spawning grounds in the rivers of Asia and North America to the rich feeding grounds of the North Pacific. After hatching, the young salmon, or smolts, venture out into the ocean where they feed on plankton and smaller fish. Pacific salmon remain at sea for periods of six months to five years. Adult fish spawn in fresh water, and to do so travel many thousands of miles to return to the stream where they were born. After the female lays its eggs, the adult fish die. Pollution of rivers and overfishing at sea now threatens the life cycle of the Pacific salmon. One solution has been to boost production through the use of hatcheries. Eggs from wild stocks are raised in pens, and the young fish are then released into the ocean.

Snared by a discarded drift net, this albacore tuna (below) faces a slow and painful death. The fisheries of the North Pacific are among the most productive in the world, and the use of drift nets brings in huge quantities of valuable species like the albacore. However, the success of the fisheries has led to the growing problem of discarded plastics, particularly fishing nets. Such materials entangle and kill fish, mammals and seabirds. Drift nets also cause the death of large numbers of non-target species.

On the coast of the island of Kyushu, near the port of Nagasaki, Japanese women clean the roe, or eggs, of sea urchins (above). Known as uni in Japan, sea urchin roe is an important ingredient in Japanese cuisine. Massive domestic demand for fish, shellfish and other marine products powers Japan's marine fishery. The country now ranks as the world's largest importer of marine products.

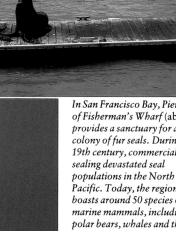

In San Francisco Bay, Pier 39 of Fisherman's Wharf (above) provides a sanctuary for a colony of fur seals. During the 19th century, commercial sealing devastated seal populations in the North Pacific. Today, the region boasts around 50 species of marine mammals, including polar bears, whales and the rare Guadalupe fur seal.

South-East Pacific

The coast of the South-East Pacific region stretches for about 10,500 kilometres (6,500 miles) and its ecosystems vary from the tropical mangrove and coral coasts of the Gulf of Panama to the cold, rocky shores of Chile's fjord region. Numerous fast-flowing rivers cross the narrow coastal plain carrying large amounts of sediment (and in some cases, pollutants) down from the highlands to the waters of the South-East Pacific. The continental shelf is also narrow, no more than 6.5 kilometres (four miles) wide in the south, extending to a maximum width of 28 kilometres (17 miles) off the coast of Ecuador.

Ocean curents and fisheries

Offshore, the cold, nutrient-rich waters of the Antarctic Circumpolar Current are dominant. It approaches the southern tip of the continent from the west and splits into two major branches, the Humboldt Current and the southward flowing Cape Horn Current. The Humboldt Current follows the coast northward and splits into two components; one follows the coast and the other circulates offshore.

The Peruvian Current (the branch of the Humboldt Current which runs northward along the Peruvian coast) is one of the most productive marine systems in the world. Its pelagic fishery contributes almost ten per cent of the world's catch. More than 16 per cent of the total catch of the Pacific Ocean is caught off the coasts of Chile, Peru, Ecuador and Colombia. In 1980, the total catch of fish and crustaceans was more than 6 million tonnes. By 1985 this had increased to more than 9 million tonnes for Chile and Peru alone.

The potential sustainable fisheries yield is estimated at 12.6 million tonnes annually. Almost all of this total comes from just three pelagic species: anchovetta (*Engraulis ringens*), sardine (*Sardinops sagax*) and jurel (*Trachurus symmetricus*). These fish are dramatically affected by El Niño events, a temporary change in ocean currents which lowers the levels of nutrients available. In 1970 the Peruvian and Chilean catch of anchovetta amounted to 13 million tonnes. This fell to only 1.2 million tonnes following the 1972-3 El Niño, recovered temporarily, and then dropped again during the 1982-3 El Niño to 1.4 million tonnes.

In addition to the pelagic fishery, hake, shrimp, prawns, crabs, scallops, clams, oysters and mussels are harvested, for local consumption and export. In Panama, a fleet of 250 boats catches 7,000 tonnes of shrimp per year. In Ecuador, 94 square kilometres (36 square miles) of land along the coast have been turned into shrimp farms.

Human impacts

A high proportion of the population of the countries in this region live on the coast, and marine resources provide these countries with much of their hard currency earnings. Renewable resources such as the pelagic fisheries and non-renewable resources such as oil provide substantial development income, but the exploitation and processing of such resources has led to problems of pollution and environmental degradation. Pollution problems affect shellfish beds, and mine wastes smother beaches. As human populations increase, the environmental problems will grow and become more intense. Recognizing the need for coastal zone management and the protection of their environment, the countries of the South-East Pacific were among the first to develop and adopt a regional Convention and Action Plan for the protection of their unique marine and coastal resources.

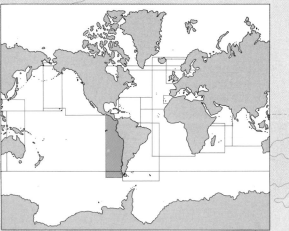

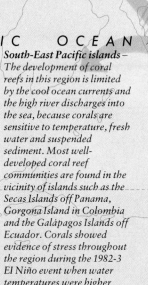

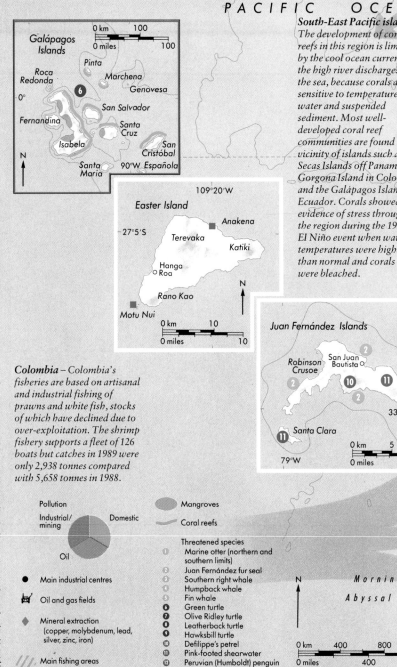

South-East Pacific islands – The development of coral reefs in this region is limited by the cool ocean currents and the high river discharges into the sea, because corals are sensitive to temperature, fresh water and suspended sediment. Most well-developed coral reef communities are found in the vicinity of islands such as the Secas Islands off Panama, Gorgona Island in Colombia and the Galápagos Islands off Ecuador. Corals showed evidence of stress throughout the region during the 1982-3 El Niño event when water temperatures were higher than normal and corals were bleached.

Colombia – Colombia's fisheries are based on artisanal and industrial fishing of prawns and white fish, stocks of which have declined due to over-exploitation. The shrimp fishery supports a fleet of 126 boats but catches in 1989 were only 2,938 tonnes compared with 5,658 tonnes in 1988.

Pollution
- Industrial/mining
- Domestic
- Oil

Mangroves

Coral reefs

- Main industrial centres
- Oil and gas fields
- Mineral extraction (copper, molybdenum, lead, silver, zinc, iron)
- Main fishing areas
- Protected areas

Threatened species
1. Marine otter (northern and southern limits)
2. Juan Fernández fur seal
3. Southern right whale
4. Humpback whale
5. Fin whale
6. Green turtle
7. Olive Ridley turtle
8. Leatherback turtle
9. Hawksbill turtle
10. Defilippe's petrel
11. Pink-footed shearwater
12. Peruvian (Humboldt) penguin

Whale migration

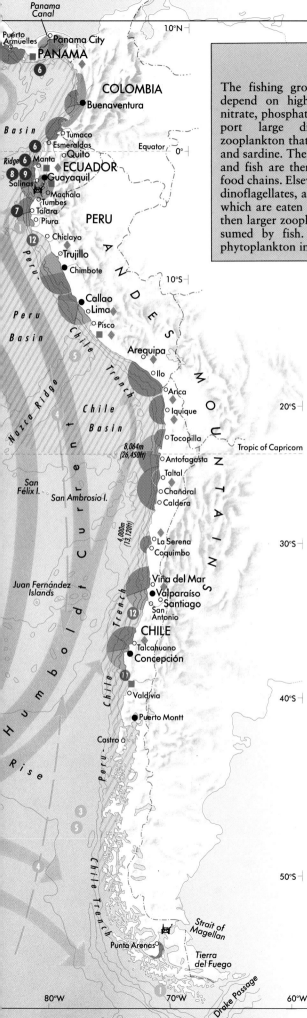

THE COMPACT FOOD WEB

The fishing grounds of the South-East Pacific depend on high levels of nutrients, including nitrate, phosphate and silica. These nutrients support large diatoms, which nourish the zooplankton that are directly eaten by anchovetta and sardine. The links between primary producers and fish are therefore fewer than in most ocean food chains. Elsewhere small phytoplankton, often dinoflagellates, are fed upon by tiny zooplankton, which are eaten by small predatory zooplankton, then larger zooplankton, before finally being consumed by fish. The high productivity of the phytoplankton in this area, which fix 1,000 grams of carbon per square metre (0.2 pounds per square foot) per year, combined with the compact nature of the food chain, results in efficient energy transfer and high fisheries production.

Apart from being caught for food and fishmeal, the large numbers of anchovetta and sardines provide food for many species of larger predatory fish, marine mammals and seabirds, including the guanay or cormorant (*Phalacrocorax bougainvillei*). The droppings of the quanay, also known as the "guano bird", provided a major source of phosphorus for agricultural fertilizers before the development of "artificial" fertilizers.

Independence Bay, Peru – *Independence Bay is a natural habitat of the calico scallop (A. purpuratus). Estimates of the biomass of this species vary from 41,200 to 72,200 tonnes. After the harvesting of the scallops, the shells are dumped in the bay. This leads to high levels of sulphur and decreases oxygen availability in the habitat of this important shellfish species. Large numbers of the remaining scallops have died as a result.*

Ite Bay, Peru – *Mining activity inland results in discharges to Ite Bay of 36.4 million cubic metres (1,285 million cubic feet) of sediment per year. This changes the distribution of coastal sediment types and causes declines in rocky shore shellfish production. Two mussel species, Perumytilus purpuratus and Semimytilus algosus, have disappeared as a result.*

Valparaíso harbour – *The source of oil pollution in Valparaíso harbour is oil refineries, oil terminals, storage tanks, and 1,500 vessels which use the harbour on a regular basis. In 1975 the vessel Northern Breeze spilled 440 tonnes of oil of which 200 tonnes affected a 46-km (29-mile) stretch of rocky and sandy shore. In addition to oil, Valparaíso Bay is polluted with domestic waste from the city of Santiago and by various industrial and domestic discharges from the city of Valparaíso. Consequently, the levels of mercury, cadmium and lead in the water and sediments exceed acceptable levels.*

The marine otter (above), or chingungo (Lutra felina), feeds on crustaceans and molluscs – mostly crabs and cuttlefish, but also some fish. The chingungo will also stray into rivers and estuaries on occasion to hunt for freshwater prawns (Criphiops caementarius). The creature's range once extended throughout the South-East Pacific from Ecuador to Cape Horn. Numbers have been greatly reduced by hunters who prize its soft pelt and by fisherman who claim that the otters have damaged fisheries in the area. The otter is now a protected species in Peru and Chile.

OVERVIEW

Fisheries

Pelagic: anchovetta, pilchard, mackerel
Coastal demersal: hake
Artisanal: mixed fish and shellfish

Coastal development

Extensive, conurbations and industrial centres along narrow coastal plain

Coastal ecosystems

Highly varied, tropical to sub-antarctic, mangroves, rocky intertidal, fjords, small estuaries
Productivity: high
Biodiversity: medium

People and Problems

The Pacific coast of Latin America has been greatly influenced by human activity. This ranges from tourist and recreational use of the beaches to offshore dumping of mine wastes, oil pollution and the discharge of industrial and domestic wastes including untreated sewage.

The major concentrations of population are along the narrow coastal plain. Fewer people live in the higher, harsher Andean region. This has resulted in extensive contamination of coastal waters through municipal waste discharge. Colombia has the lowest rate of domestic effluent discharge at just over 6 million cubic metres (212 million cubic feet) a year while Peru discharges in excess of 100 times that amount and Chile more than 700 million cubic metres (24,720 million cubic feet) a year. With the exception of semi-enclosed bays such as the Valparaíso and Concepción harbour areas in Chile, the Gulf of Guayaquil in Ecuador, Buenaventura and Tumaco Bays in Colombia and Lima Bay in Peru, problems of contamination and pollution from domestic discharges are generally restricted to areas immediately surrounding the source. This pollution is a locally critical problem since bacterial and other forms of contamination affect the shellfish industry. Humans who consume the contaminated shellfish can develop diseases such as gastroenteritis and cholera.

Industrial activity

The strong dependence of Peru, Ecuador and Chile on marine resources, and the high productivity of the offshore fisheries have resulted in the establishment of industrial fish processing plants. These plants, which produce fishmeal and oil, discharge organic wastes and polluted water directly to the sea. Valparaíso and Concepción Bays in Chile receive virtually the entire country's industrial waste discharge, amounting to around 244 million tonnes of industrial effluent a year.

Discharge of heavy metals from mining operations is also a problem, although largely confined to coastal areas of Peru and Chile. This results in contamination of shellfish, coastal sediments and waters with high levels of copper, cadmium and in some areas mercury and lead. Contamination sometimes exceeds toxicity limits, causing shellfish to die. Elsewhere, heavy metals in the shellfish exceed those recommended for human consumption.

The region has 17 major oil terminals and nine coastal refineries. In Colombia and Ecuador oil is produced inland and moved by pipeline across the Andes to Pacific coastal refineries and terminals. In Peru and Chile production is from offshore platforms, 84 in Peru and 23 in the Straits of Magellan in Chile. Oil pollution in the region is largely the result of accidents and oil spills. Between 1965 and 1978 the region had a rate of spillage 3 times as great as any other maritime region. Discharges from shipping result in losses of some 200 tonnes of oil a year at the Pacific Port of the Panama canal which handles on average 2.5 million tonnes annually for refuelling the estimated 1,900 ships which use the canal. The large fishing fleets associated with the offshore pelagic fishery are also responsible for much of the oil pollution associated with major harbours in Chile, Peru and Ecuador.

Threatened species

Conservation efforts in the area concentrate on a relatively small number of species. These include the endangered marine otter (*Lutra felina*), the southern

fur seals (*Arctocephalus* spp.), southern sea lion (*Otaria byroni*), and the Peruvian penguin (*Sphenis-cus humboldti*). Some coastal national reserves and parks provide a measure of protection for these species but the survival and reproduction of some species are adversely affected during El Niño years. The fur seals, all of which are protected under the CITES Convention include the Juan Fernandez fur seal (*Arctocephalus philippii*) from Chile, and the Galápagos fur seal (*A. galapagoensis*) both of which have highly restricted distributions. The widespread species *A. australis* is found from Peru right the way around the South American coastline to Brazil. The Peruvian penguin (also known as Humboldt's pen-guin) (*Spheniscus humboldti*) occurs in the area of the Humboldt Current which determines the distribution of the anchovies and sardines on which this species feeds. The preferred habitat is offshore rocky islands and its range extends into Peru, which is the most northerly extent of penguin distribution around the world.

Santiago fish market (below) provides a spectacle of colour and diversity with urchins, clams, barnacles and other shellfish offered for sale alongside demersal fish and large eels. Much of the coastal fish catch is consumed locally and fish in Santiago comes from the coastal ports of Valparaíso and fishing communities along the coast. Fisheries production is affected by other human activities based on the coast. Pollution affects shellfish production and quality whilst the high demand for fresh marine products is resulting in overfishing of some shellfish beds near towns and cities.

The waters off the Peruvian coast, (far left) are one of the most productive fisheries in the Pacific. The concentration of anchovetta in the productive zone of upwelling off the South American coast makes them a suitable target for large-scale industrial fishing. During normal years larger catches of up to 50 tonnes are obtained, but during El Niño years production declines and the fishing industry stagnates.

Anchovetta and sardine (left) are unloaded at a fishmeal and oil plant on the Peruvian coast. Annually around 20 million tonnes of such small pelagic fish are used world-wide to produce oil and fishmeal for livestock feed. By the year 2000 the estimated world shortfall in fisheries production for human consumption will equal this amount.

El Niño

In 1972 and again in 1983 the offshore fisheries of the South-East Pacific region were devastated by major disruptions to the ocean current systems. Known as El Niño ("the child" – because the phenomenon often becomes apparent around Christmas), the changes include a rise in surface water temperature, a rise in sea level and a decline in marine productivity.

The El Niño phenomenon is now recognized as forming part of a widespread change in tropical ocean circulation patterns. The El Niño Southern Oscillation (ENSO) occurs every ten years or so in an unpredictable manner. It has dramatic effects on the weather of the tropical belt, altering monsoon patterns, rainfall and agricultural production in India, Australia and South-East Asia.

The causes of El Niño are a large-scale change in the ocean-atmosphere interaction. In the South-East Pacific region, the eastwardly moving Equatorial Current dominates the Humboldt Current during these events causing oceanographic changes off the Latin American Coast. The temperature of the surface water increases by between 2° and 3°C (3.6° and 5.4°F), the sea level rises by 40 to 50 centimetres (16 to 20 inches) and the levels of nutrients available in the surface waters are reduced – with devastating consequences for the ocean pelagic fishery.

Impacts on humans

El Niño affects not only the oceanic conditions but also the coastal zone and land-based activities. Raised sea levels and alterations to the rainfall pattern affect agricultural production, human health and frequently lead to flooding. In Peru for example, protracted and extreme droughts during the 1982-3 event affected areas inland, while the coastal regions were subjected to heavy rainfall, wave swells and raised sea level, flooding the low-lying coastal land. In Colombia, cattle production was adversely affected, while banana production in Ecuador was significantly reduced. Malaria reached epidemic levels in coastal wetland areas. The economic damage from the 1982-3 event was estimated at US$3,480 million, 70 per cent being losses in the productive sectors and 20 per cent being damage to coastal infrastructure.

Coastal marine impacts

In the sea, changes to surface temperature have profound effects on marine ecosystems. During the 1982-3 El Niño, water temperatures around 1.5°C (2.7°F) higher than normal bleached and killed large areas of coral around the Gorgona Islands and other Panamanian reef systems. In Peru, the demersal fish lorna (*Sciaena deliciosa*) moved from their normal range 20 kilometres (12 miles) offshore to the edge of the continental shelf 150 kilometres (90 miles) further out to sea. Molluscs such as the Peruvian scallop (*Argopecten purpuratus*) become more abundant during El Niño, since spawning and larval survival are enhanced under warmer conditions. The 1983 catch of this species reached 10,000 tonnes compared with normal yearly landings of 1,000 tonnes.

Falling fish stocks

The failure of the nutrient-rich Humboldt Current to

Comparison of these two satellite images (right) reveals the difference in ocean temperature between El Niño years and normal years. Blue indicates cool (0-12°C/32-54°F), green indicates intermediate temperatures (13-24°C/55-76°F) and yellow/red/purple indicates warm temperatures (25-30°C/77-86°F). An image from January 1984 (top) shows normal sea surface temperatures. The warmest waters are found in the western Pacific, while a tongue of cooler water projects westwards from the South American coast along the Equator. An image from January 1983 (bottom), taken at the height of the biggest El Niño this century, shows far warmer conditions. During El Niño events, the cooler waters of the Peruvian Current are absent from the surface, and warmer water intrudes into the eastern Pacific.

Many Galápagos iguanas (main picture) die during El Niño when water temperatures reduce seaweed production.

Brown pelicans (Pelecanus occidentalis) (far right, top) suffer mortalities during El Niño when fish production crashes.

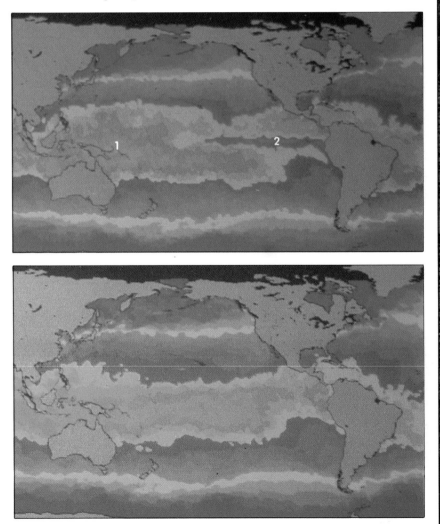

reach the sea surface at its normal northerly position reduces primary production during El Niño years. This results in a dramatic collapse in the pelagic anchovetta and sardine stocks normally characteristic of the offshore fishery. El Niño events in 1972-3 and again in 1982-3 reduced the anchovetta catch to around one sixth and one six-hundredth of the normal landings respectively.

As fish stocks decline, the fish, birds and mammals which depend on them for food die in large numbers. Following the 1972-3 El Niño, populations of the guano-producing cormorant (*Phalacrocorax bougainvillei*), the booby (*Sula variegata*), and the brown pelican (*Pelecanus occidentalis*) had declined to some 6 million from an estimated population of 30 million in 1950. A further decline followed the 1982-83 event which reduced the population to an estimated current level of only 300,000 individuals. An increase in the frequency of El Niño events is likely to have further drastic effects.

PREDICTING EL NIÑO

El Niño Southern Oscillation events cause widespread changes to climate and sea level conditions throughout the tropics. In turn, these environmental changes result in substantial economic losses in many countries. As a result, international efforts supported by many governments as well as the United Nations are being devoted to increased understanding of the mechanisms which cause El Niño. These programs aim to allow El Niño events to be predicted in advance. Two programs, TOGA, the Tropical Ocean Global Atmosphere, and WOCE, World Ocean Circulation Experiment, have been set up to collect data on ocean circulation and the interaction between the oceans and atmosphere with a view to modelling how the system works. So far, our understanding of how the world's oceans affect global climate is still at a primitive stage and prediction of events such as El Niño is not as yet possible.

Southern Ocean

The Southern Ocean, the great unbroken expanse of circumpolar sea linking the Pacific, Atlantic and Indian Oceans, surrounds the unique continent of Antarctica. Its waters are ruled by the winds of the Roaring Forties, the Furious Fifties and the Shrieking Sixties, and its southern boundary is the ice cliffs and rocks of the Antarctic coast. The continent itself forms a hub around the South Pole, with most of the land lying below latitude 70°S. Two deep indentations – the Weddell Sea and the Ross Sea – break into the near-circular landmass, with open water extending to beyond 77°S in summer. Floating ice shelves at the heads of these seas extend to 80°S. The Antarctic Peninsula juts north towards South America.

The shores of Antarctica are fringed by seas that are uniformly ice-covered. In winter, 20 million square kilometres (8 million square miles) of sea have an ice crust. Even in summer the coastal waters bear 3 million square kilometres (1.16 million square miles) of ice. This fluctuating ice fringe can be taken as one boundary of the Antarctic, but most biologists use the Antarctic Convergence Zone – an invisible frontier in the sea – where the cold surface waters spreading outward from the continent meet warmer surface seas in a frontal zone at about 50°S.

The ice cap

Today, Antarctica contains over 90 per cent of the Earth's ice. This represents about 70 per cent of the planet's fresh water. The ice has accumulated to an average depth of about 2,000 metres (6,500 feet) over the continent as a whole, with more than 3,000 metres (9.850 feet) at many points above the low-lying rock floor of the continent. If all this ice melted, global sea level would be raised by 60 metres (200 feet). Freed of the great weight of the ice, the rock surface of Antarctica could rise by 200-300 metres (650-1,000 feet).

Glaciers move slowly towards the sea and feed floating ice shelves. Known to pioneer explorers as "ice barriers", the shelves are 200-300 metres (657-984 feet) thick and border the oceans over hundreds of kilometres to a submerged depth of 150-250 metres (490-820 feet). They cover the head of the Ross Sea, the head and west side of the Weddell Sea, and a number of points around the Antarctic coast. In winter, massive icebergs float among the sea ice. This creates a danger to shipping and mobile oil installations, which become trapped in the surface ice, unable to move out of the path of the icebergs.

Only a narrow coastal fringe, less than two per cent of the landmass, lies between the Antarctic ice cap and the sea. It is on this tiny area of land that most of the wildlife of the Antarctic lives and breeds, and where more than 70 scientific research stations have been set up. The almost unpolluted Antarctic environment allows monitoring of phenomena such as global warming and atmospheric pollution. The continent's important oil and mineral deposits have attracted interest, but exploitation has so far been voluntarily banned.

The arrival of humans in the Antarctic began a process of environmental change. On a local scale, the impacts have been considerable. Wastes such as sewage, laboratory effluent, fuels and lubricants, old machinery, storage and packing containers, vehicles and equipment have all been discarded and discharged into the environment. Some offshore dumping has also taken place. Air, soil and water have been contaminated by vehicle exhausts, noise and soot.

CCAMLR and CCAS – The 1980 Convention on the Conservation of Antarctic Marine Living Resources (CCAMLR) has been used to control fishing in Antarctic waters. The 1972 Convention for the Conservation of Antarctic Seals (CCAS) included hunting bans, quotas and reserves. It has never had to be called into force because the sealing industry has not been re-established.

Research stations

Mineral deposits
(silver, gold, copper, iron, manganese nodules, nickel, lead, platinum, tin, uranium, zinc, coal)

Areas of potential oil and gas exploration

Areas of krill concentrations

Minimum summer sea ice limit

Antarctic convergence
(Polar front)

Protected areas

Threatened species
Southern right whale
Blue whale
Fin whale
Humpback whale

Whale migration

Selected seal breeding sites
(Ross, leopard, crabeater, Weddell, elephant or fur)

Selected penguin breeding sites
(Adélie, king, chinstrap, gentoo, macaroni, royal or rockhopper)

Noise pollution – Flying aircraft, particularly helicopters, over or close to breeding colonies of penguins or other seabirds can cause severe disturbance. Explosive charges used during underwater seismic experiments can disrupt the lives of birds, seals and whales, particularly when set off at depth. One particularly worrying development is the use of low-frequency sound generators to study temperature gradients in the sea. These sounds are transmitted for great distances and may interfere with communication between baleen whales.

Protected areas – Specially Protected Areas (SPAs) were selected according to two criteria: outstanding scientific interest; and rarity of the ecological systems. These criteria were later expanded to five: (i) to safeguard representative samples of the major Antarctic ecosystems, and the variations they display in relation to soil, climate, and other factors; (ii) to emphasize areas with unique complexes of species; (iii) to include areas which are the type, locality or only known breeding habitat of any plant or invertebrate species; (iv) to cover areas with especially interesting breeding colonies of birds or mammals; and (v) to set aside areas to be kept inviolate as reference sites for the future.

The crabeater seal (above) is the world's most abundant seal, with an Antarctic population of around 15 million. This one species (Lobodon carcinophagus) makes up an estimated 80 per cent of world seal biomass. The crabeater seal's teeth are adapted to form an efficient filter – ideal for catching its favourite food, krill. The seal also hunts for invertebrates which gather around pier structures. The crabeater seal is capable of sprinting across the ice at speeds of up to 25 km per hour (16 mph). This is achieved by means of alternate flipper movement and sideways thrusting of the pelvis while the tail flippers and head are held high.

Penguin protection – Six Adélie penguin (Pygoscelis adeliae) colonies have been disturbed by a runway which has been built near the French base at Dumont D'Urville. This project was begun in 1983 without informing the other Treaty nations and without an environmental assessment, both of which were required under the Treaty. Opposition has included a resolution from the French Academy of Sciences, diplomatic contact from the New Zealand government, an IUCN resolution calling on the French government to consider alternatives, and a campaign by Greenpeace. Construction work stopped when the airstrip was almost finished. If it were to be used, the noise and activity would cause further disruption to the wildlife of the area.

Tourism – Two to three thousand tourists visit Antarctica each year, attracted by the scenery and abundant wildlife. Many are now disembarking on the continent, and the Palmer Station, a US research base on the Peninsula, has become such a popular destination that a quota has been introduced. Damage caused by visitors includes disturbance to animals and fragile ecosystems, disruption of research activities and pollution.

Map labels:

Bouvet Island
30°E
Lazarev Sea
Riiser-Larsen Sea
Napier Mountains
Cooperation Sea
Kerguelen Plateau
SOUTHERN OCEAN
INDIAN OCEAN
Amery Ice Shelf
Lambert Glacier
2,000m (6,560ft)
200m (650ft)
4,000m (13,120ft)
Davis Sea
60°S
70°S
80°S
...TICA
South Pole
Transantarctic Mountains
Ross Island
Victoria Land
Shackleton Ice Shelf
Wilkes Land
Dumont D'Urville Sea
120°E
2,000m (6,560ft)
4,000m (13,120ft)
Balleny Islands
Macquarie Island
150°E
Campbell Island
80°
Auckland Islands

Life in the Frozen Seas

The icy seas and frozen wastes of Antarctica present one of the most inhospitable environments on Earth, yet the Southern Ocean is home to large numbers of seabirds, seals and whales. This abundance of life depends on the biological productivity of the Southern Ocean. It is estimated that the total annual production of plant matter in surface waters south of the Antarctic Convergence is 610 million tonnes. The microscopic plants (phytoplankton) support zooplankton, about half of which is made up of krill, which in turn sustain the region's fish, squid, birds, seals and whales.

Phytoplankton productivity depends on sunlight, but is sensitive to the wavelength received. In theory, depletion of the ozone layer in spring (the "ozone hole"), may increase the amount of ultraviolet radiation reaching surface waters, which could harm phytoplankton and reduce productivity. This may have adverse effects on plankton, and higher levels of the food chain that have yet to be convincingly proved.

Seabirds and seals

The Antarctic region is home to a variety of seabirds and seals. Most of the birdlife is concentrated in the sub-Antarctic zone, but three penguins – the emperor (*Aptenodytes forsteri*), the Adélie (*Pygoscelis adeliae*), and the chinstrap (*Pygoscelis antarctica*) – one giant petrel (*Macronectes giganteus*), seven other petrels and McCormick's skua (*Catharacta maccormicki*) breed on the continent itself. Outside the breeding season many of the petrels and albatrosses move with the westerly circumpolar winds, circumnavigating the globe between latitudes 40° and 60°S. The breeding grounds are densely packed because the extent of ice-free land suitable for seabird colonies is extremely limited.

The Antarctic seals are also limited to a few species but are extremely abundant. Of the six species, the crabeater seal (*Lobodon carcinophagus*) is the most numerous, with a population estimated at around 15 million. The Ross seal (*Ommatophoca rossii*) and the leopard seal (*Hydrurga leptonyx*) are also species of the pack ice; and the Weddell seal (*Leptonychotes weddellii*) breeds on ice and occasionally on shore in the coastal zones. The remaining two seals, the elephant (*Mirounga leonina*) and fur (*Arctocephalus gazella*) are essentially sub-Antarctic, land-breeding species which extend into the Antarctic zone. In parts of the sub-Antarctic there is overlap with the Kerguelen fur seal (*Arctocephalus tropicalis*). Although there is evidence that some populations of elephant seals are decreasing, all other species are believed to be either stable or increasing in numbers at present.

Whales

Seven species of filter-feeding baleen whales and eight species of toothed whale inhabit the ocean south of the Antarctic Convergence, although none is confined to these waters. The baleen whale stocks of the southern and northern hemispheres are separate, but both have an annual winter breeding period in tropical seas, before migrating either south or north to feed in polar waters in summer.

It is estimated that there are about 500 blue whales (*Balaenoptera musculus*) left in the Antarctic, although they may once have numbered about 250,000. The number of sei whales (*Balaenoptera borealis*) is more uncertain because much of their range has not been covered by the surveys, but they have probably been reduced to a quite similar extent. Humpback (*Megaptera novaeangliae*) and right whales (*Balaena glacialis*) originally numbered around 100,000 each but currently number in the low thousands. Right whale numbers are thought to be increasing in three of their breeding areas. Sperm whale numbers remain unknown because reliable survey techniques have not yet been implemented in the Antarctic. The minke whale (*Balaenoptera acutorostrata*) is estimated to number about 500,000 in the Southern Ocean during summer and is the only baleen whale still hunted there, but since catches to date have totalled less than 100,000, it can be presumed not to have been substantially depleted by whaling.

Estimates of the surviving numbers of blue and fin whales (*Balaenoptera physalus*) are based on very few actual sightings and the margin of error in the estimate could be up to a factor of five in either direction. It will be several decades before firm evidence of recovery of these species will be obtained.

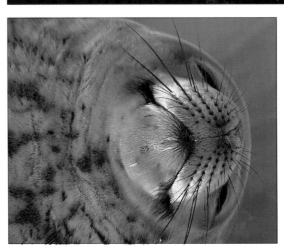

The ice of the Southern Ocean (top) plays an important role in the Earth's heat balance by reflecting solar radiation back into space.

Superbly adapted to the Antarctic environment, the Weddell seal (above) can dive to more than 600 metres (2,000 feet) and remain underwater for over an hour.

Adélie penguins gather in huge colonies (right). They overwinter on pack ice, and move south to breeding sites on exposed rocks. The young spend their first two years at sea or on the pack ice.

The Climate and the Treaties

Bases such as this one on
Seymour Island (right) are
currently the source of many
environmental problems in
the Antarctic. During
construction, the local habitat
may be radically modified,
while the generation of heat
and power once the base is
operational results in exhaust
gases, dust, noise and waste
heat production. Disposal of
wastes is also a problem,
because oil and toxic wastes
from shore-based
experimental stations are
released into the marine
environment. The most
serious pollution problem lies
in the disposal of solid wastes.
Most bases have dumps of
worn-out equipment,
packaging materials and other
items which are no longer
required. Most bases are sited
in locations where they can be
easily supplied, regardless of
possible damage and
disruption to the local
environment.

Antarctica is the world's coldest continent. In the central regions average temperatures rise briefly to 30°C (86°F) in the two warmest months, and sink to around −65°C (−85°F) between April and September. Snowfall is distributed very unevenly, and increases from the centre of the continent outward. Much of the snow borne in the "blizzards" that harassed pioneer explorers is drift, carried on winds that whip up into extremely powerful downdraughts – wind speeds on the coast are sometimes four or five times greater than on the central plateau.

A number of coastal locations have a milder climate, acting as "oases" in the cold desert, with warmer summers, patches of ground exposed by snow melt, higher precipitation, and even some small lakes that lose their ice cover in the warmest months. In such places, average temperatures may range from −1 to +1°C (30° to 34°F) in the summer months of December and February, dropping to only −10° to −20°C (14° to −4°F) in July and August. These data tell only part of the story, since during the long daylight hours of the Antarctic summer, direct warming by radiation creates microclimates much more favourable to life.

The greenhouse effect and the ozone hole

Antarctica's remoteness does not give it immunity from the atmospheric pollutants produced by industrialized countries. Of these, carbon dioxide and methane are of particular concern because they contribute to the greenhouse effect, which is predicted to raise global average temperatures significantly over the next 50 years. This warming could have a major impact on global sea level. If the massive Antarctic ice sheet were to melt, an unlikely event, the sea level around the world could rise by up to 60 metres (200 feet). Thawing of even a small part of the Antarctic ice cap could cause a significant increase in world sea level but supporting evidence for this is scant.

The marked depletion of stratospheric ozone above the Antarctic region in the spring season has become known as the ozone hole. This is caused by the free chlorine atoms released by the breakup of chlorofluorocarbons, which are used in refrigeration, the manufacture of foam insulation, and industrial solvents. There is mounting evidence that the ozone hole is expanding and has the potential to disturb stratospheric weather patterns in the southern hemisphere. The ozone hole may allow increased penetration of ultraviolet radiation. It is not known how significant this effect is likely to be on phytoplankton productivity in the Antarctic Ocean, where sea ice protects the waters during spring, when the ozone hole is most pronounced.

The Antarctic Treaty

The Antarctic Treaty was negotiated in 1959 by 12 nations to ensure that the continent is used for peaceful purposes to further international cooperation and scientific research. It banned nuclear testing, disposal of toxic wastes and military activities. No country was given territorial rights, but all previous territorial claims in Antarctica were preserved. Other countries become consultative parties if they are engaged in substantial scientific research. More than 20 nations are represented on the continent. The articles of the Treaty are not laws, but guidelines, and viewed as moral obligations. The Treaty prohibits taking species without a permit, and gives guidelines on managing Specially Protected Species and Areas. Treaty parties have also adopted recommendations to designate Sites of Special Scientific Interest (SSSI).

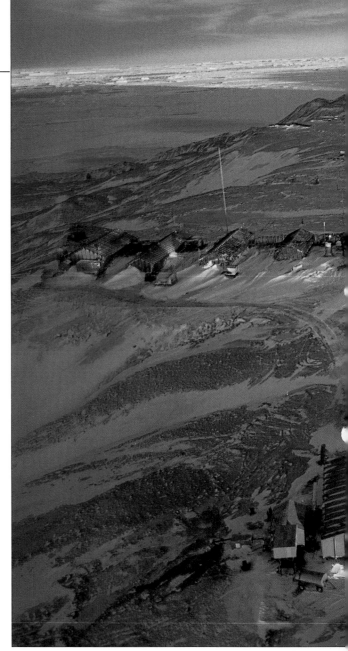

A bank (above) on King
George Island in the Chilean
sector serves tourists as well as
scientists researching in the
region. Under the Antarctic
Treaty all non-governmental
visits are classed as tourism.

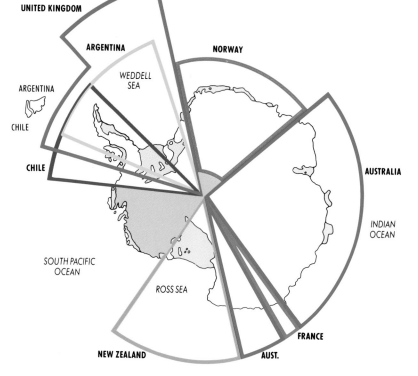

Large supply aircraft (above) *provide a lifeline for scientists working in Antarctica, but can be very disruptive in the quiet environment. The noise of large aircraft taking off and landing is known to have caused serious disturbance to penguin and seal colonies, resulting in a decline in numbers in some areas. The aircraft usually require long runways of hard rock which have to be blasted flat, causing considerable damage to the environment.*

Territorial claims (below) *were recognized but suspended under the 1959 Antarctic Treaty. The balance between claimant and non-claimant states with interests in ensuring the peaceful use of Antarctica is achieved through biennial meetings of the consultative parties which recommend to their governments measures designed to further the principles and objectives of the treaty. Such principles, which enter into force on the agreement of the consultative parties, serve as guidelines for the future actions of claimant states.*

A blizzard (left) *piles snow onto the deck of a supply ship on its way to an Antarctic base. Battling against the elements is a daily problem for scientists researching on the* *continent. Conditions tend to be worse in coastal areas where offshore winds keep temperatures very low and where blizzards hamper any movement.*

The Convention for the Conservation of Antarctic Seals came into force in 1978. It regulates seal catch levels, protected species, the opening and closing of sealing seasons and zones, and it establishes three seal reserves. The fuller (1980) Convention on the Conservation of Antarctic Marine Living Resources (CCAMLR) came into force in 1982 and established a decision-making Commission and an Advisory Scientific Committee.

The Convention on the Regulation of Antarctic Mineral Resource Activities (CRAMRA) was opened for signature on 25 November 1988, but has not yet been ratified. This controversial Convention establishes objectives and institutions to regulate possible mineral exploitation. In 1991 a new protocol for comprehensive conservation measures was agreed by the Antarctic Treaty parties.

Activities in Antarctica have to comply with legal obligations on shipping safety and pollution control. International organizations also have procedures governing scientific research programmes.

UNITED KINGDOM

ARGENTINA

NORWAY

WEDDELL SEA

ARGENTINA

CHILE

CHILE

AUSTRALIA

INDIAN OCEAN

SOUTH PACIFIC OCEAN

ROSS SEA

FRANCE

NEW ZEALAND

AUST.

The Challenge of Conservation

N o part of the oceans remains untouched by human activity. Although the open oceans have been little affected so far, coastal and inshore waters have been polluted, their environments degraded and their resources over-exploited. Human demands on the marine environment will continue to increase year by year. The challenge for this generation is to develop strategies for more sustainable use and conservation of the oceans and their margins.

The great whales symbolize for many the need for marine conservation.

Oceans: The New View

Anyone seeing planet Earth for the first time from space would be struck by the fact that it is dominated by water. From a point directly above the South Pacific one might see only a few islands, since most of the continental landmasses are grouped closely into the hemisphere opposite that point. We are conditioned not to see things from this ocean view since maps and illustrations of the world almost always centre on the land – as do many of those in this volume! Marine creatures, as well as people who spend their lives at sea and on the coast, see things differently. The land is not the centre of their world but its edge.

This situation follows, of course, because people live on the land. With few exceptions, humans have stood with their backs to the sea. Until the last century the oceans remained a place of mystery and peril, or at best strange and exotic, and on a human scale, boundless. We have looked to the heavens first and only later into the sea. Human footprints were on the moon nearly two decades before a remotely operated television camera could cruise along the decks of the sunken *Titanic*. Pioneering research on the oceans really began at the turn of this century and two major changes have profoundly affected our understanding of, and relationship with, the oceans and their resources.

The first is our recently acquired ability to exploit marine resources on a vastly greater scale and at a faster rate than ever before. Since the early 1960s, rapid advances in ocean engineering have revolutionized human exploitation of the oceans. The first such development, the use of factory ships, led to the near devastation of the great whales in the period between 1930 and 1970. More recently, long-range fishing fleets and engineering advances permitting exploration and exploitation of continental shelf minerals – mainly petroleum – have led to major impacts on ocean systems. Sea bed mining, although not yet utilized on any great scale (for economic reasons) could cause impacts in the future.

The second major development has been a change in jurisdiction over the ocean realm. Beginning in the 1960s, a new Convention on the Law of the Sea has been negotiated which establishes the rights and obligations of coastal states in controlling activities in their offshore waters. Traditionally, national jurisdiction was limited to 3 or 12 miles offshore for various activities. Under the new treaty, states can declare rights of jurisdiction over an "Exclusive Economic Zone" (EEZ) extending up to 200 miles offshore. Prior to these recent developments, the oceans were considered common property. These newly confirmed rights carry with them obligations to establish the legal and administrative procedures and infrastructure needed to manage this area.

The Convention has not been ratified by enough countries to enter into force, but when it does, many countries will not have the infrastructure to implement its provisions. To a great extent, this problem stems from our innate and biased view of the oceans as a vast, limitless and unknown entity. More needs to be done to change this attitude in order to gain a "new view" of the oceans. The challenge is to increase efforts to identify the real threats to marine and coastal environments, to communicate information about those threats to the public and to governments in a clear and understandable way, and to strengthen worldwide understanding through better education and training programmes.

The Ngerukewid Islands Wildlife Preserve, Palau.

Systems, Processes and Diversity

The oceans have been forming and changing for billions of years. The major oceans like the Atlantic, Indian and Pacific as well as the enclosed and semi-enclosed seas such as the Baltic, Mediterranean and the Caribbean that are their extensions have not always been the same size or in the same spatial relationships with each other. This continuous change is a result of sea floor spreading and continental drift. On the deep ocean ridges, partially molten material rises and spreads outward, forming new oceanic crust and pushing the continental plates apart. In other areas where plates are forced against each other, crustal material is forced downward and melts in the interior. The rates at which these changes occur are so long compared with human time scales (modern

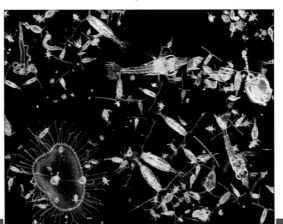

Marine plankton (left) form the basis of living marine systems. Diatoms are eaten by zooplankton, including small copepods, worm larvae molluscs and crustaceans.

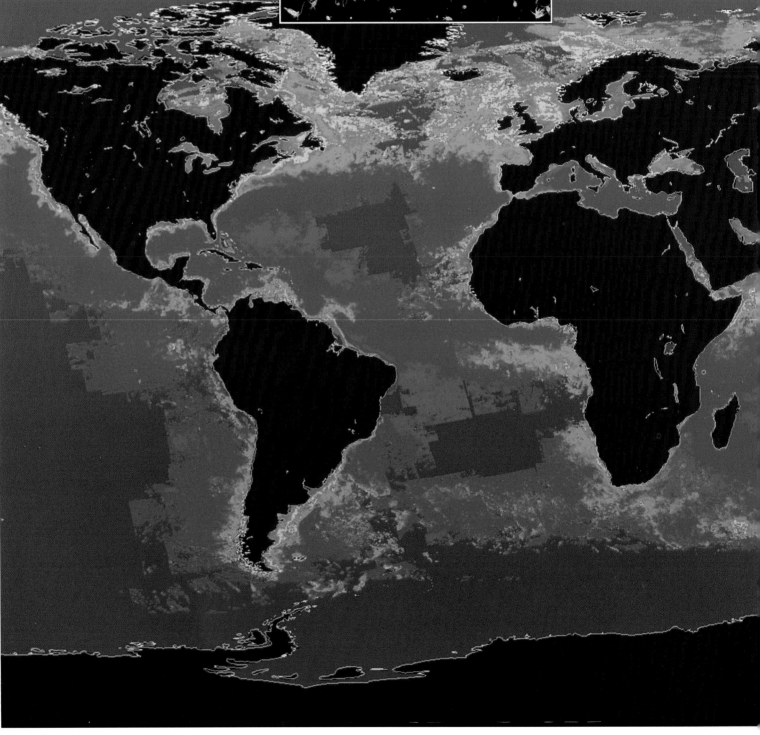

The satellite image (below) shows global phytoplankton production for July-September 1979.

man has only existed for the last 150 thousand years) that they are practically imperceptible. In fact, they were only convincingly described in the 1960s. Nonetheless these dynamic movements and recycling of material have contributed to the present day composition of the oceans and atmosphere, which in turn are basic to our life-support system.

Physical systems and processes

Waves, tides, currents, salinity, temperature, pressure and light intensity are some of the physical factors that dominate everyday ocean conditions and are the ones with which we are most familiar. Also more familiar, in particular to climatologists and oceanographers, are the constant interactions between the

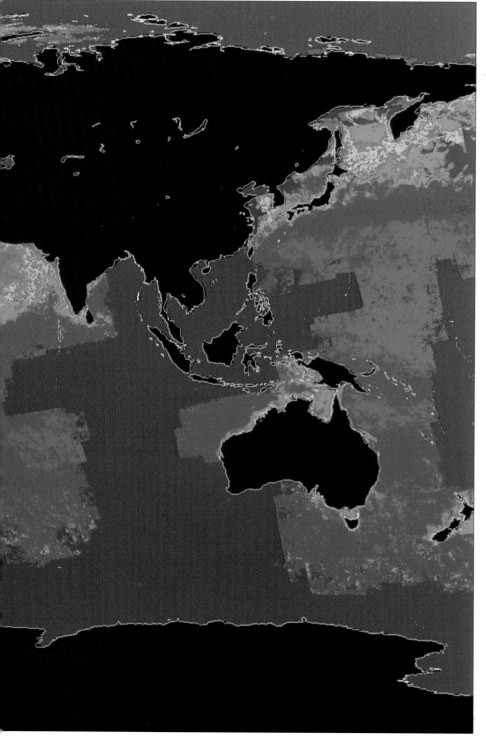

atmosphere and the oceans. The movements of the atmosphere, the heat exchange between the atmosphere and ocean, and the rotation of the earth are the major driving forces for great ocean currents like the Gulf Stream and the Humboldt and Benguela Currents. In some cases the combined interaction of atmosphere and ocean causes deep, nutrient-rich water to rise to the surface. In these areas, in particular where they are near continental shelves, there is enhanced primary productivity which in turn is the base of all marine food webs. Ocean-atmosphere interactions also result in the evaporation of water and its recondensation in the hydrological cycle, another process basic to life. All of these processes occur in a timescale ranging from a few hours, for ocean storms, to a few centuries as in the case of ocean currents. These processes form the backdrop to the present composition of life on both land and sea.

Biological processes and diversity

Life in the oceans is highly diverse. It ranges from microscopic, single-celled plants to the large fish and marine mammals such as whales. The interface between land and sea, the coastal zone, is a band of highly diverse ecosystems and habitats which are among the most biologically productive on earth. These include intertidal mudflats, rocky shores, sandy beaches, mangroves, salt marshes, estuaries and other wetlands, sea grass and seaweed beds, and coral reefs. We recognize this diversity but our understanding of the way these systems function is limited. Our knowledge of the diversity of open-ocean communities is less complete than for coastal areas. For example, deep-ocean thermal vent communities were only discovered in 1977.

Groups of living organisms are interrelated and dependent on each other and are components of a variety of food webs. Some, like those of the polar oceans, are quite simple, others are much more complex like those in the North Atlantic or in tropical reef systems. Ecosystems with differing levels of complexity respond differently to the many kinds of human intervention. Removal of key species through harvesting may change species diversity, hence the strategies for successful marine conservation and management will vary from place to place. Fisheries management needs to include the concept of whole ecosystem management.

Human influences

This diversity of marine living organisms operates on different time scales, with phytoplankton having generation times in days, zooplankton in weeks or months, and fish in years. While human activities and actions have little apparent impact on longer-term geological processes, there is increasing evidence that we can and do cause profound impacts on the shorter-term processes of the biological sectors of the oceans. This is particularly true in coastal areas and semi-enclosed seas where nutrient levels are increasing due to pollutants which in turn cause eutrophication. Human impacts through such changes as the "greenhouse effect" may now be influencing processes with a longer time scale and we need to understand the linkages between the processes and systems and marine biodiversity. A sound scientific understanding of the temporal and spatial limits to processes affecting both living and non-living components of the ocean world is needed if rational management and conservation of the marine environment are to be any more than impossible ideals.

Divers (left) *photograph a great white shark* (Carcharodon carcharias) *off Australia, an example of research that a developed country can afford, but many developing countries cannot.*

Scientific research (below) *on corals in the Red Sea. Coral reef systems are common throughout the tropics. They are highly diverse and provide the basis for many artisanal fisheres.*

decades of intensive research and monitoring as to whether or not the abundance of North Sea fish stocks is regulated or controlled by harvesting rates or environmental variables; in the meantime stocks continue to decline!

Monitoring human impact

The situation concerning long-term monitoring of pollution control is considerably worse. Monitoring has informed us of the rates and nature of coastal water degradation, yet action to control the sources of pollution is rarely taken. The functions of long-term monitoring might be taken as being twofold. Firstly such programmes provide the necessary information to enable us to better understand marine systems and processes, and secondly they provide warning of trends which may result from human actions such as the dumping of wastes, or the discharge of sewage.

Environmental monitoring must therefore be backed by the political will to enforce adequate controls and the legal instruments, either national or international, that set acceptable standards of environmental quality, rates of discharge or other agreed targets. A failure of any of the three components results at best in ineffective action and at worst in no action at all.

The commendable actions of the North Sea countries in monitoring various physical and biological indices provides a sound database for remedial action; however the lack of political will to enforce agreed standards and practices means that correcting the errors of the past is difficult. In the case of the Mediterranean Basin, monitoring, combined with the political will to improve environmental quality, outstrips the capacity of many countries to comply with agreed pollution control measures. In contrast, the lack of data available on Antarctic living marine resources makes implementation of the terms of the Convention on the Conservation of Antarctic Marine Living Resources difficult. In the latter case the priorities of scientists working in the Antarctic do not necessarily conform with the management needs and the challenge is therefore to redirect priorities of both science and management, such that they become mutually supportive and reinforcing.

Relating science and management

The persistent view that science can be divided into pure and applied branches is counter-productive and leads to anomalous situations. Physical oceanographers, for example, collect information in such a way that it is incompatible with fisheries data and unusable by fisheries biologists. Such sectoral approaches to science make rational management difficult but more importantly foster the development of narrow sectoral specialists at a time when holistic, integrated views of the oceans, biosphere and Planet Earth are urgently needed.

The consequences of specialization in narrow sectors of science become more obvious in developing countries where the numerically smaller manpower base inhibits the proper application of science to the solution of environmental problems and conservation issues. The pursuit of knowledge purely for its own sake, while a laudable objective, is a luxury which developed countries may be able to afford but developing countries cannot. The future responsibility of global marine science must be to contribute to the solution of environmental problems, if humanity is to achieve a long-lasting and sustainable relationship with the oceans.

Current understanding of the animal and plant communities of the oceans, and the manner in which the physical environment influences biological processes in the ocean, is far behind our knowledge and understanding of such phenomena on land. The need to improve the state of global marine science is not only a prerequisite for sustainable use of marine resources but also vital to repairing past damage and environmental degradation. Marine science must be seen by both practitioners and users of the information as a vital tool in rational management of the oceans.

Monitoring variability

Decisions concerning future types of use or levels of harvest can be made only on the basis of adequate information concerning the way in which natural systems work. All too often monitoring of the state of the environment is seen as an end in itself, a second-class occupation for technicians rather than a priority for "real" science. But producing models which enable prediction of ocean processes such as El Niño requires considerable volumes of routine measurements taken over weeks, months and decades. Without this background research our ability to understand, model and predict the outcome of ocean processes is severely constrained. A greater investment in monitoring of various kinds is required to provide the necessary understanding upon which to base sound future directions for the conservation and protection of habitats, species and populations.

Even in cases where data have been collected over long periods our understanding may still be rather limited. Arguments still continue, for example, after

Living Within Our Means

In a report of the Food and Agriculture Organization of the United Nations published in 1967, it was stated that "at the present rate of development few substantial unexploited stocks of fish accessible to today's types of gear will remain in another 20 years". We now have ample evidence that this statement was indeed prophetic. Many long-established fisheries have declined, for example cod and haddock in the North Atlantic, and salmon in the North Pacific. To compensate for such declines the industry increased its overall effort, developed highly sophisticated techniques for locating schools and introduced more efficient fishing gear. In some cases the increased efforts resulted in greater yields, but in retrospect these proved to be temporary and subsequent yields have declined. It is probable that in many cases the stocks had already been fished beyond a sustainable level and the increased effort simply depleted them further and more rapidly.

To meet the increasing world demand for marine products the industry turned from more traditional species such as cod, haddock, salmon and tuna to previously less preferred or unexploited resources such as squid, mackerel and shellfish including mussels. It has also shifted its focus away from the northern to the southern hemisphere in search of new stocks such as orange roughie and Antarctic krill. In many parts of the world we have exploited wild populations of fish until they could no longer support harvesting. For example, the roughie is a deep-living fish associated with sea-mounts. It has only been exploited for about 10 years but is already threatened because of trawling methods that take all classes, leaving no fish of reproductive age.

Open or limited access?

The root cause of our continued "hunter-gatherer" approach to marine resources is due to the traditional view that they are common property available to anyone having the desire and capability to extract or use them. The oceans and their resources were considered so vast in scale compared with the human capability for exploitation that they seemed largely unthreatened. Thus the traditional approach has been to allow the users of ocean resources to regulate themselves according to their own needs. This approach no longer works because competing demands for these resources are leading to more and more international conflicts. The new Law of the Sea contains many clauses aimed at resolving such conflicts. Conservation of marine living resources is impossible without sound, scientifically based management regimes. The development of such management regimes is itself dependent on setting agreed limits, in terms of both access and levels of harvest. Achieving such agreements requires concerted global action. In the case of wide-ranging species such as tuna and billfish, for example, many International Tuna Commissions do not cover the full range of individual stocks whose movements cover areas outside the Exclusive Economic Zones of participating states. The failure of the UN Law of the Sea to enter into force does not augur well for achieving the goal of international management of such stocks.

Nationally, few countries limit access to marine resources which are often viewed as the solution to rural poverty in Third World countries. Limiting access to marine resources within the territorial waters of coastal and island states may well be the only mechanism by which such stocks may be conserved for future use. More recently, attempts at

farming the sea have resulted in degradation of coastal habitats and water quality, and an urgent need from the marine conservation perspective is to develop mariculture methods which are compatible with the survival of natural ecosystems and habitats.

It is clear that the demand for marine products will continue to rise as human populations grow and the natural production of living marine resources will have to be used in a sustainable manner. The challenge for scientifically based conservation is to determine sustainable levels of yield which minimize the disturbances to ecosystem processes, and to assist in the development of less damaging harvesting technologies.

Global populations and economic issues

Living within our means clearly implies the need to address two additional problems which result in adverse stress on the natural world in general and the oceans in particular. The first is the expanding world population, which places increasing demands on a declining resource base. The consequences of this will be an increase in the world prices of marine products, which will further limit their availability to meet local demands in poorer nations. These countries will export their resources to earn foreign currency and thus deprive their poorer populations of a currently widely used source of protein.

The second problem to be addressed, as noted in the Brundtland Commission report *Our Common Future*, is the urgent need for a new economic order which adequately values goods and services provided by the ocean environment, and which are currently used "free of charge". The new economic order must also encompass the issues of Third World poverty and underdevelopment. Failure to address these issues directly will render isolated efforts at conservation of particular habitats or species an uphill if not impossible task.

A pelagic sardine trawl is sorted according to size (left). Much of the world's pelagic sardine and anchovy catch is used for animal feed and oil production, rather than for direct human consumption.

Conflicts and Compatibilities

Planning for sustainable use of the oceans requires not only the recognition of natural limits to human use of the marine environment and its resources, but also an integrated and holistic approach to planning, management and multiple use of the oceans. At present fishermen, navies, coastal developers, shipping, mining and oil companies, sportsmen and tour operators all use the goods and services provided by the sea without regard to the needs, interests or plans of each other. This sectoral approach to development, use and management of the seas is reflected in haphazard and reactive national policies; fragmented decision making processes; weak or no linkages between the decisions and policies in different sectors and a failure both nationally and internationally to calculate the net benefits which would result from balanced choice between various options for development.

Integrated ocean planning
In establishing an Ocean Development Plan each coastal or island state needs to determine initially its overall development objectives and evaluate the extent to which the ocean and coastal resources might provide the means to achieve those objectives. It is imperative therefore that a full identification and evaluation of possible options is initially undertaken and it is here that the needs of conservation need to be included. A first step is the stocktaking of present resources (both living and non-living) and potential services and opportunities in terms of: waste disposal sites; a medium for transport and communication; and a source of energy or tourist income. The impacts of alternative development scenarios should be assessed and potential conflicts identified. It may well be the case that establishing a National Park proves economically more viable as a consequence of high tourist incomes than use as a waste disposal facility. Alternatively, a tourist hotel may pollute coastal waters, in turn affecting mariculture by degrading water quality. Decisions on the choice of use need to be made in the light of the relative potential contributions the different uses could make to achieving the overall development goals.

Conflict avoidance
In assessing potential uses and impacts, conflicts and compatibilities between different sectoral uses will be identified during this planning stage. Balanced decision making, based on a consideration of the economic and environmental consequences of particular scenarios of use will then be possible. Prevention of conflicts between different uses and identification of compatible development strategies and projects will lead to an integrated planning process and this will ease the burdens of rational management by preventing rather than reacting to conflicts only after they have become apparent. Socioeconomic constraints and present management capabilities may limit the range of options available in particular countries and regions, hence a staged approach to management, use and development of the ocean and coastal areas will be necessary. Fundamental to the process of conflict resolution will be the need to sustain and enhance the productivity and diversity of the ocean realm. More integrated approaches to planning and management of the marine and coastal areas will itself result in improved conservation of these environments and their resources.

Conservation implies use, but rational use based on the concept of sustaining environments, habitats and processes which results in the diversity and produc-

A Soviet submarine (left) *caught in a fishing net dramatically illustrates the conflicts which result from increased use of the seas and their resources.*

tivity upon which the continued existence of humanity itself will depend. The outdated view that conservation means preservation and a "hands off" approach to oceans and coastal areas is no longer practical in the face of increasing human demands upon the ocean and its resources. Nevertheless the establishment of areas of coastal and inshore environments where the impacts of human activities are minimized is an urgent requirement if sensitive species and habitats are to survive.

Areas where resource exploitation is limited and use is confined to ecologically sensitive tourism, for example, might serve not only as sources of foreign currency but also as sources of recruitment for depleted marine species in neighbouring areas. Such hidden benefits need to be considered in the planning process, and proponents of the conservation ethic must strive to provide adequate economic cost-benefit analyses which demonstrate the long-term value of such conservation areas.

A traditional junk (below) *in Hong Kong contrasts sharply* *with office blocks in the background.*

Management Frameworks

Historical development of frameworks for managing ocean resources reflects the innate bias that these are "open-access" – freely available to anyone with the means to use them. This in turn is a reflection of the low levels of use that occurred until recently. The principle of "open-access" can only function when demands are much lower than supply and when activities that impinge on the marine environment – such as pollution or dredging, for example – do not exceed the abilities of marine systems to maintain themselves. Until very recently the demand did not exceed the supply. This is no longer the case. Also in the past, uses of the ocean by different economic sectors (for example industry, settlement, energy, tourism and fisheries) was less extensive, which meant sectoral development plans could proceed independently because they had little chance of affecting each other. Given the advances in technology that allow more extensive exploitation of resources and ocean services, both in kind and quantity, and the increased demand that will result from rapid increase in world population, it will be necessary to further integrate ocean resource management programmes.

Integration of planning in different economic sectors and between pure marine research and management programmes at different levels is required. These must be supported by new legal and administrative mechanisms.

Planning and use of the oceans at all levels, from local communities through to national and international levels requires integration to avoid conflict and prevent degradation and *loss of sensitive ecosystems and habitats. Planning and management units must be adjusted to coincide with the limits of ecosystems and resources.* *Penaeid shrimp resources illustrate potential conflicts between alternative uses of mangrove nursery areas for forestry, agriculture and mariculture and off-shore* *trawlers which exploit the adult population. Like pelagic tuna, shrimps do not recognise legal and administrative boundaries.*

Sectorial planning results in conflict when ports, tourist resorts, mariculture and fishing interests compete for coastal access. Integrated planning is therefore vital.

The boundaries for ocean planning and management reflect neither the limits of physical ocean systems nor the distributions of living marine resources. The UN Law of the Sea grants rights to individual states over the resources within Exclusive Economic Zones. The high seas form the commons. Single populations of migratory species such as tuna may therefore be fished by several states and distant water fishing fleets. This makes setting catch limits and rational management of stocks difficult.

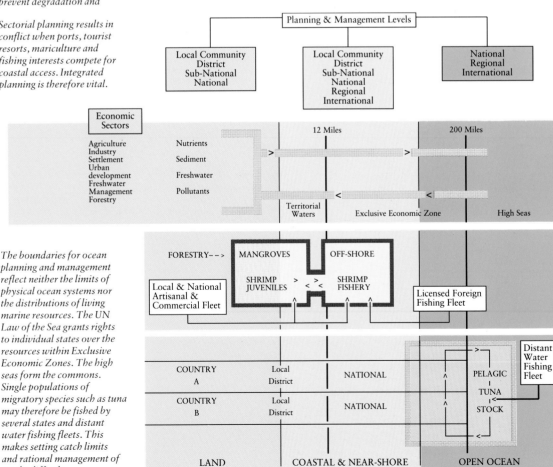

Agenda for the 21st Century

Recognizing the urgency of environmental problems and their close relationship to issues of development, Third World poverty and First World over-consumption, the United Nations has decided to convene a global conference in 1992 on Environment and Development. Two decades after the Stockholm Conference on the Human Environment, the international community will once again take stock of the state of the environment and chart a course into the 21st century.

In Stockholm in 1972, the focus lay very much on issues of environmental and ocean degradation resulting from pollution. Following the conference, the necessary actions to assess the scale and nature of such problems were rapidly put in place, while national and international actions to limit, control and regulate pollution followed soon thereafter. As a consequence of such actions we now know that although much of the open oceans are little affected by pollution at present, inshore and coastal waters are being degraded at an alarming rate – not only as a consequence of pollution but also by the actions and demands of burgeoning coastal populations.

Two significant changes in perspective have occurred in the last two decades. Firstly the concept of integrated planning and management of coastal zones has achieved wide acceptance. This more holistic approach stems from a recognition of the past failures to resolve environmental problems and concerns through sectoral approaches. By extension, it is not merely enough to view the oceans and their uses as an isolated management unit, since human actions on land may have both direct and indirect impacts upon the seas and their resources. Poor land use practices which result in inland soil erosion can also result in smothering and loss of sensitive coastal habitats. Forty per cent of all coastal marine pollution is estimated to originate from land-based sources.

The effect of global warming
More recently it has been recognized that burning fossil fuels changes the composition of the atmosphere. Such changes may result in higher sea surface temperatures and raised sea levels. This forms the basis for the second change in our perception, namely that human activities may now be affecting poorly understood global processes which function on time scales beyond that of a mere human life-span.

Such a possibility is a sobering thought, with implications for future generations. This threat demands concerted, prompt and appropriate actions at all levels of society and in all countries of the world. A new approach to ocean management must be developed which changes our approach from one of reacting to conflicts and crises to pro-active and anticipatory planning and management which avoids conflict and prevents environmental damage and future economic loss.

Integrated planning
Adoption of integrated planning for the use of coastal and Exclusive Economic Zones would not only avoid conflicts which are currently increasing worldwide, but also go a long way towards ensuring conservation of these fragile ecosystems and their living resources. A change from open to limited access to ocean resources is necessary to prevent over-exploitation. This requires changes in national and international legal and management regimes. Strengthening regional and international cooperation in the use and management of the oceans is vital and must be based on greater investment in marine science in terms of education, enhanced public awareness and institution building.

The focus for marine conservation in the 21st century must be to maintain and enhance the ecosystem processes which result in the present diversity of marine species. Such a focus is compatible with the international goal of sustainable development, which implies wise use of marine and coastal environments and their resources for the benefit and enjoyment of both present and future generations.

FUTURE STRATEGIES FOR MARINE CONSERVATION

The "New View" must recognise the importance of:
- Maintaining high water quality as essential for marine life.
- Sustaining ecosystem processes
- Sustainable harvesting of living resources
- The need to integrate multiple uses of oceans

The need for integration must address:
- Relationships between science and management
- Local and national needs and aspirations
- National and international rights and obligations
- Cross-sectoral conflicts and compatibilities

Maintaining and improving the state of the marine environment requires:
- Integrated planning to avoid conflict
- Better tools for integrated management
- Increased emphasis on "ecosystem" approaches to
  – fisheries
  – protected areas
  – conservation
- Improved coastal planning and use
- Improved control of marine pollution
- Strengthening adherence to national and international legal regimes
- Strengthening existing national, regional and international institutions
- Enhanced environmental education and public awareness
- Greater decentralization of day-to-day management responsibility to coastal communities
- Increased use of non-governmental organizations in environmental decision making.

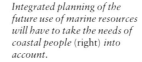

Integrated planning of the future use of marine resources will have to take the needs of coastal people (right) into account.

Threatened Marine Species

All Oceans
Mammals
E Blue whale (*Balaenoptera musculus*)
V Fin whale (*Balaenoptera physalus*)
V Humpback whale (*Megaptera novaeangliae*)

Arctic
Mammals
V Bowhead whale (*Balaena mysticetus*)
V Polar bear (*Ursus maritimus*)

North Atlantic
Mammals
E Northern right whale (*Eubalaena glacialis*)
V Bowhead whale (*Balaena mysticetus*)
V Northern bottlenose whale (*Hyperoodon ampullatus*)
Others
V Starlet sea anemone (*Nematostella vectensis*)

Mediterranean
Mammals
E Mediterranean monk seal (*Monachus monachus*)
Birds
E Freira (*Pterodroma madeira*)
E Dalmatian pelican (*Pelecanus crispus*)
Reptiles
E Green turtle (*Chelonia mydas*)
V Loggerhead turtle (*Caretta caretta*)

Wider Caribbean
Mammals
V West Indian (Caribbean) manatee (*Trichechus manatus*)
V Amazonian manatee (*Trichechus inunguis*)
Birds
E Cahow (Bermuda petrel) (*Pterodroma cahow*)
Reptiles
E Green turtle (*Chelonia mydas*)
E Olive Ridley turtle (*Lepidochelys olivacea*)
E Leatherback turtle (*Dermochelys coriacea*)
E Hawksbill turtle (*Eretmochelys imbricata*)
E Kemp's Ridley turtle (*Lepidochelys kempii*)
V Loggerhead turtle (*Caretta caretta*)

South-West Atlantic
Mammals
V Southern right whale (*Eubalaena australis*)
V La Plata otter (*Lutra longicaudis*)
Reptiles
E Green turtle (*Chelonia mydas*)
E Olive Ridley turtle (*Lepidochelys olivacea*)
E Leatherback turtle (*Dermochelys coriacea*)
E Hawksbill turtle (*Eretmochelys imbricata*)
V Loggerhead turtle (*Caretta caretta*)

West Africa
Mammals
West African manatee (*Trichechus senegalensis*)
Reptiles
E Green turtle (*Chelonia mydas*)
E Olive Ridley turtle (*Lepidochelys olivacea*)
E Leatherback turtle (*Dermochelys coriacea*)
E Hawksbill turtle (*Eretmochelys imbricata*)
V Loggerhead turtle (*Caretta caretta*)

Indian Ocean
Mammals
V Southern right whale (*Eubalaena australis*)
V Dugong (*Dugong dugon*)
Birds
E Amsterdam albatross (*Diomedea amsterdamensis*)
V Kerguelen tern (*Sterna virgata*)
E Madagascar fish eagle (*Haliaeetus vociferoides*)
Reptiles
E Green turtle (*Chelonia mydas*)

E Olive Ridley turtle (*Lepidochelys olivacea*)
E Leatherback turtle (*Dermochelys coriacea*)

E Hawksbill turtle (*Eretmochelys imbricata*)
V Loggerhead turtle (*Caretta caretta*)
Others
V Coelacanth (*Latimeria chalumnae*)

East Asian Seas
Mammals
V Dugong (*Dugong dugon*)
Birds
E Abbott's booby (*Sula abbotti*)
E Christmas frigatebird (*Fregata andrewsi*)
Reptiles
V Estuarine crocodile (*Crocodylus porosus*)
E Green turtle (*Chelonia mydas*)
E Olive Ridley turtle (*Lepidochelys olivacea*)
E Leatherback turtle (*Dermochelys coriacea*)
E Hawksbill turtle (*Eretmochelys imbricata*)
V Loggerhead turtle (*Caretta caretta*)
Molluscs
V Southern giant clam (*Tridacna derasa*)
V Giant clam (*Tridacna gigas*)

South Pacific
Mammals
V Southern right whale (*Eubalaena australis*)
V Hector's dolphin (*Cephalorynchus hectori*)
V Dugong (*Dugong dugon*)
E Hawaiian monk seal (*Monachus schauinslandi*)
Birds
V Pycroft's petrel (*Pterodroma pycrofti*)
V Chatham Island petrel (*Pterodroma axillaris*)
V Newell's shearwater (*Puffinus newelli*)
V Black petrel (*Procellaria parkinsoni*)
E Chatham Island oystercatcher (*Haematopus chathamnsis*)
V Black fronted tern (*Sterna albostriata*)
V Yellow-eyed penguin (*Megadyptes antipodes*)
Reptiles
V Estuarine crocodile (*Crocodylus porosus*)
E Green turtle (*Chelonia mydas*)
E Olive Ridley turtle (*Lepidochelys olivacea*)
E Leatherback turtle (*Dermochelys coriacea*)
E Hawksbill turtle (*Eretmochelys imbricata*)
V Loggerhead turtle (*Caretta caretta*)
Molluscs
V Southern giant clam (*Tridacna derasa*)
V Giant clam (*Tridacna gigas*)

North Pacific
Mammals
E Northern right whale (*Eubalaena glacialis*)
V Bowhead whale (*Balaena mysticetus*)
V Guadeloupe fur seal (*Arctocephalus townsendi*)
E Vaquita (*Phocoena sinus*)
Birds
E Townsend's shearwater (*Puffinus auricularis*)
Others
V Starlet sea anemone (*Nematostella vectensis*)

South-East Pacific
Mammals
V Southern right whale (*Eubalaena australis*)
V Juan Fernandez fur seal (*Arctocephalus philippii*)
V Marine otter (*Lutra felina*)
Birds
V Pink-footed shearwater (*Puffinus creatopus*)
V Defilippe's petrel (*Pterodroma defilippiana*)
Reptiles
E Green turtle (*Chelonia mydas*)
E Olive Ridley turtle (*Lepidochelys olivacea*)
E Leatherback turtle (*Dermochelys coriacea*)
E Hawksbill turtle (*Eretmochelys imbricata*)

Antarctica and Southern Oceans
Mammals
V Southern right whale (*Eubalaena australis*)
E = endangered = vulnerable

Map Sources

General references
IUCN, Gland, Switzerland

Insitut Océanographique,
Library of the Musée Océanographique, Monaco

UNEP Regional Seas Reports and Studies
various
UNEP, 1990

*Inventory of Radioactive Material Entering the Marine
Environment: Sea Disposal of RadioActive Waste*
IAEA-TECDOC-588
International Atomic Energy Agency, March 1991

Spelling
Times Atlas and Encyclopaedia of the Sea
Times Books, London 1989

Times Atlas of the World
Comprehensive 7th ed.
Times Books, London 1987

Physical Oceanography
A. Defant. Pergamon Press, Oxford 1961

Fishing
Atlas of the Living Resources of the Seas
FAO UN, Rome 1981

Coral
Coral Reefs of the World
UNEP and IUCN, 1988

Threatened birds
Birds to Watch: The ICBP World Checklist of Threatened Birds
N.J. Collar and P. Andrew,
Smithsonian Institution Press 1988

Sea grasses
The Sea-grasses of the World
C. Den Hartog 1969, Tweede Reeks Deel 59

Turtles
The Worldwide Distribution of Sea Turtle Nesting Beaches
Compiled by J. Sternberg Sea Turtle Rescue Fund
Center for Environmental Education, 1981

Animals
1990 IUCN Red List of Threatened Animals
IUCN, 1990

Habitats
UNESCO World Heritage of Information on All Natural Sites
Compiled by WCMC in collabaration with IUCN, unpub. June 1990

Biosphere Reserves Compilation 4
UNESCO, 1986

Biosphere Reserves Compilation 5,
UNESCO, 1990

Seaweed Resources of the Ocean
FIRS/T138
FAO UN

*Directory of Wetlands of International Importance
– Sites Designed for the List of Wetlands of International Importance.*

Ramsar Convention Bureau, 1990

Draft List of Marine and Coastal Protected Areas
Prepared by WCMC Protected Areas Data Unit in collaboration
with the IUCN Commission on National Parks and Protected
Areas
IUCN Marine Programme, August 1990

Physical
ATLAS OKEANOV (World Oceans Atlas)
Moscow 1974

Atlas of the Oceans
Mitchell Beazley, London 1978

Oil industry
International Petroleum Encyclopedia
Pennwell Publishing, Tulsa 1989

Pollution symbols are a synthesis of available information
extracted from an extensive number of sources.

North Sea
Atlas of the Seas Around the British Isles
Ministry of Agriculture, Fisheries and Food
HMSO, London 1981

Antarctic and Southern Ocean
Antarctique 1:5m
IGN, Paris 1969

The Greenpeace Book of Antarctica
John May, Dorling Kindersley, London 1988

Mineralische Resources der Antarktis
N.W. Roland
G. Rundschau 35, 1983

*International Agreement on Conserving the Antarctic
Environment*
P.H.C. Lucas,
AMBIO 11, 1982

East Asian Seas
Atlas for Marine Policy in the Southeast Asian Seas
J.R. Morgan and M.J. Valencia University of California Press, 1983

Mediterranean
The Environmental Program for the Mediterranean
The World Bank and The European Investment Bank, March 1990.

North-West Atlantic
*Health of the Northwest Atlantic: A report to the Interdepartmental
Committee on Environmental Issues.*
Edited by R.C.H. Wilson and R.F. Addison.

East Africa
Environmental Stress in the East African Region
Patricia Bliss-Guest.
AMBIO, 1983

Present State of Oil Pollution in the Northern Indian Ocean
R. Sen Gupta and T. W. Kureishy, 1981

Caribbean and Gulf of Mexico
Coastal and Ocean Zones Strategic Assessment Data Atlas
United States Department of Commerce National Oceanographic
and Atmospheric Administration National Ocean Service, 1985

Index

Bold type indicates the reference occurs in a caption.

Italic type indicates the reference occurs in a page heading

Acknowledgments

Illustrations: John Francis
Additional maps and diagrams: Paul Campbell, The Learning Curve
Kuo Kang Chen
Thanks to: Kerrie Keogh, Denis McWilliams, Ellen Root, Gavin Sweet and Hans Verkroost
Atlas concept and series development: Dr Mark Collins, WCMC

Advice: Dr John Twidell, University of Strathclyde
Dr John Baxter, Nature Conservancy Council for Scotland
Mr Nigel Merrett, British Museum (Natural History)
Dr Tony Rice, Institute of Oceanographic Sciences
(Deacon Laboratory)
Dr James Thorsell,
Commission on National Parks and Protected Areas, IUCN
RAMSAR Convention Bureau, Gland, Switzerland
(for information on RAMSAR sites)
Musée Océanographique, Monaco
(for research support and assistance)

Picture credits

1: Georgette Douwma/Planet Earth Pictures; 2-3: J.L. Mason/Ardea; 4-5: Francois Gohier/Ardea; 6-7: Michael Freeman/Bruce Coleman; 9: Guis-Lebrette/Figaro/Frank Spooner Library; 10-11: R. Cansdale/Tropix; 12-13: Michael Freeman; 13: Jay Freis/The Image Bank; 14-15: (b) Gavin Hellier/Robert Harding Library; 14-15: (t) Marion Morrison/South American Pictures; 16-17: Robert Harding Library; 17: Robert Harding Library; 18-19: Robert Harding Library; 20-21: Sigurg. Jonasson/Mats Wibe Lund/Icelandic Photo; 20: NASA/Science Photo Library; 23: R. Grigg; 24-25: Armstrong/Zefa; 25: Richard Matthews/Planet Earth Pictures; 26-27: Peter Scones/Planet Earth Pictures; 26: Peter David/Planet Earth Pictures; 28-29: Jean-Paul Ferrero/Ardea; 28: Mark Mattock/Planet Earth Pictures; 29: NASA/Science Photo Library; 30-31: Stan Osolinski/Oxford Scientific Films; 31: Richard Chesher/Planet Earth Pictures; 32-33: Bryan and Cherry Alexander; 33: Hires/Frank Spooner Pictures; 34-35: Gilbert van Ryckevorsel/Planet Earth Pictures; 36-37: Christian Petron/Planet Earth Pictures; 36: Tony Wharton/Frank Lane Picture Agency; 38-39: Roy Waller/NHPA; 38: Francois Gohier/Ardea; 39: Jon Kenfield/Bruce Coleman; 40-41: Ron and Valerie Taylor/Ardea; 40: Doug Perrine/Planet Earth Pictures; 41: Tsuneo Nakanura/NHPA; 42-43: J. Watkins/Frank Lane Picture Agency; 42: D. Faulkner/Photoresearchers/Zefa; 43: James D. Watt/Planet Earth Pictures; 44-45: Bill Wood/NHPA; 44: Peter David/Planet Earth Pictures; 45: D. P. Wilson/Eric and David Hosking; 46-47: James D. Watt/Planet Earth Pictures; 46: Peter Scoones/Planet Earth Pictures; 47: (b) Chaumeton-Bassot(Nature)/NHPA; 47: (t) Ken Lucas/Planet Earth Pictures; 48-49: Ocean Images, Inc./The Image Bank; 48: David George/Planet Earth Pictures; 49: Michael Burke; 50; Howard Hall/Planet Earth Pictures; 50: Ken Lucas/Planet Earth Pictures; 51: Burt Jones and Maurine Shimlock/NHPA 52-53: Francois Gohier/Ardea; 52: Hugh Yorkston/A.N.T./NHPA 53: D.P. Wilson/Eric and David Hosking; 54-55: M. R. Phicton/Bruce Coleman; 54: Laurie Campbell/NHPA; 55: Christiana F. Carvalho/Frank Lane Picture Agency; 56-57: Doug Perrine/Planet Earth Pictures; 56: G. I. Bernard/Oxford Scientific Films; 57: Ken Lucas/Planet Earth Pictures; 58-59: Gunter Ziesler/Bruce Coleman; 60-61 Eric Lindgren/Ardea; 60: John Pernetta; 61: Breck P. Kent/Oxford Scientific Films; 62-63: Roy Waller/NHPA 63: L. Campbell/NHPA; 64-65: Norbert Wu/Planet Earth Pictures; 64: Anthony Bannister/NHPA; 65: (b) Richard Vaughan/Ardea; 65: (t) Valerie Taylor/Ardea; 66-67: Ron and Valerie Taylor/Ardea; 67: (b) G I Bernard/NHPA; 67: (t) Richard Beales/Planet Earth Pictures; 68-69: Walter Deas/Planet Earth Pictures; 69: (b) Ron and Valerie Taylor/Ardea; 69: (t) Peter Scoones/Planet Earth Pictures; 70-71: Ardea; 70: Carl Roessler/Planet Earth Pictures; 71: (b) Linda Pitkin/Planet Earth Pictures; 71: (t) Valerie Taylor/Ardea; 72-73 Ron and Valerie Taylor/Ardea; 72: Peter Scoones/Planet Earth Pictures; 73: D P Wilson/Eric and David Hosking; 74-75: Robert Hessler/Planet Earth Pictures; 74: Ken Lucas/Planet Earth Pictures; 76-77: Philip Plisson/Explorer/Robert Harding Library; 77: H. Lloyd/Zefa; 78-79: Co Rentmeester/The Image Bank; 80-81: ET Archive; 80: Michael Holford; 81: Sir Benjamin Stone/Birmingham Reference Library; 82-83 Bryan and Cherry Alexander/Bruce Coleman; 82: (b) John Garrett; 82: (t) Christian/ZEFA; 83: Michael Freeman; 84-85 Fjellanger Wideroe AS; 84: Jean Gaumy/Magnum; 85: Kim Westerskov/Oxford Scientific Films; 86-87: Janoud/ZEFA; 86: Baker/Greenpeace; 87: (b) Heather Angel/Biofotos; 87 (t) Adam Woolfitt/Susan Griggs Agency; 88-89: Ocean Images, Inc./The Image Bank; 89: (b) Jon Kenfield/Planet Earth Pictures; 89: (t) J. Hartley/Panos Pictures; 90-91: McAllister/ZEFA; 91: (cl) Fred Mayer/Magnum; 91: (cr) Peter Ryan/Science Photo Library; 91: (t) Damm/ZEFA; 92-93: Kloske/Ecoscene 92: Gryniewicz/Ecoscene; 93: Luigi Tazzari/Gamma/Frank Spooner Pictures; 94-95: A.N.T. (Mark Wellard)/NHPA; 94: Bryan and Cherry Alexander; 95: NMFS/Greenpeace; 96-97: Hewetson/Greenpeace; 96: Patrick Rouillard/The Image Bank; 97: (b) Luigi Tazzari/Gamma/Frank Spooner Pictures; 97: (t) Georges Merillon/Gamma/Frank Spooner Pictures; 98-99: Dr. Nigel Smith/Hutchison Library; 103: Paul Drummond/Bryan and Cherry Alexander; 104-105: Jeff Foott Productions/Bruce Coleman; 104: Jim Brandenburg/Planet Earth Pictures; 105: Gordon Langsbury/Bruce Coleman; 106-107: Bryan and Cherry Alexander; 106: Bryan and Cherry Alexander; 107 (b) Y. J. Rey-Millet/WWF World Wide Fund for Nature; 107 (t) Bryan and Cherry Alexander; 110-111: Ira Block/The Image Bank; 110: John Egan/Hutchison Library; 111: Ted Spiegel/Susan Griggs Agency; 116-117: Adam Woolfitt/Susan Griggs Agency; 116: Larsen/Greenpeace; 117: Dr. R. Legeckis/Science Photo Library; 120-121: Malanca/Sipa/Rex Features; 120: Christian Petron/Planet Earth Pictures; 121: (b) Peter Scoones/Planet Earth Pictures; 121 (t) Adina Tovy/Robert Harding Library; 122-123: Dr Gene Feldman/NASA GSFC/Science Photo Library; 123: Venice Picture Library; 126-127: Liba Taylor/Hutchison Library; 126: Bernard Regent/Hutchison Library; 127 (b) Marc French/Panos Pictures; 127 (t) John Wright/Hutchison Library; 132-133: L. C. Marigo/Bruce Coleman; 132: Robert Harding Library; 133: Jany Sauvanet/NHPA; 136-137: Hutchison Library; 136: Robert Harding Library; 142-143: Guido Alberto Rossi/The Image Bank; 142: (b) Adam Woolfitt/Susan Griggs Agency; 142: (t) Ivan Polunin/Susan Griggs Agency; 143: Michael Friedel/The Image Bank; 144-145: R. Berriedale-Johnson/Panos Pictures; 144: J. Mackinnon/Planet Earth Pictures; 145: (b) Hutchison Library; 145: (t) Georgette Douwma/Planet Earth Pictures; 148-149 Luca Invernizzi Tettoni Photobank/BKK/Robert Harding Library; 148: (b) Gavin Hellier/Robert Harding Library; 148: (t) Nancy Durrell McKenna/Hutchison Library; 150-151: S. Sreedharan/WWF World Wide Fund For Nature; 151: Liba Taylor/Hutchison Library; 154-155: Frilet/Sipa Press/Rex Features; 155: (b) A.N.T./NHPA; 155: (t) Erwin Christian/Zefa; 156-157: Roger Brown/Oxford Scientific Films; 157: (b) John Pernetta; 157: (t) Peter Scoones/Planet Earth Pictures; 158-159: Ron and Valerie Taylor/Ardea; 158: Ron and Valerie Taylor/Ardea; 159: (b) John Pernetta; 159: (t) Kim Westerskov/Oxford Scientific Films; 164-165: Grace/Greenpeace; 165: (b) Trevor Smith/Robert Harding Library; 165: (t) Robert McLeod/Robert Harding Library; 168-169: Tony Morrison/South American Pictures; 169 (b) Tony Morrison/South American Pictures; 169 (t) Robert Francis/South American Pictures; 170-171: Frans Lanting/Bruce Coleman; 170: Photri/Robert Harding Library; 171: Tony Morrison/South American Pictures; 174-175; Photoresearchers/ZEFA; 174 (b) P. V. Tearle/Planet Earth Pictures; 174 (t) Ben Osborne/Oxford Scientific Films; 176-177: D. Parer and E. Parer-Cook/Ardea; 176: (l) Mecky Fogeling; 176: (r) E. Mickleburgh/Ardea; 177: D. Parer and E. Parer-Cook/Ardea; 178-179: Francois Gohier/Ardea; 180-181: Michael McIntyre/Hutchison Library; 182-183: Dr Gene Feldman, NASA GSFC/Science Photo Library; 182: D. P. Wilson/Eric and David Hosking 184-185: Kelvin Aitken/NHPA; 185: Christian Petron/Planet Earth Pictures; 186-187: G. Le Cossec/Explorer; 188-189: R. I. Lloyd/Hutchison Library; 188: Rex Features; 190-191: Rangar Axelsson/Gamma/Frank Spooner Pictures; 190: Carl Roessler/Bruce Coleman; 192-193: Ted Spiegel/Susan Griggs Agency